Hitler's Man in Havana

HITLER'S MAN IN HAVANA

Heinz Lüning
and Nazi Espionage
in Latin America

Thomas D. Schoonover

THE UNIVERSITY PRESS OF KENTUCKY

Copyright © 2008 by Thomas D. Schoonover

The University Press of Kentucky
Scholarly publisher for the Commonwealth, serving Bellarmine University, Berea
College, Centre College of Kentucky, Eastern Kentucky University, The Filson
Historical Society, Georgetown College, Kentucky Historical Society, Kentucky State
University, Morehead State University, Murray State University, Northern Kentucky
University, Transylvania University, University of Kentucky, University of Louisville,
and Western Kentucky University.
All rights reserved.

Editorial and Sales Offices: The University Press of Kentucky
663 South Limestone Street, Lexington, Kentucky 40508-4008
www.kentuckypress.com

12 11 10 09 08   5 4 3 2 1

Maps created by Eric Truesdell and Jacob Wasilkowski at the University of Kentucky
Cartography Lab

Library of Congress Cataloging-in-Publication Data

Schoonover, Thomas David, 1936–
  Hitler's man in Havana : Heinz Lüning and Nazi espionage in Latin America /
Thomas D. Schoonover.
    p. cm.
  Includes bibliographical references and index.
  ISBN 978-0-8131-2501-5 (hbk. : alk. paper)
  1. Lüning, Heinz, 1911–1942. 2. World War, 1939–1945—Secret service—Germany.
3. Espionage, German—Cuba. 4. Spies—Germany—Biography.
5. Spies—Cuba—Biography. I. Title.
  D810.S8L867 2008
  940.54'8743098—dc22   2008013205

This book is printed on acid-free recycled paper meeting the requirements of the
American National Standard for Permanence in Paper for Printed Library Materials.

Manufactured in the United States of America.

 Member of the Association of
American University Presses

To two colleagues who have inspired this project:

Louis A. Pérez Jr., who proposed the project in April 2001 and listened to me repeatedly thereafter, and

Walter LaFeber, who has discussed this and other projects with me for decades.

Contents

Foreword

Latin America was one of the few parts of the world that was not directly involved in World War II. As air raids and land campaigns laid waste to cities and countryside in Asia, Europe, and Africa, Latin America appeared to have remained at the margins of the drama that engulfed the vast portion of humanity. Certainly, this has long been the conventional historiographic wisdom. The received knowledge is not, of course, without some basis. Measured by the magnitude of the loss of life and the destruction of property, the Latin American experience during the war years was relatively tranquil.

But the story of Latin America and World War II is more complicated. In recent years, the works of Thomas Leonard, Leslie Rout and John Bratzel, and Max Paul Friedman, among others, have directed renewed attention to Latin America during the war years. This scholarship has provided a greater appreciation of context and consequence and the nuanced ways in which the war insinuated itself into the conduct of daily life. No less important, new attention has been drawn to the ways in which the war was "fought" in Latin America.

Thomas Schoonover's fascinating study of Heinz Lüning in Havana makes one more contribution toward an understanding of the ways in which Latin America served as site and setting for the greater war of the world. At first glance, Lüning's story seems to be no more than an inconsequential episode of the war. And, indeed, in many ways, and certainly in a comparative sense, the Lüning affair never rose to any level higher than an episode incidental to the global conflict, with the added allure of tropical intrigue not unlike the imagined mystique associated with Casablanca. In the case of Lüning, it was Havana: stereotyped as a romantic Caribbean seaport, something of an exotic New World center of

international espionage, a saga of a Nazi spy and Nazi spy hunters, intelligence and counterintelligence intrigue, bars and brothels, corrupt politicians—all in all, heady stuff. There is sufficient drama in the Lüning
affair to arouse the curiosity of even the most casual espionage buff.

In fact, there is much more to the Lüning story. The need to protect
the Caribbean sea—lanes against German submarine warfare was vital
to the uninterrupted Allied supply of raw materials from Latin America,
most notably petroleum and bauxite, of course, but also sugar and coffee: the military success on the war front and the morale of the home
front depended on it. No less important, while the Caribbean was distant
from the decisive maritime dramas unfolding in the Pacific and Atlantic, it was, nevertheless, a vital strategic transit site for Allied trans-
oceanic shipping through the Panama Canal. A two-front war could be
sustained only by secure access to two-ocean shipping lanes. Lüning's
activities in Havana—the principal port in the West Indies—could not
but be perceived as a threat to the security of Allied merchant and
naval vessels.

Taken as a case study, the account of the life and death of a German
spy in Havana during the early 1940s, moreover, serves to shed light on
facets of multiple levels of daily life in the practice of espionage during
World War II: how intelligence services went about the business of spying, and how counterintelligence services went about the business of
catching spies. Schoonover's compelling account of invisible ink, secret
mail drop-off sites, intercepted transatlantic correspondence and tapped
telegraph messages, secret rendezvous and illicit liaisons, all conducted
in the guise of the mundane and ordinary comings and goings of everyday life, provides palpable corroboration of the aphorism that things are
never quite what they seem to be.

The detailed texture of Schoonover's study provides insight into the
ways in which foreign counterintelligence services forged collaborative
practices, the ways in which they shared information and acted in con-
cert, the methods they used in common, and the occasions when they
worked at cross-purposes with each other. Contained within the Lüning
story is a fascinating account of the ways in and means with which the
Cubans (Servicio de Investigaciones de Actividades Enemigas), the

Americans (FBI), and the British (Secret Intelligence Service) worked together to disrupt the activities of a common foe.

The account of German wartime espionage also offers a deeper understanding of the workings of Cuban national politics and North American power, of trade and commerce, of the complexities of wartime relations in the Americas. Fulgencio Batista had only recently exchanged his military uniform of general for the civilian suit of president and relocated his office from army headquarters to the presidential palace. The power he had seized in a military coup in 1933 had been validated by national elections in 1940. These were the halcyon days of Cuban-U.S. wartime cooperation, a time when Batista won the admiration and sympathy of prominent U.S. officials that would serve him well a decade later when he seized power illegally in 1952, thereby setting the stage for the Cuban Revolution and Fidel Castro.

As often happens in the real-life stories of the men and women involved in the shadowy drama of international intrigue and shady deeds justified in the name of national interest—and especially during times of war—the Lüning affair had more than its fair share of elements of farce. The account of Ernest Hemingway clumsily supervising a private counterintelligence network of eighteen operatives is charming. The premature arrest of Lüning in Havana, with the intelligence services of three countries working at cross-purposes, is possessed of slapstick elements. There was, indeed, something of a hapless aspect to Lüning's activities in Havana. As Schoonover indicates, Germany's principal agent in Havana had not adequately mastered the most rudimentary basics of espionage. This did not, however, deter him from persisting in his functions as a spy. Inept in the preparation of secret ink, incompetent as a radio operator, he misplaced correspondence and missed drop boxes. He transmitted intelligence messages from a radio that did not work. From the distance of sixty-five years, the Lüning affair often takes on the appearance of something akin to a comic drama. Lüning's arrest, trial, and conviction were not entirely unexpected. His execution by firing squad in November 1942 had, as Schoonover indicates, less to do with his activities as a spy than with policy needs in Washington and political expedience in Havana. Lüning was the only German spy executed in Latin America.

Lüning's short-lived espionage misadventures in Havana are surely the stuff of a well-written novel. And in the case of Lüning, art has, indeed, been modeled on life. As the fates would have it, one of the intelligence analysts in England involved directly with the Lüning affair was Graham Greene. As Schoonover persuasively suggests, Greene's access to the details relating to the real-life drama of Lüning in Havana provided the writer with more than adequate material for the creation of James Wormold, the protagonist of the novel *Our Man in Havana.*

Then there is the story of Captain Mariano Faget y Díaz, one of the principal Cuban counterintelligence officers during World War II. Ten years later, when Fulgencio Batista again seized power by way of a military coup, he organized the Buró de Represión de Actividades Comunistas and appointed then Colonel Faget to head it, charged with the task of suppressing all opposition to the Batista government. After the triumph of the revolution in 1959, the Faget family fled the island, eventually settling in Miami. In 2000, Faget's son, Mariano Faget Jr., then the subdirector of the Immigration and Naturalization Service in Florida, was charged with and convicted of espionage for passing information to agents of the Cuban government.

The chronicle of Lüning in Havana also provides scholars an opportunity to study in detail the conduct of intelligence and counterintelligence operations during the early years of World War II. At first glance, it would have seemed reasonable to expect that the records pertaining to a previously obscure case of a German spy in Havana early in the war would have been opened and available to historians without restrictions, without limitations. But, alas, such was not the case, as Schoonover discovered early in the course of his research. Virtually all the U.S. records that he consulted were made available through the arduous and often exasperating procedures required under the terms of the Freedom of Information Act (FOIA). But the added cost, time, and energy necessitated by FOIA procedures did not produce access to the complete files bearing on the case. More than sixty-five years after the capture, trial, and execution of Lüning, vast portions of U.S. counterintelligence records pertaining to him remained classified. Hundreds of pages of documents were denied outright; hundreds of others were entirely or partly blacked out.

These procedures raise troubling questions for historians. Is it reasonable to expect that these denied documents will someday be made entirely available to scholars, without restrictions? Or must historians assume that existing records will remain beyond their scrutiny forever? If in the Lüning case, an affair of limited reach and marginal impact sixty-five years ago, vast quantities of records were denied—even under the FOIA—what type of access to records can historians reasonably expect to obtain in order to study the decisive and momentous developments of the twentieth century? And when?

Schoonover's study provides insight into both history and the process of researching and writing history. The narrow focus of his work implicates a wide scope of doing history. In the Lüning affair, Schoonover offers the reader history as a case study and a case study of writing history. Both offer cautionary tales.

Louis A. Pérez Jr.
University of North Carolina, Chapel Hill

Preface

On August 31, 1942, the combined efforts of British, Cuban, and U.S. counterintelligence captured a German Abwehr (intelligence) agent, A-3779, Heinz August Adolf Sirich Lüning (aliases: Lumann, Enrique Augusto Luni, Rafael Castillo, Manuel González, and numerous other code or cover names). U.S. and Cuban officials treated Lüning as the German master spy in the Americas. Presumably, he was one of the chief managers of the German espionage service in the Western Hemisphere. This Allied counterespionage success was represented (in self-serving exaggeration) as a first significant reversal of Allied misfortune. This story, veiled behind secrecy for over sixty years, is worth exploring because it forms a part of the campaign in the winter of 1942–1943 that halted the Axis successes. The Lüning story played out in the period when the Allies were able to push back from the edge of defeat.

The events and personalities involved in the story of Lüning offered intrigue, drama, and humor. Four objectives motivated me in this project. First, there was an intriguing, yet largely unknown, relation between German U-boats, U.S. and British security and intelligence activity in the Gulf of Mexico–Caribbean area, and U.S.-Cuban relations during World War II that needed to be told clearly (from declassified SIS files). (The U.S. Special Intelligence Service, or SIS—not to be confused with the British Secret Intelligence Service, commonly known as MI6—was an agency linked to the FBI.) The stakes were considerably higher than merely Allied shipping security in the Caribbean region. The Allies (the United States, the British Empire, France, the Soviet Union, China, and other, smaller countries) considered the east-west shipping routes through the Caribbean and the Panama Canal as necessary for their two-ocean, two-front war. They also used north-south shipping routes in and near the Caribbean to move essential strategic raw materials and food items to the United States and, in some cases, on to Britain, China, and the Soviet Union.

Second, I wanted to describe the life of a common intelligence field agent—his training and his activity. In this case, the German field agent told the story to U.S., Cuban, and British agents who conducted extensive research to verify and amplify his version. This story differed then from the numerous upper-echelon Abwehr officers whose published memoirs were unfiltered narratives of their successes and rare failures.

Third, I discovered how political figures from various countries treated, manipulated, and twisted a simple intelligence agent's story for their personal benefit. The pursuit, capture, and execution of Lüning allowed specific U.S. and Cuban officials to win praise, rewards, and influence, even when they had little role in tracking him down.

And, fourth, I was intrigued with a novelist-spy's vision of what a specific field agent might do. In this case, the novelist had some counterespionage background as a field agent and also as an agent handler for Britain's MI6. There seemed to be a link between the real field agent Lüning and Graham Greene's fictional field agent James Wormold in *Our Man in Havana.* I found the link in the startling parallels between the activities of the two spies. Although Lüning has been largely forgotten by history, he may live on, unbeknownst to readers, in one of the most popular espionage novels of all time.

For different reasons, finding the Abwehr (the German foreign intelligence agency) agent in Cuba was not simple in 1942, nor had it become any easier in 2002 when I began a four-year quest to obtain FBI material on Heinz August Lüning. In 1942, the Allied agents had Lüning's secret ink writings but could not find the writer; sixty years later, I knew the writer-agent but could not easily get to see the written FBI material about his activity and arrest. Lüning entered Cuba on September 29, 1941. After eleven months of routine and unsuccessful spying, he was arrested on the morning of August 31, 1942.

At the end of World War II, Theodore Koop, the assistant to Byron Price, the director of the Office of Censorship, recalled Lüning as "a grave threat to the United Nations [the Allied nations, not the postwar international government]."[1] Koop wrote a book in 1946, *Weapon of Silence*, that exaggerated and distorted Lüning's operations into a primary challenge to U.S. counterintelligence during World War II. Tellingly, Koop never offered a single specific piece of valuable information from Lüning's intercepted messages to illustrate his importance as an agent. In 1946, Mary Knight, a secretary to Byron Price, also told about intercepted cables, secret ink messages, and Lüning's radio contact (known to the Office of Censorship to be nonexistent) with U-boats. She implied that the U.S. censors did the work.[2] Koop, Price, and Knight publicly supported the same theme. In fact, British censors intercepted Lüning's secret ink messages, and Lüning never radioed while in the Americas. The reality of intelligence and counterintelligence in the 1930s and early 1940s was routinely less romantic than Koop's, Price's, and Knight's images suggested. In the immediate postwar years, all three distorted Lüning's part in his story. Still, in 1942, Axis espionage and U-boat activity posed a potentially very serious danger to the Allied war effort.

Since the records of Lüning's activity and his capture and interrogation seemed sparse at first, I suspected that this study would produce only an article summarizing the modest amount we know about the case. The original idea of a small to mid-sized book was resurrected when a shot-in-the-dark Freedom of Information Act request in late 2001 for FBI headquarters' materials on Heinz August Lüning revealed a large file—four thousand pages. Two fast-track requests brought me about a thousand detailed, informative, and interesting pages. A third request for the remaining materials that looked interesting and useful in this extensive collection took two and a half years to obtain approval. Work on the project was burdened by antiquated, self-serving rules guarding these old records. Although Lüning had died over sixty years earlier and everyone involved in the case is dead or at least eighty-five years old, much of the material is still kept secret.

Lüning's story was subject to spin, manipulation, and distortion. Various participants sought to gain advantage from his capture and death. Their conduct had less to do with his actions and more to do with the real and perceived success of German and other Axis land and sea campaigns classes for one day and gave a marvelous (and well-attended and well-received) talk on Cuban cultural ties to the United States in the 1950s. During the day, he researched the university's archives on U.S. sugar interests with regard to Cuba in the 1950s. At night, we wandered mentally through U.S. foreign relations with Latin America, Cuban history, and the project I was then engaged in, which became *Uncle Sam's War of 1898 and the Origins of Globalization* (University Press of Kentucky, 2003). After over three decades examining U.S. and European relations with Mexico and Central America, I had my attention directed by Lou to Cuba and the Caribbean.

At one of these evening talks, Lou recalled reading many Cuban newspaper and magazine stories about a German spy—Heinz August Lüning, although he did not recall the name—who was uncovered, captured, and executed in Havana in 1942. Since I worked in German as well as Spanish and English, Lou suggested this as a potentially interesting topic (he mentioned the likelihood of making the *New York Times* best-seller list, near-certain movie rights, and years of large royalty checks to grab my attention). From his vast memory, he recalled stories about loose canaries in Lüning's room to protect him from having to open the door to an unexpected visitor, a prostitute–bar girl who formed a close relationship with him, many aliases and cover names, and the only execution (by firing squad) of an espionage agent in Cuban history, at least until that time.

A quick survey of the printed material on German World War II espionage in Cuba and Latin America uncovered a few brief items on Lüning and his capture. The prospects for this story were intriguing. Within ten weeks, I had mined the U.S. Justice Department, the Military Intelligence Division, the State Department, and some miscellaneous materials in the National Archives at College Park, the German Military Archives in Freiburg (it houses the records of the Abwehr [or Amt Ausland/Abwehr des Oberkommandos der Wehrmacht, OKW (Supreme Command of the Armed Forces)], the German intelligence and counterintelligence agency), and the Auswärtiges Amt [Foreign Ministry] in Berlin. Soon I added numerous items from Cuban newspapers and magazines and the *New York Times*. Within six months, I had a modest amount of material, and I was hooked. During the research, I discovered that, as interesting as Lüning's personal story was, his detection, arrest, and execution had a greater importance in World War II history.

This modest volume required a large group of helpers. The background search drew on the staffs of the University of Louisiana at Lafayette's Dupré Library, the Library of Congress Reading Room, the Staatsbibliothek in Berlin, the British Library, and the University of North Carolina (Chapel Hill), Duke University, Cornell University, and University of Erlangen-Nuremberg libraries. Since destruction of records and excessive secrecy burdened the search for Lüning's path, I called on the staffs of the National Archives (Washington, D.C.), the FBI Headquarters' FOIA section, the Militärarchiv in Freiburg, Germany, the Auswärtiges Amt in Berlin, the Staatsarchiv Hamburg, and the Public Records Office/National Archives, Kew Gardens, London, to help piece together the story. Friederike van der Linde of the Standesamt [Civil Registry] Bremen-Mitte, Katrin Urbin of the Standesamt Hamburg (Eimsbüttel), Lars Worgull of the Staatsarchiv Bremen, Karen Kloss of the Cook County Clerk of Court's Office in Chicago, Maura Rogan of the Winnetka Historical Society (Winnetka, Ill.), and Amy Rupert of Rensselaer Polytechnic Institute, Troy, New York, located material on the Lüning family and the Bartholomae (Lüning's wife's) family for me. Petra Bendel, the head of the Zentralinstitut für Regionalforschung of the University of Erlangen–Nuremberg, offered me a home away from home. Dr. med. Luiz C. DeAraujo nursed some sick photographs back to life for me. Over the past three-plus decades, Dr. med. Ulf Garmsen and his wife, Sabine, have always welcomed me into the Hamburg area. My colleague Enrique Rodríguez (his grandfather died on a vessel sunk by a German submarine) in Havana supplied information and photographs.

Graham Greene's novel *Our Man in Havana* probably drew on the Lüning story. Greene's books are everywhere, but the principal collections of the papers of this alleged "anti-American" are in Boston College, Georgetown University, and the University of Texas, Austin. The staffs of these Greene collections all helped me review the materials they held. One unexpected joy of this project came from the realization that I had to read about Greene and to read or reread his autobiographies, novels, and stories. Like the spy he was, perhaps for decades, Greene has stealthily entered the lives of many in the world over the past eight decades. My Norwegian (Scandinavian) ancestry assures me that he deserves some belated recognition from the Swedish Nobel Prize Committee for Literature for its oversight.

Of course, as with all my scribbling, I turned to others for advice, to test my ideas, to help clarify my language. As the dedication indicates, Louis Pérez and Walter LaFeber have inspired and aided this work. Both read an advance draft closely and with benefit to my manuscript. I owe them the large personal debt that friendships produce. My good friend Max Paul Friedman read an advance draft carefully and offered me numerous and valuable suggestions to improve the organization and style of the book. I am fortunate in his friendship. Max and I share a brotherhood—we both married Berlin girls. Other friends have read the manuscript and helped me make it better: Richard Frankel, Thomas Aiello, and Ralph Lee Woodward. My wife, Ebba Schoonover, has heard and read more about Heinz Lüning than any woman except Lüning's wife, Helga. This time, I believe Ebba's labor was rewarded with a story full of intrigue, irony, satire, humor, and incredible twists. Ebba also took the photographs of buildings in Bremen and Hamburg relevant to Lüning's life. Steve Wrinn was long eager to acquire this project, even when it was only a set of ideas in my mind. He sensed with enthusiasm the possibilities. I am glad that I ended up with him, Anne Dean Watkins, Melinda Wirkus, William McKay, and Joseph Brown to complete this project. I hope it is as successful as Louis Pérez and Steve Wrinn foresaw.

Acronyms/Glossary

AA, Auswärtiges Amt = German Foreign Ministry
Abwehr = German counterintelligence, intelligence
Abwehrabteilung = German Defense Bureau
AO, Auslandsorganisation = German Nazi Party Foreign Bureau
AST, *Abwehrstelle* = German major intelligence station
BIC = British Imperial Censorship
BSC = British Security Coordination
CIAA = Office of Coordination of Inter-American Affairs
COI = British Coordinator of Operations Intelligence
FBI = Federal Bureau of Investigation
FDR = Franklin Delano Roosevelt
Falange = Spanish fascist party
Gestapo, Geheime Staatspolizei = German State Secret Police
ISOS = British Intelligence Section, Oliver Strachey
MID = Military Intelligence Division
MI6 = British counterintelligence (also Secret Intelligence Service)
Nazi, Nationalsozialistische Deutsche Arbeiterpartei = German
    National Socialist Workers' Party
NEST, *Nebenstelle* = German branch station of AST
OKW, Oberkommando der Wehrmacht = German Supreme Command
    of the Armed Forces
ONI = Office of Naval Intelligence
OSS = Office of Strategic Services
PAAA, Politisches Archiv des Auswärtigen Amts = German Political
    Archive of the Foreign Ministry

RSHA, Reichssicherheitshauptamt = German State Central Security
  Bureau
Reichswehrministerium = German National Defense Ministry
SD, Sicherheitsdienst = German Security Service
Section V = British MI6 unit responsible for counterintelligence
SIS = Special Intelligence Service (FBI overseas)
SOE = British Special Operations Executive
SS, Schutzstaffel = German elite defense corps of the Nazi Party
TR = Theodore Roosevelt
Wehrkreis = German military district

Hitler's Man in Havana

Pushed to the Edge of Defeat in 1942

The Lüning episode had characteristics of the contemporary "weapons of mass destruction" phenomenon. It was seized as an opportunity to manipulate opinion and to produce beneficial rewards and consequences for these manipulators. Political, military, and counterespionage leaders sought praise, prestige, and power for their institutions. It is not possible to accurately assess the significance of the Lüning episode without recalling the increasingly threatening and ultimately violent history around the world from 1931 until the U.S. entry into World War II after December 7, 1941. Rising tension and overt hostility marked East Asia, North Africa, and Europe in these years.

In Asia, specifically in places where Asian and Western interests met, a brutal, long-term conflict simmered between China (with support from the United States and Britain) and Japan. After decades of competition for greater influence and access to that region's land, resources, and labor forces, the Western nations watched in September 1931 when the Japanese army, following a series of incidents, clashed with Chinese troops in Manchuria. Despite efforts to negotiate the differences between the Chinese and the Japanese governments, the Japanese army argued for further conflict. This conflict alternated between simmering and boiling for the next fourteen years.

In January 1932, the Japanese army invaded Shanghai. Hard fighting and minor clashes followed, especially near Shanghai and along the

3

Manchurian border with China, until a larger violent incident occurred between Chinese and Japanese troops at the Marco Polo Bridge on July 7, 1937. In late 1938, the Chinese Nationalist leader Jiang Jie-shi (pre-Pingying form, Chiang Kai-shek) retreated into China's interior, one thousand miles up the Yangzi (Yangtze) River, at Chongqing (Chung-king). This confrontation sharpened in mid-1939 when Chinese soldiers trapped about three hundred Japanese troops (part of the embassy guard returning to Beijing [Peking]) in a devastating cross fire. For the next two years, the war in China became incredibly brutal and cruel.

The Chinese defeats increased in 1939 and 1940. The record of defeats also spread to the future Allied powers in Europe and the Mediterranean. After the Axis powers (Germany and Italy) tested their military weapons and tactics in Spain and North Africa, Germany initiated the major conflict of the twentieth century on September 1, 1939. It overran Poland. In 1940, the German military conquered Norway, Denmark, the Netherlands, Belgium, and France before launching a massive air assault on Great Britain—the Battle of Britain. The few German submarines available for service began a devastating attack on the shipping of Britain and its allies. Italy joined in the conflict with attacks on French and British Somaliland, Egypt, and Greece. In Asia, the Japanese created a puppet Chinese government in Nanjing (Nanking) and compelled the British to close the Burma Road in order to isolate Jiang Jie-shi. The Japanese hoped to compel him to surrender or negotiate from weakness.

After two years of Axis advances and Allied surrenders or retreats, matters turned worse in 1941. The German military gained control of Yugoslavia and Greece and pushed the British imperial forces in North Africa back beyond the border of Egypt, to within several hours of Cairo, the Nile, and the Suez Canal. In June 1941, the German army destroyed large parts of the Soviet Union's land forces and drove the remainder back to the outskirts of Moscow and Leningrad and into the Ukraine. However, Moscow and Leningrad did not fall, and the German army retreated. An increased number of German submarines, aided by a few Italian ones, conducted destructive campaigns on the shipping of Britain and its allies in the Mediterranean Sea and the Atlantic Ocean (about 4.3 million tons of Allied merchant vessels, or a quarter of all Allied losses during World

War II [1939–1945] in all theaters to all forms of attack). In 1941, German U-boats threatened the survival of the United Kingdom. They sank more ship tonnage than the British and their allies built or acquired.

Meanwhile, the Japanese military advanced south through Indo-China during 1941. It controlled the whole area by late 1941. The final major act of 1941 was the Japanese air assault on Pearl Harbor. Simultaneously, the Japanese military attacked the Philippines, Hong Kong, and Malaysia. The nations of the world quickly activated their respective alliance structures—the Axis powers and the Allies.

The danger to the Allied nations was magnified in 1942 as the upward curve of Allied losses soared. The year 1942 was the most ominous in World War II for the Allied alliance. The Allies stood on the edge of defeat. Their strategic losses grew almost exponentially. In the Asian-Pacific arena, Japanese forces seized Burma, Singapore, Dutch Indonesia, the Philippines, and most of the islands of the western, southern, and central Pacific and conducted scouting activity on Australia's north coast. In 1942, the German military returned to its attack on the Soviet Union. It revitalized its siege of Leningrad, again approached Moscow, and moved through all of the Ukraine to capture Stalingrad on the Volga River in the southeast. Almost all of the European Soviet Union was under German domination.

In 1942, German U-boats sank almost double the tonnage of Allied ships they had destroyed in 1941. These shipping losses were so severe that Winston Churchill periodically halted the flow of Lend-Lease supplies to the Soviet Union. Of course, Josef Stalin became deeply angered. Churchill and U.S. leaders recognized that, if the Soviets were defeated or made peace with Germany, there would be extremely serious consequences for the British Isles. U.S. planners called a Soviet collapse a "catastrophe" that would place the United States in a "desperate" situation.[1] However, it was necessary to stifle German U-boats in order to keep the Soviet Union engaged with the German military. Sinking the U-boats, driving them from the oceans, or severely hampering their activity lay at the heart of a successful Lend-Lease program to sustain the Soviet army's engagement of between 80 and 90 percent of German military forces. The buildup of U.S. forces in the Mediterranean and Northern European theaters depended on dominating the U-boats. In

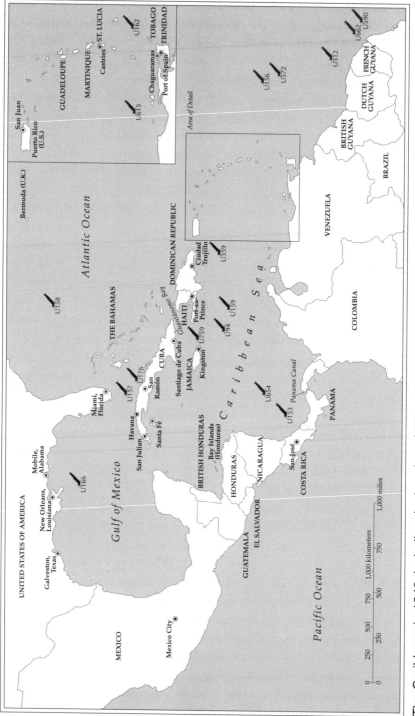

The Caribbean in 1942, including the location of U-boat losses.

North Africa, the German-led forces continued to threaten British control of Egypt and the Suez Canal. The potential danger from the U-boats lent Lüning and his alleged spy network significance.

As serious as these losses were, the Allied leaders faced other challenges. The Allied powers had become even more dependent on the manpower and resources of the fractured remains of their empires. Drawing on these widely scattered resources required ever-increasing use of international sea-lanes. However, that use was dramatically challenged by Axis submarines. In 1942, destruction of Allied vessels shot up to 7.8 million tons, or about 43 percent of all Allied losses in the war. The threat to the Allied capacity to conduct war was real.

Allied leaders were rightly concerned about German U-boats and Axis espionage in the Gulf–Caribbean–Central American isthmus region. Axis espionage and submarines endangered Allied survival. Just in the greater Caribbean, Axis submarines sank over 3 million tons of Allied shipping (over six hundred vessels) in a ten-month period, February–November 1942. Thus, in ten months in the tiny but strategically valuable space of the Caribbean, the Axis U-boats sank ship tonnage equal to 17.5 percent of all Allied losses throughout the war on all the seas and oceans. This rate of loss was dangerous for the Allied survival. In addition, losses on these shipping routes seriously threatened the Allied ability to conduct a strategic, two-ocean war against the German and Italian forces in Europe and North Africa and the Japanese military in the Pacific and Asia. The Allies needed to maintain the strategic movement of ships, manpower, and supplies through the Panama Canal, and the U.S. government needed to secure the flow of vital raw materials from South America across the Caribbean to the United States. Cargo traffic in the Caribbean included large quantities of aviation fuel, almost all the aluminum used to construct airplanes in the United States, and coffee and sugar for the K rations that fed the U.S. military. Stifling U-boat activity would greatly influence the ability of the U.S. war industries to supply Lend-Lease aid to its allies in Europe and Asia. The Allied intelligence agents believed that the Axis submarine campaign depended on a well-functioning German intelligence organization in the Americas.

Heinz August Lüning in the door to his jail cell. Courtesy *Carteles* and *True Detective* magazines.

► 1 ◄

A Troubled Life

In September 1942, the recently captured Nazi Abwehr agent in Havana Heinz August Lüning was considered a master spy and the most important spy captured in the Western Hemisphere. Initially, the FBI-SIS suspected that this Nazi headed a spy network that was instrumental in German U-boat successes in the Caribbean and the Gulf of Mexico. This perception made Lüning a serious threat to the Allied campaigns in Europe, North Africa, and the Pacific and to the Allied ability to draw on the foodstuff, refined petroleum, and minerals required to fight the war effectively.

Over the next two years, the FBI-SIS undertook to investigate every person, not just in Cuba but also in the Americas, who had any relationship to Lüning. Since he had married his stepsister (from a prominent Chicago family), agents interviewed or conducted surveillance of relatives from his and his wife's families as well as people around his extended family. This wide net included Fred Astaire and Douglas Fairbanks Jr. Until mid-1945, agents interviewed people in Cuba, the United States, the Dominican Republic, Honduras, Mexico, Argentina, and Chile and sought information from U.S. officials in other American nations in their pursuit of an espionage network with Lüning at the center. The FBI-SIS persisted because high-ranking U.S. officials had alleged his central role in Nazi intelligence. The FBI-SIS, British MI6, and Cuban espionage agencies never found any evidence to indicate that Lüning was doing vital work. His life as a spy was routine and uninteresting (in terms of the work), with a touch of incompetence.

Lüning's youth and upbringing did not suggest a career as a spy. He was born in Bremen on March 28, 1911, to a German father (Stephan August Lüning, b. December 12, 1876, Bremen) and an Italian mother (Elise Adelheit Duncker, Stephan's second wife). His life followed a restless path. Heinz was orphaned young. Although he had gained entrance to a gymnasium (the secondary education required to attend a university in Germany), he was not promoted in the spring of 1924 (possibly due in part to the serious illness of his mother). The next year shattered his life. His beloved mother died on December 21, 1924, and, at the same time, he was set to fail the class again. A second failure meant a permanent dismissal from the school. Instead, he withdrew. His father found him a place at the Pädagogium Pestalozzi, a private school, approximately equivalent to a midlevel secondary school—a *Realschule*. He would not be allowed to study at the university and would need to find a position in business.[1]

An additional shock struck Heinz five years later. His father committed suicide on November 10, 1929. His father and an uncle, Gustav Adolf Lüning (b. December 17, 1878, Bremen; d. November 28, 1945, Hamburg), had shared a tobacco-importation business. For a year and a half after his father died, Heinz visited his uncle and aunt in Hamburg, but he lived with his father's third wife, Marie Ella (maiden name Stolte). In early 1931, he moved permanently to Hamburg. Gustav, a rather wealthy Hamburg import-export and tobacco merchant, and his wife, Olga Sophie Bartholomae (b. June 1884, Winnetka, Ill.; d. June 6, 1961, Hamburg), a German American from Chicago, who was in her second marriage (previously she was a Magdeburg), adopted Heinz. In Hamburg, he attended a commercial school for a year. Then he worked for two and a half years as a merchant apprentice for Albert Schilling, an American businessman and acquaintance of Gustav's, at the import firm of Clasen Berger and Company.[2]

Five years after Heinz moved to Hamburg, the Lüning family confronted embarrassment. Heinz had impregnated his stepsister Helga. In April 1936, Heinz traveled to New York City with his fiancée (stepsister), Helga Barbara Magdeburg (b. 1909; d. Hamburg?), the daughter of his

German cities relevant to Lüning's life.

aunt Olga by her first marriage. The Hamburg elite family of Gustav and Olga Lüning had acted to shield the family name and reputation when it sent the young couple to distant New York City for a wedding. The couple married in Manhattan—five thousand miles from Hamburg— on May 8, 1936. Family relations became complicated. Olga became Heinz's aunt, stepmother, and mother-in-law. Helga was his stepsister, cousin, and wife. The bridal pair stayed in the Manhattan apartment of Philip Bartholomae (b. July 3, 1880, Winnetka, IL; d. January 5, 1947, Winnetka), Olga's brother. He was a playwright of some renown on Broadway between 1911 and 1926.[3]

Once married, Gustav, who owned the Dominican Tobacco Company, sent Heinz to Santo Domingo twice to find suitable work for him in a family business, to obtain knowledge of tobacco, and to learn Spanish. Several weeks after the marriage, Heinz headed to Santo Domingo on business before returning to Hamburg. Uncle Gustav had refused funds for Helga to travel with Heinz; there was no reward for embarrassing the family. Helga returned to Hamburg in the company of Uncle Philip. Six months after the wedding, on November 16, 1936, she gave birth to a son, Adolf Bartholomae Lüning (d. December 6, 1997, Hamburg). Under such circumstances, Gustav tried diligently to find a suitable place for Heinz in his various businesses. After three months in the Dominican Republic, Heinz returned to Hamburg.[4]

In early 1943, Philip Bartholomae told FBI agents a different story about the marriage and Heinz's relationship to the Bartholomae family. Seven years after the event, Philip, suffering mental disease from tertiary syphilis, recalled his version of the Heinz-Helga wedding. In his recollection, Heinz was "no good at all in business" and the family was unhappy with the forced marriage. He contended that Heinz had been sent to Latin America to separate the couple and to allow for the possible breakup of the marriage.[5]

Whether to separate Lüning from Helga or to prepare him to support his family, the uncle sent him to the Dominican Republic again in April 1937. After five more months of Spanish and tobacco training, he went to New York City for three months to improve his English. While in Santo Domingo, Heinz completed the paperwork to obtain residency in Santo Domingo. He did not wish to return to Germany, but the German government blocked funds for Helga (and their infant son) to travel to New York in 1937. Lüning returned after his uncle promised him passage back to the Americas. So Heinz Lüning, modestly educated, an indifferent worker, and a fun-loving young man (he pursued wine, women, and song, according to his friends), learned some Spanish and English but apparently little about tobacco.[6]

Later, after Lüning's capture, the SIS interviewed seven people from the Dominican Republic who knew Lüning in 1936 and 1937. The information from these wartime interviews, regarding distant prewar conduct, requires cautious use. The circumstances of the war and Lüning's arrest probably heightened memories of suspicion and increased the likelihood of interlinking past and present. For example, one interviewee noted that Lüning and his Dominican friends suspiciously "spent many evenings together in deep conversation." Some observers alleged that Lüning was an intimate friend of Fritz Hartmann's, an "undesirable alien deportee" who, according to the SIS interrogator, was believed to be in an internment camp in Texas in 1943. Lüning also met Paul Thumb, a former German military officer who did scientific and naturalist work in the Dominican Republic and Cuba. Thumb visited the Dominican Republic repeatedly in the mid- and late 1930s. The FBI-SIS considered him an "inspector of the Gestapo and a Nazi party member of some consequence." He eventually departed to an uncertain location. Later, U.S. government officials failed to locate him.[7]

Not surprisingly, Lüning met other Germans during his visits to the Dominican Republic. One of Lüning's best friends there was Ernest Gallus, supposedly a German Jewish refugee. The two often sat in Duarte Park in the evening, according to one interviewee, "where they used to converse at great length, but in low tones so that they were unable to be overheard." U.S. investigators discovered—although the value of the discovery is unclear—that Gallus's son, Ernest Jr., was a great friend of Walter Kahn's, who had been under FBI surveillance for some time.[8] So the FBI-SIS learned that Lüning knew someone (supposedly Jewish) whose son had a friend whom the FBI was watching. The SIS interrogators pursued every suspicion, even those by association.

After Lüning's execution, a German national who was a prewar resident of the Dominican Republic offered his perspective on his friend Lüning. One has to keep in mind that memory is an imperfect tool. This person, after consulting other acquaintances of Lüning's in the Dominican Republic, claimed erroneously to have traveled with Lüning to Trujillo, the Dominican Republic, on the passenger ship *Claus Horn* in early 1937 (possible). During the twenty-four days on the ship, they became friends "as Lüning was what is called a good chap; he liked a drink, was generous, and liked a joke even at his own expense." This source also claimed erroneously that Lüning offered a big fiesta when a cable arrived announcing the birth of his first child (impossible). Lüning's only child was born in November 1936.[9]

This German national recalled time with Lüning in the Dominican Republic: "We always spent an evening together, having a good time with girls and drink." In his judgment: "Lüning was, regarding his high school education, from a wealthy family; much traveled; but mentally a weakling. I never heard an intelligent word or phrase from him. He had no kind of general knowledge of history, literature, art, geography, or anything else. He had no political convictions, so he wasn't a Nazi either. I still remember some jokes of the hundreds he told about the Nazis. . . . The only thing he was looking for was girls, girls, and more girls, together with drinks. . . . Although he bought big quantities of tobacco, he didn't know a bit about the leaf. There are people who doubt if he could distinguish between a tobacco leaf and a cabbage leaf. However, he had some good fellows working for him." And this informant added: "His Spanish was awfully bad; he improved it a bit, but I never heard him speak even a fairly good Spanish." But the Guatemalan Lola Ardela de Tejar, who tutored Lüning in Hamburg for several years, claimed that he ultimately spoke a respectable Spanish.[10]

An SIS agent, reviewing the statements from the seven people interviewed in the Dominican Republic, arrived at a harsh conclusion. He surmised that Lüning was "a degenerate sent to the Dominican Republic by a wealthy uncle to get him out of Germany. In the Dominican Republic, subject [Lüning] bought tobacco and chased women." Still, while he bought tobacco, his "main activity was in running around with women."[11] Despite his conduct in the Dominican Republic, Lüning remained, oddly but strongly, committed to his family—wife, child, and the uncle and aunt who had adopted him.

If Lüning could arrange to move his family out of Germany, he could look to well-to-do family and in-laws in Milwaukee, Chicago, and Beverly Hills, California, for support. In 1942, a rumor suggested that he drew on the fortune of his wife's family while in Cuba. The FBI investigation of the family of Olga Bartholomae revealed fascinating background stories. Olga's father, George Bartholomae (b. 1851, Heidelberg; d. Chicago), a brewer who immigrated from the area around Heidelberg in July

1870 and became a successful brewer and beer importer in the Chicago area, married Emma Lassig (b. 1858) on September 12, 1878. Emma's father was Moritz Lassig (b. 1831, Rochlitz, Saxony, Germany; d. January 7, 1902, Chicago), the well-to-do president of the Lassig Bridge and Iron Works Company. The American Bridge Company of Chicago acquired Lassig Bridge prior to becoming a chief component of U.S. Steel on its creation by J. P. Morgan and Andrew Carnegie in 1901. American Bridge was valued at $70 million for the merger.[12]

Thus, the four children of George and Emma stood to inherit appreciable wealth from the brewery business and from the sale of Moritz's Lassig Bridge and Iron Works. Olga and Philip had two sisters, Ida (b. 1883, Chicago?; d. Munich?) and Ella (b. January 5, 1888, Winnetka, IL; d. May 1967, Winnetka). Ella never married and lived in Chicago. Heinz apparently never met her; he had not accepted an invitation to visit Chicago in 1937. Ida, like her siblings, had been educated for several years in Germany, near the family estate outside Heidelberg. Members of the family returned to Germany quite frequently. Ida, like Olga, settled in Germany, where she married a Baron von Stengel, who died before World War II. The von Stengels had four daughters. During and after the war the widow lived in Munich.[13]

Of the American relatives, Heinz knew Philip best. The relationship was not close, however. The FBI had mistakenly concluded that Philip's hosting of the wedding and the honeymoon implied a close relationship. Actually, Philip hosted the wedding as a favor to his sister. Still, his success in the New York theater world created a plausible basis for suspecting financial support for Heinz when he became a spy in Havana. The tale of Philip is bizarre. He finished his schooling in Germany near Heidelberg (apparently with an *Abitur*, the German secondary diploma required for university study) and entered Heidelberg University for a year. On returning home, in 1899, Philip "Dolly" (his college nickname) Bartholomae began studying civil engineering at Rensselaer Polytechnic Institute in Troy, New York. The institute's yearbook noted, most likely with humor, that, in his first week in Troy, he was engaged to five young ladies and continued on that path afterward. Oddly, he and his sister Ella both died unmarried. Years later, Fred Astaire, a longtime acquaintance of Philip's, pondered whether Philip had homosexual tendencies. Philip's senior yearbook contained his words of wisdom (or humor): "I would rather be handsome than President." In his third year at Rensselaer (1901–1902), his grandfather Lassig died. Since Philip preferred the theater to engineering, he left Rensselaer at the end of 1902 in the middle of his senior year and sought a career in New York City.[14]

Philip's parents refused to support his theatrical ambitions, so he struggled. For a while he worked at Brentano's Book Store in New York City. Occasionally, he wrote sketches for vaudeville. As a small sign of his potential, he sold one to the legendary Sarah Bernhardt that became part of her show for a season. Then, after eight years of struggle, he became a strange "overnight" success when his first play, *Over Night*, was a hit in early 1911 with 160 performances. His career boomed.[15]

Between 1911 and 1926, Philip wrote or cowrote fifteen theater productions that reached Broadway. At some point he received a major inheritance—the theater press referred to him as a "millionaire-producer" before World War I. Three of his comedies played on Broadway, but his theatrical reputation and his bank account swelled from contributing to the story line, and occasionally some lyrics, for twelve Broadway musical productions. He worked with premier people in premier theaters. Between 1913 and 1926, he joined Sigmund Romberg, Jerome Kern, Guy Bolton, John Boles, Fred and Adele Astaire, and others for productions at the Lyric, J. J. Shubert, Princess, Booth, Casino, and other theaters. Among his more successful shows were *Little Miss Brown* (1912, 84 performances), *Girl O' Mine* (1914, 255 performances; revived, 1918, 48 performances), a musical version of *Over Night* called *Very Good, Eddie* (1915, 341 performances; revived, 1975–1976, 307 performances), *Over the Top* (1917, 78 performances), *Tangerine* (1921, 361 performances), and *Kitty's Kisses* (1926, 170 performances). Most of these shows had touring companies. *Very Good, Eddie* and *Little Miss Brown* each had two.[16]

Several of Philip's shows were performed abroad. In 1916, a London West End production of *Very Good, Eddie* lasted only a month. A production developed in Australia ran for fifteen weeks in Sydney and Melbourne. The 1975 Broadway revival of *Very Good, Eddie* ran for over four hundred performances in London's West End.

Philip worked with John Murray Anderson and A. Baldwin Sloane on the *Greenwich Village Follies of 1919* (232 performances). Like its model, the Ziegfeld Follies, the Greenwich Village Follies became an annual review on Broadway. For his most successful musical, Philip and Guy Bolton wrote the book for Jerome Kern's music in *Very Good, Eddie*. This musical was a highly regarded Princess Theater show. The eminent theater historian Gerald Boardman called it "the mold out of which powered a half-century of American musical comedy." In his autobiography, Richard Rodgers claimed that *Very Good, Eddie*, which he saw numerous times, strongly influenced his decision to write musicals. In late 1917, Philip had another high point. He and Harold Atteridge wrote the story and lyrics for *Over the Top*, a Sigmund Romberg and Hermann Timberg musical. This production gave Fred and Adele Astaire their first Broadway break. For a time, Fred Astaire shared Philip's living quarters. Philip's success allowed him to join the highly exclusive Lamb's Club.[17]

Not long after they worked together, the careers of Philip Bartholomae and Fred Astaire diverged. Astaire began a star-studded career in Hollywood. Philip's career declined after the mid-1920s. Sometime in the late 1920s, Philip was diagnosed with hereditary tertiary syphilis. He began treatment in the United States, but, in April 1930, he traveled to Germany for treatment. He responded well but never regained his artistic talent. About 1940, he moved to Beverly Hills, California, and became a scriptwriter for Metro Goldwyn Mayer. Renewed success eluded him. He lived on inheritances from his family and the income from his own fifteen years of success on Broadway and elsewhere.[18]

The FBI investigated whether Philip had supplied funds to Lüning or engaged in possible espionage activity for the Nazis. Sixteen years after his last Broadway success, the FBI interviewed some of Philip's acquaintances from his Broadway days regarding the playwright's loyalty and his possible espionage ties to Lüning. Agents monitored Philip's mail for sixty days but found nothing incriminating. Then they interviewed numerous people, including Fred Astaire, apparently Douglas Fairbanks Jr., John Boles, and the FBI agent Edward Martin Lane, a former theater actor who had used Philip Bartholomae as a reference when he applied to the FBI. Fred Astaire considered Philip a bit unbalanced, but he never heard him say anything favorable about the Axis or un-American. Finally, FBI agents interviewed Philip on several occasions. He claimed that he met Lüning only twice: once when his niece Helga and Heinz Lüning got married and then, later, in Hamburg during Philip's 1936 trip to Germany to view some of the Olympics (Heinz went to Santo Domingo for three months after his marriage and returned in the early fall of 1936). Philip volunteered that Lüning "was very stupid and bombastic." The FBI found no evidence that Philip had pro-Axis sympathies. To the contrary, he had volunteered his services in World War I and II to the U.S. government, to British Emergency Relief, and to the USO.[19]

In addition to the Chicago Bartholomaes, Heinz had a paternal uncle, Julius John Adolf Lüning (b. August 17, 1873, Bremen; d. 1947, Milwaukee), who had lived briefly in Chicago at the turn of the century and then for four decades in Milwaukee. Among the U.S. relatives, in addition to Olga, Heinz Lüning had had personal contact with his uncle Philip but only indirect contact with his uncle Julius Lüning and his aunts Ella and Ida Bartholomae. Still, the FBI interviewed and investigated all the relatives living in the United States during World War II. There was no indication of espionage or conduct favorable to the Axis powers on the part of any relative living in the United States.[20]

The evidence also indicated that Heinz Lüning disliked the Nazis. In the 1930s, he saw war coming and wished to avoid military service, in large part because he did not sympathize in any manner with the Nazis. Well-known for anti-Nazi jokes, Lüning was alienated from the Nazi Party, its leaders, and its programs. He expected to avoid military service until he could flee Hitler's Germany with his family. During his SIS interrogations, he expanded on his antiregime views. About 1930, he claimed, he had joined the Hamburger Sportverein [Sports Club], only to resign in 1934 because Nazi members came to dominate the association. The Hamburger Sportverein and the German Arbeiterfront [Workers' Front], an employee organization, were the only organizations he had joined in Germany. He denied any relationship with Nazi-led organizations. Other family members also opposed the Nazi movement. Uncle Gustav was anti-Nazi, and another uncle, a minister, was imprisoned on three occasions for anti-Nazi activities. Heinz confessed to one blemish. While in Santo Domingo in 1937, he had paid a $2 fee to the Nazi front leader to keep his name off a blacklist of businesses and to avoid difficulties with the German government. More revealing, in his view, in 1937, he had completed the paperwork for residency in Santo Domingo. In his mind, his family had remained behind "as hostages" in Hamburg during his second trip. Since he expected Nazi conduct to lead to war, Heinz assumed that his mother's Italian citizenship and his Dominican residency might keep him out of the German army.[21] At the very least, these conditions should confuse and delay the German bureaucrats.

While the developing tension between the Nazi-Axis alliance and the rest of the world disturbed Lüning, he also had to earn a living. In the late 1930s, he seemed headed for a career working for his uncle, who, in the meantime, had acquired a general merchandising export firm, B. Schoenfeld and Company. After sending Heinz to Santo Domingo twice to learn about tobacco, Uncle Gustav recognized his nephew's limitations. From 1937 to 1941, Lüning was a sales representative for the B. Schoenfeld general merchandising firm, not the Dominican Tobacco Company.[22] Since both Heinz and Helga were blood-related family members, Gustav strove to find a position that would keep Heinz's family in a materially comfortable situation.

In an ongoing effort to fit into the Lüning family's largest business, the Dominican Tobacco Company, Heinz continued to study Spanish in Hamburg with the tutor Lola Ardela de Tejar. Ardela, born in Guatemala in 1909 and educated in a Spanish convent, had married a German and moved to Germany. Four years later, her husband died. She returned to Guatemala but soon decamped for Germany when an affair in her homeland turned sour and potentially dangerous. To earn a living, she taught Spanish to Germans in Hamburg. In 1938, Lüning became a pupil and then a friend. Ardela was invited on several occasions to Uncle Gustav's residence, where Heinz lived with Helga, called "Mammy," and their son, Adolf, called "Hunky." Ardela found Lüning a restless individual who preferred Latins to Germans. Although his Spanish was not fluent, she considered him a good student. She recalled his complaints about the military atmosphere in Germany and his desire to leave the country.[23]

However, by late 1939, Germany was at war. In Hamburg, Lüning—who disliked Hitler's racist and militaristic pronouncements—abhorred the thought of military service.[24] Ardela confirmed that the German government denied Lüning passports for his family several times. To help him leave, she introduced him to Majín Herrera A., the Honduran consul, who sold black market passports. The price, ten thousand reichsmarks each (and Heinz needed three), was beyond Lüning's means. His uncle refused to advance him such a large sum. Lüning failed to negotiate a reduced price. His quest became dormant.[25] Later, Ardela suggested that he join the Abwehr as a convenient method for a Spanish-speaking German to find service abroad.[26] Lüning seized on this idea.

This idea also appealed to Uncle Gustav. A Hamburg acquaintance and attorney, Hans Joachim Koelln, had Abwehr contacts. In January 1941, about a month after Lüning stated his wishes to Koelln, a certain Alfred Hartmann (apparently an alias as there is no known relationship to the Fritz Hartmann in Santo Domingo) of the "Propaganda and Information Office" visited Lüning at the B. Schoenfeld firm. Then, in May 1941, Hartmann called Lüning to arrange a series of cloak-and-dagger meetings. At the first meeting, Hartmann inquired about Heinz's language skills and arranged a meeting the next day at his own office. Heinz, who spoke Spanish, Italian, and Portuguese and knew some English, was anxious to go to the Western Hemisphere. Hartmann mentioned service abroad and a Honduran passport. The Abwehr would support Heinz's travel abroad in exchange for information about trade, prices, and commerce. Lüning agreed even though no country or duty station was mentioned. At this time, Hartmann learned that Lüning had visited only Santo Domingo and the United States. He avoided Lüning's queries about taking his family with him on any assignment. Lüning was asked to return the next day for instruction. At this point, he was given the code name "Lumann." Lumann's training took place at the Abwehr academy in Hamburg.[27]

In the 1930s, Heinz had acquired limited skills as a merchant in tobacco and general merchandise. His future rested with his uncle's firms because he demonstrated little commercial ability. He saw a war coming and wished to avoid it, in part because he did not sympathize with the

Nazis. Later, the SIS was intrigued by Lüning's ability to avoid the draft in Germany during 1940 and 1941. Lüning mentioned several strategies. He used his mother's Italian citizenship and his residency papers from the Dominican Republic to cloud the issue. Still, his chief strategy was to flee Germany. That strategy was stymied when the German government denied him and his family exit permission and the Honduran consul demanded thirty thousand reichsmarks for three passports. He grasped Ardela's recommendation that he join the Abwehr, which needed agents in Latin America. In the end, Lüning accepted Abwehr service in the Caribbean to escape military service for the Nazi government.

2

The World
He Scarcely Knew

Despite being considered by several Allied officials the most important Nazi spy caught in Latin America during World War II, Heinz Lüning knew little about the region where he was to do his secret work and meet his end. Nor did he understand well the strategic security importance of Cuba and the greater Caribbean. He had visited New York City and Santo Domingo in 1936 and 1937 for family reasons, not out of curiosity and interest in Latin America. Even later, Heinz served the Abwehr, not out of special interest in Latin America but as an unexpected option to escape undesired military service for the Nazi state. He exhibited little interest in matters beyond his personal and family well-being. Initially, knowledge of Spanish became the vehicle for shielding the family name and escaping military service, but, in 1941, it led to his death. In this story, one ill-fated move led to another.

Although Heinz generally opposed war and violence, he probably did not reflect on the deeper historical currents that led to the war that ended his life. Serious reflection would have been inconsistent with his disinterest in knowledge and his carefree search for pleasure, as the seven acquaintances from Santo Domingo, his tutor Lola Ardela, and his own testimony during the SIS interviews suggested. Once the Hamburg AST (*Abwehrstelle*, the major intelligence station) decided to send

Heinz to Havana, the events of World War II, the history of the Caribbean, U.S. relations with the Caribbean, and the value of the Gulf of Mexico–Caribbean region for the strategy and conduct of World War II shaped his future. So did a variety of influences from past New World versus Old World conflicts.

The cataclysmic death, destruction, and social turmoil of World War II have burdened the explanatory capacity of historians. They do not consider World War II the product of particular short-term circumstance. To the contrary, they have rummaged through the prior decades or generations, if not centuries, to make sense of the massive destruction of human life and property. However, most of the search for causes has involved European racism and nationalism, Mediterranean affairs, or the consequences of European colonial and imperial ambitions. It seems helpful to look beyond nationalism—in its rational or irrational manifestations—and to contemplate the power of broad ideological and institutional forces (classical laissez-faire liberalism and technological-industrial mass production) rising first in the North Atlantic community and then spreading into the world to produce conflict.

Internationally, from the mid-nineteenth century to World War I, the leaders of the North Atlantic societies nudged these young, unstable, industrializing nations toward increased international competition and risk taking (colonialism, colonial wars and revolts, imperial acquisitions, social imperialism [achieving domestic objectives through international activity], and informal empire). New international forms developed to control economic factors: land, labor, raw materials, foodstuffs, consumer markets, and investment opportunities. The incorporation of new areas and economic factors into a global arrangement would, presumably, facilitate increased economic growth, social and political stability, well-being, and security. The leaders of North Atlantic countries, confronting the instability from the rapid and profound technological changes, juggled risk and reward as they sought foreign policies that responded to domestic and foreign events in a competitive framework. The friction from dramatic socioeconomic change heated up internal and external tensions and conflict.

The central events in the North Atlantic world during the era from

the conflict over Texas in the 1830s and 1840s until World War I outlined a mosaic of crises that spread over large chunks of time and geography. These numerous events included revolutions, wars, and a long,
worldwide depression (1873–1897). The mounting social and economic
discontent and disruption caused by that depression culminated in a series of armed crises, especially on the periphery of the world economy,
and particularly during the depression of the 1890s and its aftermath.
This era of conflict encompassed various revolutions and wars in Central
America, Mexico, the Caribbean, East Asia, South Africa, the Mediterranean area, and Russia as well as the subsequent world war. The world
war between 1914 and 1918 shifted, for a short time, the bulk of human
and property destruction from colonial or peripheral regions to the European and North Atlantic communities. This world war had repercussions, however, almost everywhere around the globe.

The U.S. government also faced the consequences of the contradic-
tions of the classical liberal economic order (competitive, free markets)
and its subsequent disorder. U.S. leaders attempted, in part, to resolve
the dilemmas of the malfunctioning political economy through expansion west of the Mississippi River, then out to some Pacific islands, south
into Mexico, Central America, and the Caribbean islands, and north
into Alaska. From the 1890s to 1930, the U.S. government pursued ever
more aggressive and active policies abroad.

As the nineteenth turned to the twentieth century, Theodore Roosevelt (TR) and his friends and supporters articulated the U.S. imperial
role. The Roosevelt Corollary (1904–1905) to the Monroe Doctrine (a
U.S. policy statement from 1823 that denied European territorial expansion in the Western Hemisphere, the transfer of existing European
colonies to non-American nations, or the transfer of European political
systems to the New World) proclaimed U.S. authority to define law, order, and financial sovereignty in the Americas. Later, the Senator Henry
Cabot Lodge Corollary (1912) limited the territorial sovereignty of Latin
American nations. This unilateral declaration denied Latin American nations the right to even lease their national land when the United States
declared that such action affected its security. U.S. leaders presumed
that liberal development, aided by the constraints of these two corollar-

ies, would produce material success and security for the United States and the Latin American countries, followed by political, social, and economic transformation. Of course, U.S. economic circles would enjoy priority in the transformation of Latin America. Many of the economic, financial, political, or military winners worked with U.S. (or European) businesses to supply raw materials, foodstuffs, investment opportunities, or labor services for U.S. (or European) firms. There were narrow incidental benefits for Latin American leaders and societies. In other words, the U.S. government would define and build free market societies south of the Rio Grande that materially satisfied U.S. and host-country citizens, in that order. U.S. authority (or guidance) would help the Latin American nations contribute to the alleviation of faulty or insufficient U.S. wealth accumulation and distribution.

TR's successors in the political and economic areas followed similar paths in the 1910s and 1920s. U.S. banking, manufacturing, and financial and commercial ties with Latin America became numerous, sizable, and intricate. One scholar concluded: "During the 1920s [U.S.] overseas economic and political expansion was virtually unrestrained, particularly in Latin America."[1] Worldwide in the 1920s and 1930s, lingering disputes remained in Europe and Asia.

Exploitation and its discontent survived World War I. Americans faced the dangers in the Americas from the goals and conduct of an Axis alliance—German, Italian, and Japanese. The Janus focus of President Franklin Delano Roosevelt (FDR) was Germany-Europe and Japan–East Asia. Japan posed some threat to the Philippines and Hawaii, but it was viewed as principally interested in China, Manchuria, and Southeast Asia—areas of key importance to U.S. expansionism. In addition, around the world, unresolved religious, ethnic, economic, and security issues from previous generations intensified in the Great Depression, contributing to the tension that erupted in the Second World War.

Two significant developments marked U.S.–Latin American relations in the interwar years. First, in the 1920s, U.S. leaders struggled to comprehend and respond to Latin America's lack of support for the U.S. government during World War I. Many Latin American leaders had found U.S. prewar conduct denigrating, disrespectful, and intervention-ist. In the 1920s and early 1930s, the State Department worked to develop a suitable political response. This introspection framed the Good Neighbor policy of the early 1930s, a course aimed to demonstrate the respect and goodwill of the United States toward its Latin American neighbors and to reject intervention in their internal affairs.

Second, a series of policies developed around the U.S. perception of a direct threat to the Americas from the rise of fascist governments in Japan, Spain, Italy, and Germany. The long history of conflicts between the United States and Latin American nations made it difficult for U.S. leaders to convince their counterparts to the south to accept their interpretation of the dangers posed by the Axis. Many U.S. leaders acknowledged a Japanese threat to the West Coast but generally considered that possibility less immediate. The influence of Spain, linked to the millions of Spanish migrants and their descendants who had made their home in the Western Hemisphere over the preceding four hundred plus years, was weakened because it had engaged in civil disorder for much of the 1930s and a brutal civil war in the last three years of that decade. The Italians were viewed principally as Mediterranean-area expansionists. Germany represented the major threat.

The chief danger came from the Nazi (acronym for National Socialist German Workers' Party) movement, led by Adolf Hitler. Nazi expansionism, belligerent and racist, was viewed as dangerous to the Americas. Lüning too rejected Nazi racism and expansion. FDR and U.S. officials, aware of weaknesses in U.S.–Western Hemisphere defenses, thought that Nazi military expansionism, starting from Italy's Mediterranean base, might threaten numerous points in the Western Hemisphere. Some U.S. officials worried about the potential Nazi use of Iceland. More U.S. officials suspected that, operating from areas that Mussolini's government hoped to acquire in or near North Africa (Dakar, the Canaries, the Azores, the Cape Verde islands), Germany could attack the northeastern bulge of Brazil at Recife-Pernambuco. For a while in 1941, the U.S. government contemplated preempting the perceived German threat to Brazil by sending twenty-five thousand men to occupy the Azores. Yet, before December 11, 1941, FDR needed a stronger justification to take preliminary military steps against Atlantic islands or North Africa. Since Northwest Africa was comparatively close to the northeastern areas of Brazil, he explored the idea that the Monroe Doctrine covered West Africa.[2]

The U.S. government saw threats even closer than Brazil. The Caribbean posed a more immediate danger to U.S. security, but U.S. war preparations moved slowly there. The greater Caribbean region, including the Panama Canal, attracted serious attention only after war erupted in Europe. Once war started in late 1939, the United States reevaluated its security and began a rapid fortification of its Caribbean possessions. This concern for security spread throughout the Caribbean. Then, the U.S. vital interest in securing the Panama Canal and the Gulf-Caribbean sea routes stimulated increased military and counterintelligence activity. As the war deteriorated for the Allied powers, Axis threats to the Gulf-Caribbean area received increased attention. During 1940 and 1941, Germany unleashed devastating U-boat activity in the Atlantic, including the South Atlantic. Clearly, if the United States entered the war, U-boats would endanger all shipping routes using the Gulf-Caribbean also. Hence the concern that a German spy network in the Caribbean could guide U-boat attacks. The need to strengthen defenses in the Caribbean, however, strained the demands for scarce U.S. forces in the Pacific and Atlantic. Ultimately, U.S. leaders, realizing that the Caribbean could supply much of its own defense force, relied heavily on Puerto Ricans.[3]

Defending the Caribbean would not be easy. The Nazi defeat of France in 1940 complicated U.S. security. U.S. security in the Americas had to consider Vichy French (Vichy France, a small part of old France, was tied to Nazi Germany) war vessels in North Africa and in Martinique and Guadeloupe in the Caribbean. Since the Vichy government was dependent on Nazi Germany, the future course of its army and navy was uncertain. Thus, these Vichy French naval forces threatened all territory, protectorates, and commerce in the Gulf-Caribbean region and, of course, ship routes using the Panama Canal. Ultimately, the Vichy French agreed to neutralize their war vessels rather than risk destructive Allied attacks.[4]

Among the islands of the Gulf-Caribbean, Cuba, the largest and most populous, was the key to U.S. security. Unfortunately, between

1898 and World War II, the U.S. government had established a record of disrespect for Cubans and Cuban governments. U.S.-Cuban relations had pursued a particularly tense and ambivalent course since U.S. forces had occupied the island from 1898 to 1903. In the first decades of the twentieth century, Cubans and U.S. officials were frequently at odds. The leaders of Cuba, under intense pressure from the U.S. government in 1903, had reluctantly allowed it to obtain a strategic naval base at Guantánamo Bay. The U.S. government commonly relied on force. Its military intervened in Cuba in 1906–1909, 1912, and 1917–1923. It threatened intervention at other times. U.S. efforts to force an "honest" cabinet on Cuba in the 1920s encountered ignominious defeat and embarrassment for the U.S. government.[5]

After World War I, U.S.-Cuban relations shifted emphasis from political to economic ties. For much of the nineteenth and twentieth centuries, the stability of Cuban society had been closely linked to the quantity and price of sugar and the distribution of the income from sugar sales. The "dance of the millions," windfall revenue for a few Cubans from the sharply elevated sugar prices during World War I, created an elite of unearned wealth who sought to preserve their good fortune through alliance with political factions that used corruption and force. Cuban relations with the United States in the 1920s were marked by huge loans and a sharply falling sugar price. After 1923, the U.S. government apparently lost its fear of foreign aggressors in the Caribbean, so it opted for a hands-off policy and tolerated a corrupt, brutal regime in Cuba as long as it affected only Cubans.[6]

The world economic crisis after 1929 troubled U.S.-Cuban relations. The depressed sugar price and revenue of the 1930s exacerbated matters. The Cuban share of the U.S. sugar market declined from 49.4 percent in 1930 to 25.3 percent in 1933. The severe unemployment and financial disorder in Cuba encouraged President Gerardo Machado's government to implement ever tighter police control rather than lessen the graft and corruption. With a government unresponsive to the hard times, Cuban society was moving toward a violent, uncontrolled civil rupture.[7]

In the 1930s, unemployment, poverty, maldistribution of income, and monoculture with sugar fostered "nearly intractable" economic-social problems in Cuba. As the historian Thomas O'Brien, a specialist in U.S.–Latin American economic relations, noted: "In 1933, near starvation wages [still] prevailed in the Cuban sugar industry." Frequent discontent among the sugar entrepreneurs and laborers with the quantity and price of sugar or the fairness of the distribution of sugar income led to violent civil disorder. In 1933, workers struck. Rural labor discontent spread throughout the mills and plantations, and, at times, the rural guard joined the workers. The workers seized plants and mills, many U.S. owned. Many U.S. managers fled. The Good Neighbor policy encountered much ill will in Cuba. Yet, in 1933, with the United States in a deep domestic crisis, FDR found little time for foreign relations. He wanted Cuba quieted. As U.S. concern with rising tension and civil unrest in Cuba mounted, FDR met with Argentinean, Brazilian, Chilean, and Mexican diplomats to ameliorate Latin American sensibilities. His policies aimed to promote stability, not intervention in Cuba.[8]

The respected Cuban historian Luis E. Aguilar succinctly summarized the crucial events of the late 1920s and early 1930s. For him, the revolution of 1933 was a key event: "By the mid-1920s Cuba had already entered a revolutionary period from which she emerged deeply and radically transformed: a popular revolutionary party had been formed; a constitution emphasizing social legislation had been adopted; a new sense of nationalism prevailed; and the necessary forces for an economic revival were present. Some of the programs and ideas which seemed radical and new to those who ignore Cuban history evolved to a great extent from the ideals and frustrations of the revolution of 1933."[9] And these events had an effect beyond Cuba's border.

This revolution drew a U.S. reaction with cataclysmic consequences for Cuba. The U.S. undersecretary of state and Latin American specialist Sumner Welles, FDR's trusted and highly regarded friend, overthrew Gerardo Machado in 1933 with the threat, not the actual use, of U.S. military power. To force Machado's hand, Welles used words and funds to encourage disaffection among Cuban politicians and army officers and gathered U.S. naval forces off Cuba's coast. After Machado's departure, the Good Neighbor policy guided U.S. leaders to abandon the Platt Amendment (which gave the U.S. government unlimited rights of intervention in Cuba) in April 1934. Guantánamo, a strategically valuable naval base, remained the only U.S. site in Cuba. Still, FDR followed Welles's recommendation and kept U.S. ships and marines in Cuban waters to support the regime replacing Machado. The U.S. government, however, disapproved of the victory of the reformist president Ramón Grau San Martín. It withheld recognition of his government because U.S. entrepreneurs and Cuban political and military elites disliked him. He was deposed. In need of some order in Cuba, U.S. officials reluctantly supported Colonel Fulgencio Batista but looked for a more acceptable figurehead. Their choice, Carlos Mendieta, proved acceptable to the Cuban army and the elite for the late 1930s.[10] Repairing the Cuban-U.S. relationship became increasingly important as the war moved toward the Caribbean.

The danger of war in Europe challenged the noninterventionist aspect of the Good Neighbor policy, not just in Cuba. U.S. leaders, aware of the poor support in Latin America for U.S. policy during World War I, valued friendly, cooperative governments in Latin America. Still, the approaching war in Europe increased the need for U.S. access to select raw materials and military bases. Latin American businesspeople, mired in a punishing economic decline, desperately desired economic opportunities. However, if the U.S. economy could not purchase their products, the Latin American leaders hoped that European nations, even Hitler's Germany, would. As a counterstrategy, FDR's administration sought policies to control the sales and distribution of Latin American resources and to reduce the role of Germany in Latin American economic life.[11] FDR considered Hitler the principal threat to world peace.

Commercial matters posed a problem. The U.S. government could not encourage the sale of U.S.-manufactured goods commonly desired by Latin American elites and entrepreneurs. The U.S. economy needed to divert more industrial production to its own preparedness and to its friends (soon to be allies) in Europe and Asia. In this situation, the occasional Latin American experimentation with import substitution (developing domestic production of items normally imported) met little U.S. resistance. However, Latin American import substitution during the war altered domestic conditions. It increased domestic industrialization and urbanization, strengthened the labor movement, and fostered a rising middle class.[12] A decade or two later, these transformed Latin American political economies posed special postwar problems for the U.S. political economy.

While the outbreak of war in Europe affected economic relations in the Americas, it also nudged on great-power espionage and counterespionage activity. Intelligence activity and material well-being were both important issues. Before 1939, the United States, Great Britain, and Germany had maintained only modest intelligence or counterintelligence operations. This was true even in Latin America, a region that was near the United States, had close traditional British imperial and economic ties, and had large German and Italian immigrant populations. The clouds of war invigorated information gathering and espionage in the Americas. After 1939, the German, British, U.S., and Cuban intelligence agencies gradually increased operations in Cuba.

Aggressive Nazi foreign policy in the 1930s did not place immediate political or military demands on Latin America. Initially, the German leaders primarily desired trade in raw materials. Later, they expected a gradual increase in propaganda activity and political influence. The many German settlers in Latin America who had preserved their culture would generate some local sympathy for German policies. Thus, the Nazi leaders appealed for the support of the *Reichsdeutsche* [born in Germany] and *Volksdeutsche* [blood descendants of Germans]. Their media campaigns aimed to use public influence to build economic access to Latin America for Axis business interests. "The Nazis' main drive," according to one scholar, "centered on commercial expansionism."[13] By 1938, Germany had an effective program of political, military, and economic penetration of Latin America.

Latin America became the first area of U.S. resistance to the Axis powers. Some U.S. leaders feared that the Axis intended to use the old and new immigrants in the Americas for propaganda and espionage. The Spanish were judged less of a risk because, after a brutal and destructive civil war (1936–1939), Spain was too weak and divided to export fascism to Latin America. Still, the tens of thousands of Falangists (the Falange was the Spanish fascist corporatist party] and Falange supporters in Latin

America posed a potential danger to U.S. security. The novelist Ernest Hemingway considered the Falangists in Cuba particularly dangerous.[14] These Falange sympathizers in the Americas often supported German interests. The large number of refugees of the Spanish Republic, however, served as a counterweight to the Falange support.

In the late 1930s, U.S. officials were alarmed over increasing Axis activity, economic competition, and propaganda in the Americas. As U.S. concerns grew, the U.S. government closed down German and German American activities in the United States. By 1940, those principal German sympathizers in the United States were considered under control, but not those in Latin America. Excluding the very numerous, but politically divided, population with Spanish roots, at least 8 million residents of Latin America were native-born citizens or blood descendants of native-born citizens of Axis nations. All totaled, Italy had 6 million emigrants and their offspring in Latin America; about 250,000 Japanese and about 2 million Germans and German descendants also lived there. The value of the Italians for the Nazi program in Latin America was uncertain. The Japanese immigrants, principally in Brazil, Peru, and Mexico, were widely unpopular. The *Reichsdeutsche* were found everywhere but principally in Argentina, Brazil, and Chile. About 250,000 Germans resided in Argentina, 1 million in Brazil, 50,000 in Chile, 20,000 in Paraguay, 10,000 in Uruguay, and 16,000 in Central America (half in Guatemala and most of the rest in Costa Rica). Some of the descendants of the *Volksdeutsche* were German on both sides of their parentage; others were of mixed ethnicity. Some exerted significant economic influence. For example, Germans or German descendants controlled much of the coffee crop in Central America. For many U.S. observers, the most recent German immigrants—suspected of including many Nazi agents or sympathizers—were the most troubling.[15]

From the late 1930s through 1941, the U.S. public interpreted three aspects of German policy as a threat: (1) the Tripartite Pact, a 1939 military alliance between Germany and Italy that Japan joined in 1940, was interpreted as a bid for world domination by authoritarian and militaristic states; (2) German officials accelerated the commercial and human penetration of Latin America; and (3) various incidents between U.S.

and German naval vessels in the Atlantic were interpreted as signs of German militarism creeping west. The naval incidents might help Nazi antidemocratic authoritarianism gain a grip on the Americas.[16]

The success of the German army in Poland, the Netherlands, Belgium, France, Denmark, and Norway from late 1939 to mid-1940 boosted Germany's prestige and image. This improved reputation concerned U.S. officials. The relative ease of Hitler's conquests in Western Europe from April to June 1940 prompted the foreign ministers of the American republics to meet in Havana from July 21 to July 30, 1940. Secretary of State Cordell Hull and Undersecretary Sumner Welles approved a resolution that converted the unilateral Monroe Doctrine into a collective shield under a different name—*hemispheric defense.* An attack against one would be viewed as a threat to all.[17]

FDR led an exuberant opposition to the Nazi threat. Scholars and critics frequently scrutinize this conduct using a calculated, analytic framework. Once convinced that the Nazi regime intended war and conquest, according to a specialist on FDR's foreign policy, "Roosevelt led the anti-Hitler campaign." FDR was adamant that Hitler sought world domination, so the United States and its allies needed control of the seas. The Good Neighbor policy, which pretended to combine U.S. and Latin American interests, responded to the reality (or fear) that the Nazis might one day menace the United States or the Americas.[18]

Some observers thought that many U.S. officials misread German intentions in the Americas. In their view, the Germans were initially after trade, propaganda, and information. In the mid-1930s, the Yale professor William Burchard saw little evidence of German political or ideological expansionism in Latin America. The socialist Norman Thomas noted: "Actually there is much crude and primitive fascism in Latin American countries, but most emphatically it is not pro Italian or pro German."[19] So, in the 1930s, and until early 1941, some observers saw the U.S. fear of a fifth column as more of an obsession than a reality.

Many Americans shared another concern. Hitler's irrational conduct made his word untrustworthy. This untrustworthiness inspired FDR's conduct. Some scholars have noted that FDR never found evidence of Nazi sabotage or political acts in Latin America prior to the attack on

Pearl Harbor. And he exaggerated various incidents and episodes in order to elicit aid for the Allies. However, the irrational and unpredictable Hitler demanded opponents who exaggerated his conduct and ideas in order to prepare for the startling, illogical, and bold conduct that he repeatedly confronted them with. By 1941, it was clear that Hitler's public promises of Germany's limited objectives and peaceful aspirations did not indicate his intent and had no value. His mind-set and conduct demanded policies of maximum opposition, not a minimum response.[20]

From the perspective of logical, rational evaluation, critics who urged caution seemed to raise valid points. But Hitler consistently broke promises. Contrary to German international commitments, he unilaterally rearmed Germany, marched into the demilitarized zone between France and Germany, annexed Austria, occupied the Sudetenland (an area in the former Czechoslovakia with many people of Germanic origin and cultural characteristics), occupied the rump Czechoslovakian state, and manufactured a war against Poland. In the minds of many Western observers and officials, Hitler did not follow normal, rational conduct. The longer he was in power, the less rational and more willfully he acted.

A leading scholar of Germany's World War II intelligence services, David Kahn, detailed Hitler's unreality rooted in will, self-delusion, and arrogance. Kahn's argument, here in greatly reduced form, is persuasive. In 1941, Hitler believed that he could defeat the Soviet Union quickly and, thus, force Great Britain to an agreement. He declared war on the United States after Pearl Harbor because he dismissed U.S. industrial might. In self-delusion and arrogance, he argued that German quality production trumped U.S. (and Allied) quantitative superiority. His authority rested on charismatic faith and willpower. Both these qualities are alien to reason, Kahn noted, but reason is an essential element of intelligence. Not surprisingly, the utilization of German intelligence failed frequently in the war.[21] Hitler marched to the beat of a different drummer. It made no sense to apply Aristotelian logic when evaluating the conduct of such an emotional megalomaniac.

Key aspects of National Socialist ideology raised serious problems for German objectives in Latin America. German diplomats in Latin America questioned the appropriateness of party material with regard to "race politics." The widespread racial mixing among Europeans, Indians, and Africans made racial politics unacceptable to most Latin Americans. Some Germans advised reducing the nation's political objectives and working more in the economic and cultural areas.[22] However, the Nazi leaders showed little willingness to adjust their racial policies for Latin America. Thus, the Nazis' racial views limited their prospects for acquiring influence in Latin America.

U.S. policies regarding the Nazi threat received some sympathy south of the border, but Latin American diplomats remained very sensitive to prior episodes of U.S. abuse of power and to the U.S. drive for domination. Of course, security in the Americas was not assured. The unstable internal conditions in some Latin American nations could aid Nazi objectives. Political division in any country opened opportunities for Axis spies, saboteurs, and subversives. Increased Axis influence in any Latin American country could reduce vital raw-material deliveries north to the Allied nations.[23]

While Hitler had difficulty winning the political confidence of Latin American governments, he had a more serious confidence gap in military strategy with his naval leaders. Geopolitically, his grand strategy diverged from that of the German naval leadership. He focused on land war rather than sea operations. Thus, the German naval leaders Admirals Erich Raeder and Karl Dönitz planned a naval strategy that Hitler would support only abstractly, never with adequate funds and materials, as long as his land and air forces had not achieved his goals on the European continent. The U.S. leaders, meanwhile, revisited the doctrine of Admiral Alfred Mahan (the renowned U.S. naval warfare strategist of the late nineteenth and early twentieth centuries) and reconfirmed the value of the sea routes. In the prewar era, U.S. leaders had marked the Caribbean for permanent U.S. defense bases in Puerto Rico, Guantánamo (Cuba), and Chaguaramas (Trinidad).[24] The defense of ocean shipping lanes and the Panama Canal was a fundamental element of U.S. strategy.

Reports of Latin American political factions sympathetic to the fascists were disturbing. Feeding on the irrational fear associated with profascist activity, economic and political groups in the Americas could readily twist a real concern about possible fascist incursions into irrational witch hunts. The image of the Axis threat was malleable in the hands of some Latin American leaders. Politically, the U.S. fear of fifth columns encouraged witch hunts in the Gulf-Caribbean countries. Local political leaders, claiming to pursue a fifth column, snagged their opponents more often than they did subversives.[25] While U.S. military and many political leaders worked to win the war, some local businessmen and business-friendly politicians used the opportunity to weaken or eliminate resistance to contemporary and future political power and economic accumulation.

Some private U.S. corporations understood how to benefit from the feared German commercial penetration of the Americas. By the mid-1930s, it seemed evident that some conflict between the United States and Germany for political or economic control of the Western Hemisphere was inescapable. Some U.S. firms (e.g., airlines) extracted permanent advantages while the fear of Nazi activity reigned. U.S. airlines had received favored treatment after World War I. But the perceived crisis of rising German involvement justified increased assistance to them, especially Pan American Airways, in their struggle with Lufthansa in the 1930s. In early 1942, the diplomatic historian Irwin Gellman noted: "The United States [had] effectively crushed any vestige of Axis influence in Latin American airlines."[26] The U.S.-German conflict in Latin America often compressed strategic, military, economic, and intelligence aspects into one course of conduct.

The U.S. government found it convenient and beneficial to do business with several Latin American dictators during the 1930s. Since stability and order in the Caribbean region became more desirable as the likelihood of a major war increased in Europe and across the Pacific in East Asia, U.S. leaders found fewer reasons to complain about stable, authoritarian governments in the region. Strongmen like the Dominican Rafael Trujillo, the Nicaraguan Anastasio Somoza, the Honduran Tiburcio Carías Andino, the Guatemalan Jorge Ubico, and Batista identified superficially with the Good Neighbor to gain U.S. support and enhance their authority. All these dictators offered friendly authoritarianism in places considered vital for U.S. security and shipping in the Caribbean.

On the eve of a world crisis, national security and economic needs benefited, while the lack of progress toward democratic, humanitarian governments was rationalized away.[27] Survival trumped democracy—even if the threat to survival was exaggerated and the need to curtail democracy was distorted.

For the most part, Latin American governments cooperated with U.S. war efforts. As the United States moved toward involvement in the war, U.S. relations with Cuba grew in significance. Even before Cuba declared war on the Axis, U.S. officials thought that that country took prompt, effective action against enemy aliens. After consulting local leaders and U.S. officials, Batista smashed pro-Falangist operations. He banned the Cuban Nazi Party in September 1940, and, according to British security officials, he "intern[ed] 700 Germans and 1370 Italians." These British officials, however, considered the Cuban steps to curtail Axis aliens superficial and ineffective. To their knowledge, a small bribe gained the release of any detained German.[28]

Even prior to December 1941, Cuba cooperated spontaneously and extensively in the political, economic, and military spheres. It declared war on the Axis powers already on December 9, 1941. After December 1941, U.S.-Cuban arrangements tightened. Later, on September 7, 1942, the U.S. and Cuban governments concluded a comprehensive agreement coordinating military and naval measures for the duration of the war. Cuba imposed compulsory military service and leased several sites for air bases to the United States, including a major base near Havana valued at $20 million. And the Cubans eliminated Lüning's spy ring. For Cuban cooperation, there were rewards. It led to large Lend-Lease grants for the Cuban military and more accommodating U.S. policies toward Cuban sugar. Already during 1941, the Export-Import Bank had placed $36 million aside to finance the purchase of the Cuban sugar production. The Cubans exaggerated the danger from Lüning—that his network had an agent in Panama—and inflated their role in capturing him.[29]

In the interwar and early war years, intelligence agencies in Germany, the United States, Britain, and Cuba expanded to confront the rising great-power tension and talk of war. The German intelligence service aimed at a different target; it developed skills in tactical deciphering and information gathering. The U.S. and British counterparts concentrated more on higher level deciphering and information gathering. The Versailles peace settlement after World War I had compelled Germany to disarm, and its intelligence service all but disappeared. A small Abwehrabteilung [Defense Bureau] of the Reichswehrministerium [National Defense Ministry] was created on January 1, 1921. The Abwehrabteilung's small staff and workload increased slowly in the 1920s. Gradually, it expanded into active information seeking and counterintelligence.

The Abwehr's slow growth was not just a consequence of international restrictions. A professional, independent Abwehr within the OKW [Oberkommando Wehrmacht, Supreme Command of the Armed Forces] did not fit Nazi plans. In 1934, the Abwehr chief, the naval captain Conrad Patzig, was forced to resign as a consequence of ongoing disputes with the Gestapo [acronym for Geheime Staatspolizei, State Secret Police] leadership and other Nazi Third Reich agencies. Patzig's replacement, Admiral Wilhelm Franz Canaris, managed to stamp the agency with his personality and objectives without directly challenging the SS [Schutzstaffel, the elite security corps of the Nazi Party and, later, the German government], the chief of German police and interior minister Heinrich Himmler, or Reinhard Heydrich, the head of the SD [Sicherheitsdienst, the German Security Service]. Himmler, Heydrich, and General Heinrich Müller (the head of the Gestapo) sorely wanted to subordinate the Abwehr to the SD. However, Heydrich, who would have headed the combined security force, apparently found it awkward to unseat his friend, fellow violinist, and former commanding officer Canaris. These two had a good relationship and remained neighbors in Berlin until Heydrich's death.[30] Personal relations played a role to preserve Canaris's post.

Despite the internal conflict among the German intelligence agencies, the Abwehr grew in 1940 and 1941 in response to the struggle to control the British use of the Atlantic Ocean and the German need for information to serve the Western and Eastern European fronts. In the early months of World War II, German intelligence, especially the

Abwehr, had few agents in Latin America. Despite (or, perhaps, because of) persistent U.S. fears of effective Axis fifth-column activity, nothing threatening developed anywhere in Latin America. In fact, even planning for a German "regional build-up [in Latin America] did not commence until late in 1940." Hence: "The Abwehr and SD had to manage with whatever personnel they could recruit, and hope for the best."[31] The Abwehr recruited extensively for Latin America only beginning in 1941.

The Abwehr was headquartered in Berlin, but it operated over thirty principal substations. It maintained an *Abwehrstelle* [AST, chief intelligence station] in every *Wehrkreis* [military district] under German control. The general staff officer for intelligence of the district military commander directed the AST. Wehrkreis X (Hamburg) was formed in May 1935. It incorporated Hamburg, Schleswig-Holstein, Münster, Stettin, and the northern part of Niedersachsen. The Hamburg AST oversaw the Geheim-Meldedienst [Secret Radio and Telegraph Station] at Hamburg-Wohldorf. It also controlled the German censors of the *Auslandsbrief- und Telegrammprüfstellen* [foreign letter and telegraph examining stations]. Initially, the Hamburg AST had about 250 workers. But the Abwehr exploded in size once the war began, and the station grew to the point that it had 2,000 employees in 1939 and 13,000 by 1944.[32] Hamburg became one of the largest ASTs.

The questionable quality of late Abwehr recruits was reflected in Lüning's espionage labors. Germany's intelligence material about Latin America was gathered at the ASTs in Hamburg, Berlin, and Brussels. While these three posts shared responsibility for intelligence work in South and Central America, the Caribbean, and the United States, the Hamburg AST had the Americas as its primary responsibility. In addition, *Nebenstellen* [NESTs, branch intelligence stations] in Cologne, Flensburg, and Bremen supported the Hamburg AST intelligence work in the Americas.[33] Lüning was assigned to Cuba from Wehrkreis X, Hamburg AST.

The information gathered abroad had to find its way to Hamburg as quickly as possible. Mail service was not reliable once the war began, so Hamburg's radio service became a key resource. The Hamburg-Wohldorf radio station, the principal Abwehr overseas radio station, was one of the largest in Germany and responsible for contact with South America, the United States, England, Spain, and Portugal. During the war, the Wohldorf station expanded and specialized in agent-radio contacts. It employed 120 workers—one-third worked European radio contacts and two-thirds overseas contacts. Relay stations in France and Spain forwarded foreign radio contacts, especially from Central and South America.[34]

The intense competition, jealousy, and lack of cooperation among the Abwehr, the Gestapo, the SD, the Foreign Ministry intelligence officials, and the Auslandsorganisation [AO, Nazi Party Foreign Bureau] severely limited the effectiveness of German intelligence gathering. Despite the intrigues of several ranking Nazi leaders, Canaris remained chief until February 1944, when the SS leader Ernst Kaltenbrunner finally gathered command of all German intelligence agencies in the Reichssicherheitshauptamt [RSHA, State Central Security Bureau]. On April 9, 1945, just as the Allies liberated Bavaria, Canaris, imprisoned because of suspected ties to German anti-Nazi groups, was executed.[35] The inner fighting and jealousy in Germany's intelligence service remained bitter to the end.

The U.S. counterintelligence was as fractionalized and competitive as the German but not as bitter or brutal. Under FDR's directive, the FBI organized the Special Intelligence Service (SIS) to work in Latin America, but it had to compete with long-established agencies, the Military Intelligence Division (MID), the Office of Naval Intelligence (ONI), and the diplomatic corps' information gathering. Since 1924, the FBI director J. Edgar Hoover had used an ever-increasing public awareness of federal law enforcement to build an empire. He eagerly sought to win public notice and praise. His highly publicized campaigns against robbery and kidnapping (despite the fact that he did little against the Mafia, gambling, protection, extortion, murder for hire, and drugs) built a strong public image for Hoover and "his FBI." The agency expanded steadily in the 1930s. By 1939 and 1940, Hoover judged that he needed to shift his police activity and public relations efforts to antifascism. As the U.S. government moved closer to war, he believed that guiding the counterintelligence work in Latin America would win him and his FBI recognition and rewards.[36]

Despite an extensive self-produced publicity campaign, Hoover's SIS never received significant recognition. It was only a small subagency. At its peak, the SIS had about 360 agents in Latin America and the Caribbean. It played a role in 389 arrests for espionage and the identification of 282 propaganda agents, 30 saboteurs, and 222 smugglers. It aided in the interning or deporting (to the United States) of 7,064 enemy aliens. Its chief task was to encourage local counterespionage agents or police to act vigorously against Axis agents.[37]

Even before World War II, FDR was exasperated that the FBI, MID, ONI, and State Department were constantly at odds. He was displeased with the disjointed, overlapping, shotgun conduct of intelligence. To ameliorate this situation, in June 1939, Assistant Secretary of State George S. Messersmith was assigned the task of synchronizing the four agencies. Messersmith made little progress. Hoover was particularly uncooperative. He waged inexhaustible bureaucratic turf wars behind the scenes. Besides the friction and inefficiency resulting from the competition among the intelligence agencies, Congressman Martin Dies of the House Un-American Activities Committee exercised irrational but attention-getting interference with all intelligence agencies.[38]

Allied intelligence efforts to expose German espionage (including, as it turned out, Lüning's) activity in the Gulf-Caribbean were divided among the United States, Great Britain, Cuba, Canada, Mexico, and other mainland nations. Hoover expanded FBI authority even in the face of FDR's efforts to unify intelligence. In 1942, FDR named William Donovan chief of the Coordinating Office of Intelligence to coordinate intelligence gathering as the head of the Office of Strategic Services (OSS). Hoover opposed the broad mandate claimed by Donovan to conduct propaganda, espionage, counterespionage, special operations, and research. The FBI resisted coordination under Donovan and kept the SIS under its control until after the war. Later in 1942, Nelson Rockefeller, the head of the Office of Coordination of Inter-American Affairs (CIAA), maneuvered FDR into granting the CIAA control over Caribbean and Latin American propaganda to the exclusion of Donovan's OSS. The centralization of U.S. intelligence proved evasive. In Cuba, the U.S. ambassador, Spruille Braden, despite resistance, subordinated all intelligence agents to the embassy, precisely to prevent fractionalized and competitive counterespionage. He threatened to remove any intelligence official who opposed his coordination project.[39]

FDR's opposition to Germany grew increasingly determined, even though he could not persuade many others in his administration or in Congress to follow him. After the mid-1930s, as FDR urged a more confrontational policy toward the Nazis, Hitler struggled to avoid conflict with the United States. Once war began in Europe, he ordered his navy not to fire on U.S. ships, and he denied any intention of attacking either North or South America. In response, FDR ordered the U.S. Navy into close surveillance of German submarines. Even more aggressive and confrontational, in 1940 and 1941, U.S. naval vessels followed German submarines and radioed their position to the British. British air and surface units then attempted to sink these submarines. FDR considered the hard line fully justified. In a radio talk in late 1941, he declared: "What started as a European war has developed, as the Nazis always intended it should develop, into a world war for world domination. No, I am not speculating about this, I merely repeat what is already in the Nazi book of world conquest. They plan to treat the Latin American nations as they are now treating the Balkans. They plan to strangle the United States." The Nazis were moving toward the Azores and Cape Verde Islands, he warned, only "seven hours distance from Brazil."[40] While FDR's perspective rested on his observations, his feelings, and anecdotal information, after the war his judgment was supported in contemporary documents, especially Hitler's second book, unpublished until the 1960s.[41] FDR's opposition to Hitler's government remained relentless.

British intelligence, especially the Secret Intelligence Service (commonly known as MI6, the intelligence agency employed outside the empire), entered this conflict several years before the United States. British intelligence had a long history. The predecessor to the Secret Intelligence Service started in October 1909 as a foreign section of the Secret Service Bureau (known as MI1c in the 1920s). It had the task of gathering evidence of German plans for an invasion of Britain. Colonel, later Major General, Stewart Menzies became the head of the German section of MI6 in 1932. He rose in rank and reputation. Then, in 1940, Churchill unsuccessfully resisted his appointment to succeed

Rear Admiral Hugh "Quex" Sinclair as the head of MI6. Nevertheless, Churchill and Menzies worked well together during the war.[42] In the pre–World War II years, Great Britain revived its intelligence services and struggled to balance cooperation and competition among them. The tension among British information services remained during World War II.

As world political and military tension grew in the prewar and early war years, British intelligence monitored German activity in the Americas more closely. Since Britain historically drew much industrial raw material and foodstuff from the Western Hemisphere, it needed to protect its Atlantic and Caribbean lifeline, which was seriously threatened. After September 1939, German U-boats sank many British ships in the Atlantic while suffering few losses. British officials fought back but without great effect for a long time. They labored to maintain a leadership role in information gathering in the Americas. British intelligence formed a cooperative partnership with U.S. intelligence to shut down German espionage and U-boat operations in the Americas. However, once the United States entered the war, a new agreement restricted British intelligence activity to the commonwealth areas. The British could operate in Latin America only with FBI cooperation. This U.S.-British intelligence liaison went through the State Department.[43]

Before World War II, British counterintelligence was modest in size. MI6's counterespionage bureau, Section V, expanded during World War II. Its successes during the war were often linked to ISOS (Intelligence Section, Oliver Strachey), the branch that decrypted German signals' intelligence traffic. Major J. Felix Cowgill, from the Indian police, became an effective leader at Section V. His best student was Kim Philby, the head of the Iberian subsection and a close friend of the MI6 agent and novelist Graham Greene. Philby later replaced Cowgill as the chief of Section V.[44] In 1942, MI6 assigned Field Agent Greene to cope with French intrigue in North Africa from Freetown, Sierra Leone. After the Americans captured French North Africa, Greene returned to London in early 1943. Philby recruited him for Section V's Portuguese subsection.[45] Thus, Greene assumed responsibility for a post that oversaw Abwehr activity in Portugal and, by extension, in the Americas (since the Iberian

Peninsula was a principal communications point for Abwehr agents in the Western Hemisphere).

The German blitzkrieg hindered British efforts to achieve success in intelligence and counterintelligence. The German military success-es on the Continent undermined MI6 work there. For example, MI6 needed new agents for the Continent because the prewar veteran agents were compromised when Germany overran Europe. By late 1941, only Secret Intelligence Service stations in Stockholm, Madrid, Lisbon, and Berne remained beyond Nazi control. Consequently, considerable con-flict, intrigue, and tension in Allied-Axis relations were transferred to the Iberian Peninsula, which swarmed with Abwehr and MI6 agents. The Abwehr benefited from Canaris's good personal links with the Spanish dictator Francisco Franco, other Spanish officials, and some Falangist leaders. It used the Iberian Peninsula to communicate both ways with agents throughout the United States, Canada, the Caribbean, and Latin America. Thus, Greene shared supervision of counterespionage against the Abwehr in the Caribbean (including Lüning). As an important task, British intelligence on the Iberian Peninsula labored to learn about Ger-man projects in the Americas.[46]

For one of its principal tasks, British intelligence struggled to nudge U.S. officials toward England's preferred course for the United States—entering the war on Britain's side—while simultaneously competing for influence in the Americas. In the effort to favorably influence U.S. con-duct, Colonel (later Sir) William Stephenson, the Canadian head of the British Security Coordination (BSC), was a key figure. He coordinated at least three British intelligence agencies in the Western Hemisphere: MI6, the Special Operations Executive (SOE), and the Political Warfare Executive. A fourth British agency, the British Foreign Office, gathered political, economic, and social information, although seldom military in-telligence. Roughly on a daily basis, Stephenson's office at Room 3603 of the Rockefeller Building in New York City clandestinely exchanged Brit-ish intercepts of Axis messages for material from U.S. agencies. Under Stephenson's direction, British intelligence in the Americas cooperated, efficiently in many ways, even while trying to manipulate the United States toward war.[47]

Stephenson intended to manage U.S.-British relations to Britain's advantage. Soon after his arrival in the United States in early 1940, he established a good relationship with Hoover. Stephenson recognized that FDR's emotional conviction about Hitler's ill intentions made him susceptible to manipulation. One deceptive act occurred in October 1941 when FDR publicly claimed that he had a map showing secret Nazi conquest plans for Latin America. Senator Burton Wheeler tracked down the map. It merely showed U.S. airline routes and production, storage, and movements of airplane fuel. Even more damaging, it was a forgery from Stephenson, who, perhaps with the connivance of Donovan, foisted it off on FDR. Assistant Secretary of State Adolf Berle wisely warned Secretary of State Cordell Hull that British intelligence agents were "manufacturing documents detailing Nazi conspiracies in South America": "I think we have to be a little on our guard against false scares."[48] Britain wanted more than U.S. sympathy in its war effort.

FDR recognized the value of Allied cooperation in intelligence work. He agreed to the "closest possible marriage between the FBI and British Intelligence." In the year before the U.S. government joined the war, British censors sent seventy-five thousand pieces of intercepted correspondence to the U.S. government. After Pearl Harbor, this cooperation increased. Several days after Pearl Harbor, Cowgill of Section V arrived in Washington to inquire whether there were any hitches in the full and quick exchange of intelligence from the Americas. At this time, the information exchange was expanded to include the FBI and the Cuban, Canadian, and Mexican intelligence services.[49]

The British and U.S. counterintelligence services hoped to detect German agents through monitoring the vast communications between the Old and the New Worlds. To monitor mail and radio exchanges between Europe and the Americas, British Imperial Censorship (BIC), a subunit of the Controller of Postal and Telegraphic Censorship, established about twelve hundred censors at the Princess and Bermudiana hotels in Bermuda. This site, the Bermuda station (along with a smaller Trinidad station), became the center of hemispheric censorship (south of the United States) from 1940 through 1945. It monitored air and surface mail and radio traffic signals during World War II. Joint British-

U.S. cooperation routed all transatlantic mail (except the direct Brazil to Rome service) through the Bermuda station.[50]

The Bermuda station intercepted hundreds of thousands of pieces of suspected enemy correspondence. The first Lüning secret ink message was intercepted in mid-October 1941. It reported on airports in Cuba (but intended for U.S. military use), shipping, and other matters of interest regarding the United States. In 1942, BIC's intercepts ended the espionage work of three Abwehr agents: Kurt Frederick Ludwig, Heinz August Lüning, and Frederick Lehmitz. During its existence, the Bermuda station supplied material for twenty-seven espionage convictions.[51] The divided British intelligence organizations were perfectly capable of long-term cooperation, as Stephenson's labors demonstrated.

The contest within Cuban intelligence reflected the tension between professional counterespionage and the political utility of a secret information service. The able Captain Mariano Faget y Díaz (b. September 9, 1904; d. May 29, 1972, Florida), *jefe* [chief] of the Oficinas contra las Actividades Enemigas y de Control [Bureau of Counterintelligence against Enemy Activities], directed Cuban counterintelligence. The U.S. embassy and the SIS agents in Cuba held Faget's counterespionage work in high regard.[52] In fact, Captain Faget possessed shrewdness, intelligence, and a suitable work ethic.

Faget's superior was the politically ambitious and self-serving General Manuel Benítez y Valdés, who became a favorite of Batista's as the result of a crisis in 1941. In that year, the army chief of staff, Colonel José A. Pedraza, and the naval chief of staff, Angel Anselmo González, challenged Batista's authority because he had dismissed one of their allies, the police chief, Bernardo García, for "negligence" and appointed Benítez as his successor. In this tense situation, Benítez initially offered to resign to defuse the problem. When this offer was refused, he then stood by Batista. The president took heroic and determined action to terminate the uprising. Pedraza and González were dismissed and sent out of the country. Benítez rose even higher in Batista's circle. The British officials in Cuba immediately judged Benítez as a dangerous, ambitious, and shady character. Later, in June 1944, Benítez dissipated his goodwill. Convinced that he would not be Batista's designated successor, he plotted against "the Sargent-typist" (the term the British minister in Cuba used confidentially to designate Batista). Benítez was forced to resign and leave the country. In September 1944, he returned and was arrested.[53]

Benítez had a past that sparkled with adventure and self-serving greed. He had worked as a Hollywood extra in his youth, was self-absorbed, and often exercised poor judgment. Then, in 1939, serving as the head of Cuba's Immigration Department, he had sold thousands of "landing permits" for $150 each. Some were sold wholesale to agents in Europe. These documents purported to allow the holder to land in Cuba while awaiting a visa for the United States or elsewhere in the Western Hemisphere. When he refused to share the bounty with other Cuban officials, the permits were declared invalid. Many, perhaps most, of the 930 European passengers—mostly Jewish refugees—on the liner *St. Louis,* in the spring of 1939, held these invalid permits and, thus, had to return to Europe. As a favorite of Batista's, he was named the head of Cuban police and intelligence even though he knew little about intelligence work. On more than one occasion, he extracted personal advantage from Faget's work in Cuba to the detriment of Allied counterintelligence. In sum, the numerous intelligence agencies of Great Britain, the United States, and Cuba cooperated, but the U.S. and British agents distrusted some Cuban police work and specific personalities like Benítez.[54]

In Latin America, German agents were not easy to detect initially, not even the weaker ones like Lüning. The steady stream of Germans fleeing the Nazi regime after 1933 added appreciably to the numerous prior German immigrants and their descendants from the century before 1933. The new immigrants often acted as if they opposed Hitler's Germany. But, of course, not all did. The Allies knew that the Nazis slipped intelligence agents, such as Lüning (whose Honduran passport indicated that he was Jewish), into the stream of German refugees. The Allies did not know, of course, how many agents came to the Americas on false passports. A decade of the Nazi leadership's self-serving conduct suggested that a fairly large number of agents were sent to the Western Hemisphere with these improper documents. There was a related complication. Many old-time German residents proclaimed nationalistic views, although most commonly they were attached nostalgically to the imperial Germany of their youth or, perhaps, to the Weimar Republic. Naturally, Nazi officials sought support from the established resident Germans. Some old-time residents became National Socialists, but, even then, they commonly advocated a different ideological mix and set of priorities from the homeland National Socialists. Thus, the Abwehr agents were camouflaged within the large body of new immigrants and old German residents.[55]

Since Hitler ordered his government to avoid conflict with the United States, the German leadership had not expected the United States to enter the war. Therefore, Germany had not prepared many agents for duty in the American continents until after mid-1941. In December 1941, the Japanese had not warned Germany about an imminent attack on U.S. territory. Of course, Germany was unable to adjust its intelligence operations efficiently to a post–Pearl Harbor world. The German, U.S., and British intelligence services operated in the Americas with considerable internal tension and uncertain objectives in the early stages of World War II. The increasing German espionage activity, when linked to the startling success of German submarines early in the 1942 "Battle of the Caribbean," heightened U.S. concerns about Axis influence in the Americas.

▶ 3 ◀

Back to School!
Trained as a Nazi Spy

In July 1941, Hans Joachim Koelln arranged for Lüning to enter the Abwehr academy in Hamburg. From the beginning, Lüning seemed anxious to go to the Western Hemisphere. Later, after he was captured, rumors surfaced about earlier Abwehr service. There is no evidence to support this allegation and considerable evidence that it was not true. An FBI-SIS investigation rejected these unsubstantiated claims that Lüning had conducted espionage activity while in the Dominican Republic in 1936 and 1937. The FBI was convinced that Lüning entered the spy world only in 1941.[1] The Abwehr files and other evidence from his family and friends confirm that he entered service in July 1941.

Lüning was not a happy spy. He entered Abwehr service only to avoid military service. His description of training and service for the Abwehr exposed many of the less glamorous aspects of espionage. His schooling was rigorously secretive and intense. Prior to entry, Lüning signed a pledge of secrecy. He agreed to keep his Abwehr service secret even from his wife. In 1942, he told the SIS that his class had eleven other students and three instructors. Each student had a code name; Lüning's was "Lumann." Presumably, the instructors also had code names. During his interrogations in Havana, Lüning dug back into his memory. To the best of his ability, he supplied the U.S., British, and Cuban intelligence agents with the code names, detailed physical descriptions, the language capabilities, and his personal evaluation of his classmates and the instructors at the espionage school.[2] He willingly described his experience in the Abwehr academy.

The Hamburg Abwehr school commonly trained a class as individuals or in small groups. The members of Lüning's small class were trained individually. When the students were brought together, they were not allowed to talk to each other. Each day, they signed in with their code names and were checked twice daily for attendance. In the course of the war, the Hamburg Abwehr school trained about two hundred agents.[3]

During his espionage training, Lüning was exposed to a variety of skills but mastered none of them. His six-week training program covered wireless radio transmission and reception, how to mix and write in three secret inks, and Morse code. In his interrogation, he claimed the ability to transmit seventy letters per minute in Morse code during his training. His only radio transmission and reception, however, occurred with German stations in Bremen and Hamburg-Wohldorf, and even then he used printed exercise drills. He received signals only from the German station in Halle. While some radio trainees monitored night radio reception from less active stations such as Africa, Lüning never was allowed to, probably a sign that his instructors doubted his skill. Thus, during his Abwehr schooling, he never sent signals to or received them from a radio station outside Germany. As part of his training, he successfully constructed a radio set in his instructor's office. However, all the parts and materials were available. He merely assembled them. Later, in Havana, he could not rise to the challenge. He failed to acquire the necessary parts and materials to assemble a radio. The training in Hamburg also included microdot photography, recognizing and escaping shadows (people following agents), and basic knowledge of the armed forces in the country of the agent's service (especially identifying ships, planes, and tank types).[4] The only "James Bond" characteristics he learned well were how to find girls and drinks.

At the end of the course, Lüning became Abwehr agent A-3779. The A indicated that he was in the regular service, the 3 indicated that he had been trained at the Hamburg AST, and 779 was the consecutive number assigned to him. His designation suggests that Lüning had entered the service somewhat late since, presumably, the first agent trained by the Hamburg AST would have been designated A-3001.[5] However, because most Hamburg Abwehr records were destroyed, it cannot be determined whether all the numbers between 1 and 779 were assigned.

In the course of the Abwehr school's instruction, Alfred Hartmann—who, as we have seen, recruited Lüning and was now training him—recognized Lüning's limitations. Initially, he had mentioned that Lüning would learn a book code based on Pearl Buck's novel *The Good Earth* and receive the names of three people in the Caribbean as contacts: a Swiss man in Port au Prince, Haiti; the German wife of an American army officer stationed in Puerto Rico; and a gentleman in Puerto Rico. When Lüning's training revealed a person of clearly limited capacity, Hartmann altered his plans. Lüning would not receive a book code nor the contact names in the Caribbean. In fact, Hartmann instructed him not to conduct inter-American Abwehr correspondence.[6] He wisely withheld the information to minimize any damage to Abwehr activity in the Caribbean if (when?) Lüning was arrested.

Hartmann lost interest in Lüning once his limitations were evident. Only during his last days at the school did Lüning learn that he was headed to Cuba. In Lüning's mind, as he explained to the SIS, Hartmann was "in a great hurry" to get him "out of his way" and "nervous" while giving final instructions. Hartmann told Lüning: "We are interested in information from Cuba, but Cuba is Spanish controlled." That apparently meant that Spain, "a member of the Axis," conducted espionage in Cuba for Germany. To protect his cover during his stay in Cuba, Lüning should avoid Spanish Falangists, Germans, and Italians and sympathize with the democracies.[7] Avoiding Axis sympathizers should minimize Allied suspicion of him.

Special instructions made Lüning's correspondence identifiable to the Abwehr. He should write cover letters in Spanish—on business or personal matters—and use English for the secret ink messages. The signatures of all the cover letters to his secret ink messages should have first names that began with *M* or *R*. The last name was immaterial, and only the first letter of the first name was important. The form of the date on the letter identified which of the three secret inks was used. If the year was four digits (e.g., 5 July 1942, No. 6), an ink called *1942*—0.5 ounces of alcohol and ten drops of lemon juice—had been used. If the year was only two digits (e.g., 5 July 42, No. 6), the ink called *1941*—0.5 ounces of urine and ten drops of lemon juice—was indicated. If the number of the secret ink message was given in Roman numerals (e.g., 5 July 1942, No. VI), the third ink—a zinc sulfate—was used. Lüning claimed that he had used the latter only about four times. It took ten to twelve hours to bathe the paper in zinc sulfate and then to dry the paper before writing on it. For some reason, he withheld information about the third secret ink. Only in late October 1942, after the Allied labs detected a sulfate residue on some of Lüning's correspondence, did he confess to it. If the day of the message was given in Roman numerals (e.g., V July 1942, No. 6), the letter contained a microdot. However, Lüning never used this date form because his efforts to create a microdot were unsuccessful. A microdot used photography to reduce several pages of information to a period, such as the one ending this sentence.[8] When he left for Cuba, Lüning carried several microdots with information from the Hamburg AST, but he could not effectively use them.[9]

Lüning displayed his talents when fulfilling his central duty—writing secret ink messages. He wrote such messages on roughly a weekly basis but with flashes of incompetence. He misnumbered the messages and mixed the inks improperly. Secret ink writing required some technical knowledge and the skill to mix and to apply the ink effectively. Lüning appeared weak in these essential skills. He may have guarded (or forgotten) one part of the formulas because he never mentioned paradinol, a headache pill, which was commonly crushed into powder for use in German secret inks. His secret inks were not durable, perhaps because he forgot to add the paradinol. Since writing in these inks required paraphernalia and considerable time, Lüning kept canaries in the room. Much was made of this, but his family had kept birds in Hamburg. Under determined SIS questioning, he insisted that the canaries were his idea, not a product of his Abwehr schooling. Nevertheless, the excuse of loose birds allowed him to delay opening the door until he had hidden the secret ink writing materials or the radio that he worked on periodically without success.[10]

Near the end of the Abwehr training, Paul Kraus of the Hamburg Gestapo obtained a Honduran passport for Lüning, who had never visited Honduras. Dr. Majín Herrera A., the former Honduran consul in Hamburg, had had his exequatur—the legal authority to issue passports and to exercise consular functions in a foreign land—canceled a year earlier. Nevertheless, he retained blank passports, seals, and stamps and issued passport number 32, dated June 13, 1940, to Enrique Augusto Luni for a bribe of five thousand reichsmarks (roughly equivalent to $2,000 [in 1942 dollars]).[11] An unusual relationship between the Gestapo and Herrera apparently was related to the illegal documents. German counterespionage agencies welcomed legal-looking passports.

The FBI interviewed a South American diplomat, traveling with a Dominican Republic passport, who had resided in Hamburg from early 1936 until being interned in December 1941. He knew Lüning and Herrera. He recalled, for example, that Lüning had acquired a Dominican Republic tourist visa. Significantly, when the Germans interned the South American diplomatic and consular officials in December 1941, this South America diplomat noted that Herrera was not included. He heard that Herrera left for Spain sometime in 1942. A State Department official discreetly learned that, when Herrera departed for Barcelona, he left his two children in Germany to continue their schooling. Lüning's passport belonged, ostensibly, to a persecuted Jew who had fled the Netherlands after the German bombing of Rotterdam. Lüning alleged that, with sufficient money, it was easy to acquire passports from small Central and South American countries.[12] His passport bore stamps indicating that he had lived in Bremen and Hamburg for over one year. It also had the proper stamps for his departure and reentry as well as a Gestapo stamp.[13] One stamp was missing, however, and this jeopardized his departure for Barcelona to travel to Havana.

Before Lüning left Hamburg, Hartmann had advised him "to construct a story" to bridge the time gap between his imaginary flight from Rotterdam (June 1940) and his real trip to Havana (September 1941). At Hartmann's suggestion, he purchased a small notebook-diary. He then created entries that would simulate his employment as a tutor of Spanish for Germans. The notebook contained imaginary records of his students, the fees they paid, other meetings, and some addresses and notes from everyday life. The initial page showed his name and an Abwehr safe address: E. Augusto Luni, Maria-Louisa-Straße 61, III, telephone 523957. A few items in Lüning's notebook-diary, especially names of women added in Havana, came from his real life.[14] This created record book was supposed to serve as evidence of his innocuous activity in Germany prior to arriving in Havana.

The story of Lüning's travel to his duty station in Havana illustrates the low value attached to his work after he finished at the Abwehr academy. Hartmann, who doubted that there was direct passage from Europe to Havana, proposed travel to be arranged with the British firm Thomas Cooke from Lisbon, Portugal, to Buenos Aires, Argentina, and then back north to Havana. However, Lüning, with maritime experience in his family, booked the travel from Barcelona directly to Havana on September 10, 1941, aboard the Spanish steamer *Villa de Madrid.* Hartmann's proposal would have subjected Lüning to British surveillance because Cooke was a British firm and Great Britain had a close relationship with Portugal. Fortunately, the departure of Lüning's ship was delayed until September 11. At the French-Spanish border, German officials delayed him for two days awaiting confirmation that he had permission to take so many dollars out of the German-controlled region. Thus, in a further indication that Lüning's work was taken lightly, Hartmann had failed to obtain the proper stamp to permit the export of dollar currency. Lüning's permission to remove dollars arrived only two hours before the last train that could connect him to the ship in Barcelona. Finally, sailing on the delayed *Villa de Madrid,* he arrived in Havana on September 29.[15] His successful arrival in Havana owed more to his own initiative than to Abwehr effort.

Once it had determined that Lüning was not good agent material, the Abwehr had shown little regard for him. It had canceled his book code and withheld the names of the three contacts in the Caribbean. It did not bother to determine the best route to Havana or to make sure that he had the proper stamp in his passport to allow dollar export. Even his travel funds did not come from the Abwehr. The Abwehr merely converted Lüning's reichsmarks into dollars (only the government could legally convert marks to dollars); he received about $3,575 prior to departing for Barcelona (only $2,821 remained on arrival in Havana). Besides a few $50 bills, he carried mostly denominations from $1 to $20. Later, when a $10 note was refused in a Havana business, Lüning suspected that some of the U.S. currency was counterfeit. Various $10 bills bore the words *El Paso, Texas* in the lower-right-hand corner. These were either counterfeited or had circulated prior to the 1935 law that withdrew national bank currency from circulation.[16] The Abwehr even undermined Lüning when it converted some of his reichsmarks into dubious U.S. currency.

Once in Havana, Lüning was instructed to build a radio, to cable a specific open code message to an address in Mexico City, and then to open radio contact with intermediaries in Argentina and Chile. In keeping with the loss of interest in him at the end of his training, he was given only some of the wavelengths or the specific transmission times necessary to make contact in South America.[17] He was advised to place his radio antenna to communicate principally to the south—Argentina or Chile. His messages would then be relayed north to Europe. His assigned call letters were 136-VVV and 246-VVV on band 26.9. The Abwehr would contact him at 6:00 P.M. for about ten minutes on band 27.2 or 27.3. But his radio skills were weak. Even after four hours of questioning by the SIS, he had considerable difficulty reconstructing the radio code he had learned. He apparently expected some retraining from an inspector who would visit him once his radio was completed.[18] He never received the refresher instruction because the radio was never operable.

Lüning had also left Hamburg with a password phrase for this expected radio inspector-instructor, who would have identified himself with the phrase in Spanish: "Was it not I who took you out from beneath a beam during a cyclone in Ciudad Trujillo?" The inspector-instructor never arrived. Still later, when Lüning was arrested, one of the Cuban police, who had lived previously in the Dominican Republic and had perhaps seen Lüning there, inquired: "Didn't I know you in Ciudad Trujillo?" Initially, Lüning feared that this man was a Gestapo agent. He was not.[19]

After Lüning's capture, the SIS investigators quickly evaluated his ability to utilize his training. They decided that the radio was inoperative: "It had been constructed in a very amateurish fashion and could not be operated in the condition in which it was found. Several of the poorly soldered keys had been broken and the connections to the tube sockets were improperly made." The antenna was detached. At first, no one noted that the radio lacked one essential tube. Later, after a more careful examination, Cuban, SIS, and FCC experts confirmed that the radio would not operate. Their report was devastating about the incompetent radio construction. The Cuban experts were convinced that it had never operated. The SIS agents argued, however, that, if properly constructed, wired with a good antenna, and connected to an adequate power source, Lüning's radio could have sent distant communications under good weather conditions.[20] But none of these hypothetical conditions reflected reality.

Hartmann apparently had no illusions about Lüning's capacity as a spy. Yet he imparted only cursory instructions about how the agent should conduct himself in an emergency. During an SIS interrogation, Lüning voluntarily declared that Hartmann told him that, in an emergency, he should flee to the Dominican Republic or, failing that, seek refuge in the Spanish embassy in Havana. In this latter case, he should present his passport and explain his activities in Cuba to the Spanish. These were Hartmann's only instructions on possible emergency flight.[21] It seemed that it was neither desirable nor possible to save Lüning if he got into difficulty.

Abwehr agent A-3779 had a modest level of education, a brief training period, narrow and personal interests, modest intelligence, and no desire to serve Germany. Lüning could not build or operate a radio or mix any of three secret inks properly. After watching his training for six weeks, his superior at the Abwehr headquarters in Hamburg quietly judged him to be inadequate.

Nevertheless, from his post in Havana, Lüning regularly supplied information from printed media and conversations with common people because his wife, child, and aunt and uncle (who had adopted him) remained in Hamburg. While the Abwehr considered Lüning a *zuverlässig* [reliable] agent, that adjective meant that he was trusted, not that the information in his reports was reliable or valuable. As Lüning prepared to depart for Havana, the cavalier treatment from the Hamburg AST headquarters—no book code, no contact people, incomplete radio contact information, no concern about how he might travel to Havana—suggested that they expected very little from him. And he was a decoy, intentional or unintentional, because the FBI-SIS devoted enormous resources to "discovering" Lüning's nonexistent spy network.

▶ 4 ◀

Tested in Action

Despite a rather dismal record of education in his young life, Lüning had finished the Abwehr academy. This may say more about the Abwehr's need for agents than Lüning's maturity or suitability as an agent. Perhaps the Abwehr was more concerned about getting people into Latin America than locating and training qualified agents. Certainly, when Lüning entered Abwehr service after two years of wartime mobilization, the pool of potential German agents was very thin. Under pressure to get agents into Latin America once the war became global, the Abwehr had to train the best prospects it could find. Lüning's year in Havana revealed his potential.

Those who knew Lüning in the Caribbean saw no qualities of a spy in him. One of seven acquaintances interviewed in Santo Domingo pondered whether the Gestapo and the German intelligence services selected intelligent people: "We cannot believe here that Lüning was a real spy. . . . He was sent out by the Gestapo [*sic;* read: Abwehr] to be captured, to draw attention upon himself in order that the real spies could work more undisturbed. . . . Lüning had no qualities of a spy—none of them." His profile was obvious. He had only passable Spanish, was not committed to Nazi goals, and had poor work habits—his life experience had not prepared him for spying. When this informant learned that Lüning was caught after having correspondence sent to his home address rather than a drop box, he remarked that the Gestapo did not use such "childish means of communication." This acquaintance concluded: "Anyway, for anybody who knew Lüning it is ridiculous to believe that he was a spy. Either he was sent out to be sacrificed, or the efficiency of the German Intelligence Service must be equal to zero if they use a 'zero' like Lüning as a spy."[1]

Another source in Santo Domingo concluded: "The Gestapo had sent out a simple person like Lüning as a spy in order that he might be captured and draw attention from the other agents or that the Gestapo is hard up for espionage agents in the Western Hemisphere." The U.S. military attaché who interviewed several informants found the idea of Lüning as bait "interesting."[2] In fact, the Abwehr had entered the Americas very late. It assumed that the less competent of its new agents would get caught, thereby distracting attention from the more effective agents. After his training revealed his limitations, the Abwehr officials apparently sent him out as a decoy.

From the perspective of U.S. and British military leadership, the success of German U-boats in the Gulf-Caribbean needed an explanation. The Allied war effort required the termination of the German threat to north-south and east-west ship traffic in the Gulf-Caribbean area. The elevated strategic value of interoceanic transit and special products increased the importance of the anti-U-boat campaign in the Caribbean in 1942. It was unacceptable that a German spy network operating out of Havana gathered and radioed information to German U-boats. An active, effective Abwehr spy in Havana would pose a most serious threat to the Allies.[3]

During his first night in Havana, Lüning (he was known there by the name in his passport, Enrique Augusto Luni) enjoyed an evening that reflected the lifestyle he pursued during visits to Ciudad Trujillo, Dominican Republic, in 1936 and 1937. After his arrival late on September 29, 1941, he and several friends, including the Catalan Abwehr agent Ricardo Dotres and a Dr. Hornung, from the *Villa de Madrid* took a cab ride through Havana until they found a suitable restaurant. While eating, one friend suggested lodging at the Lincoln Hotel. Later, the group checked in at the Lincoln, which charged $4.50 per night. After taking room 8, Lüning went looking for entertainment. He found a girl and went to the Hotel Siboney. In addition to the evening with the lady, he discovered that the Siboney charged only $1.50 per night. Soon, he moved to the Siboney, about fifty yards from the Wonder Bar (on the Wonder bar, see below).[4] His first undertaking in Cuba involved food, drink, and a girl.

As he settled into Havana, Lüning became known as a German Jew who had escaped Nazi persecution. Later, when the SIS interrogated him, he insisted that he worked alone. While he suspected that other Abwehr agents operated in Havana, he claimed not to know a single one. All the information that he sent back to Germany came from the local press and conversations with people in the Havana harbor area. He talked to unwary sailors, harbor pilots, dockworkers, bar entertainers, bar girls, prostitutes, and other waterfront people in bars and cafés. Among his preferred haunts were the Salon H, the Bar Puerto Chico, and the Wonder Bar. He sought information about ship sailings and cargoes. Despite his efforts, he gathered and sent back little information of use. To communicate with Abwehr headquarters, since his radio never functioned, he used the three secret ink formulas that the Abwehr had taught him. His airmail correspondence went to Bermuda (where MI6 copied it) and then on to the Iberian Peninsula, but his cables were sent to the Iberian Peninsula through Abwehr people in Argentina or, more commonly, Chile.[5] Lüning's weekly messages reported incompletely on ship traffic at Havana, the movement of Allied naval vessels, the construction of several U.S. military airports in Cuba, and public economic information.[6] And, in general, the Abwehr was dissatisfied with his paltry results.

After Lüning's capture and interrogation, it became clear that his low-quality information had even less value because the British had delayed its arrival in Germany. Still, even if the British had not exercised such caution, Lüning had little useful information. Describing a likely course for his weekly secret ink messages reveals the limits of their potential as a threat to ships. Even using airmail, the messages would require three or four days to reach a drop box in Lisbon, Portugal, or Bilbao, Spain. There, an Abwehr agent would need time to expose the secret ink and transcribe the message; one has to remember that Lüning was not the only Abwehr agent writing to Iberian Peninsula drop boxes. The Abwehr agents in Lisbon and Bilbao could radio the information to Hamburg or Berlin if deemed urgent and then forward the paper text to Germany.

To continue this hypothetical time line, Abwehr headquarters in Berlin would read and evaluate the messages before forwarding the content to the Naval High Command. From there, it would go on to the headquarters of Admiral Karl Dönitz, the commander of the submarine force. Finally, Dönitz's staff needed to evaluate the information—under normal conditions already five to ten days old—and determine whether it merited special action. Since Lüning's reports frequently lacked important pieces of information, like sailing dates, sailing directions, specific cargoes, or quantity and quality of convoy protection, they would have had limited value for planning submarine missions even if they had arrived in a week or so rather than the actual time of about eight to twelve weeks. Spies like James Bond are rare. A weak agent will often pass along unclear, imprecise, and low-quality information. Lüning excelled at that aspect of his job. Despite his apparent weakness, however, until his capture, the U.S. and British counterespionage services could not be certain that he was not using alternative routes to carry duplicates of the captured dispatches or, perhaps, even more crucial information.

British censors at the Bermuda station, the principal British censorship post in the Americas, had detected Lüning's secret messages—the first such messages from a spy in Cuba—almost immediately. On October 14, 1941, for no particular reason, a wary British mail sorter at the Bermuda station placed a business letter from "R[afael] Castillo" in Havana to a Mr. Mutz at a Lisbon, Portugal, address in a stack of correspondence being sent for chemical tests. Conceivably, she had merely responded to the ominous times. The need for greater vigilance had increased as the war went badly for the British and Americans. The tests detected a 3 in the corner of a secret ink message written on the back side of the business message. The British decipherers exposed the secret ink message by placing the letter in a glass box and exposing it to a special chemical mist that allowed the censors to transcribe and photograph the exposed writing. (When the letter was removed from the presence of the chemical mist, the ink reverted to its invisible state.) This letter was the first of forty-four of Lüning's secret ink messages that were intercepted—although initially all that was known was that the sender was a Nazi agent, apparently in Havana. The visible message was written in Spanish, the secret note in English.[7]

To facilitate effective resistance to the Axis powers, over a year before the United States actually entered the war, the U.S. and British governments agreed to exchange counterintelligence information acquired in the Americas. In New York City, the British exchanged this first secret message from Cuba and other intercepts for copies of relevant materials from U.S. intelligence. Further exchanges occurred on a near daily basis. Soon, thousands of eyes, alerted to the handwriting and the recipient's name and address, scanned incoming correspondence for similar handwriting or a similar addressee. The British censors soon found eleven other messages for the "Mutz file." The writer appeared to be a careless German because German words appeared in the Spanish notes.[8] Ten months passed, however, before the identity of the writer was traced. In one sense, this discovery was not unusual. German agents working in the Americas commonly used Portugal and Spain for drop box locations. However, the story of this Mutz-file agent sheds a special light on intelligence operations in the Caribbean during World War II.

After the discovery of an Abwehr agent operating in Havana, the Allied governments were determined to locate and capture him. The British, U.S., and Cuban counterintelligence agencies suspected that this spy and, perhaps, other Axis agents were gathering information to increase the effectiveness of German submarine activity in the Caribbean area. Hoover wanted to uncover the identity of all agents operating in Havana and, perhaps, unravel the whole Axis network in the Gulf-Caribbean region. To this end, he cautioned that SIS agents not accompany Cuban police on searches or arrests but, instead, work "to discover [the German agents'] activities and contacts." British and U.S. intelligence officials considered the value of the intercepted messages. Should they release the intercepts to the drop boxes in Spain and Portugal? After extensive review, the SIS leaders decided that the messages of the Mutz file did not contain information of "instant naval or military value." The reports on shipping and convoys "cannot reach their destination in time to disclose [in a manner useful to the U-boats] the whereabouts of shipping at sea." These intercepts—about the size and strength of convoys and the nature of materials shipped—had, the SIS officials decided, only record-keeping value and should be released. Otherwise, the Abwehr would become suspicious, and "subsequent messages might be more difficult to intercept."[9] Observing this known agent offered the best opportunity to uncover other contacts and agents. The possibilities were wide open.

Lüning knew, of course, that Allied counterintelligence would search for any Axis agent in the Caribbean. Several incidents alerted him to aspects of the Allied counterintelligence work. Once, during a visit to a brothel, he saw what he assumed were two FBI agents. They were U.S. agents, in his judgment, because they seemed interested not in the women but in "something else." They spoke Spanish with an American accent and were dressed "elegantly." After a short visit, they left. The story ended.[10] However, they could have been looking for Axis agents. The author of the Mutz-file messages would certainly have been high on their most-wanted list.

In early January 1942, Lüning reported a bizarre incident. In his view, he "had [been the object of an] investigation last week." A British official (MI6 agent?), pretending to be a Cuban investigator, visited his room and inquired whether he was writing to foreign countries and, if so, which ones. Lüning admitted writing to the United States. The investigator held his papers, with a British consulate letterhead visible, so that Lüning could read the first few lines. The exposed text suggested that "Luni" was a German citizen who held a false Honduran passport.[11] Thus, the British already suspected Luni in January 1942 because of his passport and conduct in Havana. Despite their suspicions, however, they did not tie him to the secret ink writing or even to espionage work. Most likely, they suspected every person of German origin who arrived in Cuba. But numerous Jewish and other refugees from Germany in Havana held possible false passports.

The capture of any Axis agent would require cooperation among the Allied counterintelligence agents. Allied intelligence agencies cooperated most of the time, though they sometimes reached different conclusions. Lüning claimed that he wrote forty-seven secret ink messages, but he often misnumbered his secret correspondence—both leaving out and repeating numbers. The assistant to the director of the U.S. Office of Censorship, Theodore Koop, claimed that the Allied censors intercepted forty-three of forty-eight secret ink messages. However, U.S. censors intercepted only a few of Lüning's secret writings. Almost all their intercepts came from the British Bermuda station. The British intercepted forty-four of what they judged were forty-nine secret ink messages. They intercepted the items numbered 47 and 48 (but one duplicated number had not been corrected) about the time that Lüning was arrested. The forty-nine secret ink dispatches went to four drop boxes:

> Sr. Mutz, c/o Sres. Mattos Tavares and Cia., Caixa Postal 171, Lisbon, Portugal;
> Sr. José Bonger, Apartado 417, Bilbao, Spain;
> Sres. Bender, Ltda., Caixa Postal 532, Lisbon, Portugal;
> Sres. Maquinarias Industriales, Apartado 417, Bilbao, Spain.[12]

There was a firm and a private individual in Bilbao and in Lisbon.

Before Lüning's identity was uncovered, the British named the file the "Havana Secret Writing Case—Mutz-Series," after the addressee on the first intercepted message. The FBI adopted the designation the "Mutz Secret Writing Case." In addition to the Iberian drop boxes, Lüning used mail, telegrams, and cables to communicate within the Americas, mostly addresses in Chile, Argentina, Honduras, and the United States. Much of Lüning's telegram activity was not directly related to his Abwehr activity; rather, it involved his efforts to create cover businesses that also offered an opportunity to earn a living. Since he could not get his radio to work, he occasionally telegraphed intermediaries in Chile or Argentina to contact Abwehr headquarters. These intermediaries relayed his telegrams to the Abwehr. Still, the secret ink messages were his chief means of communicating with Germany.

Lüning's superiors in Europe communicated with him in writing infrequently. They had intended to send instructions by radio. The British and U.S. censors intercepted only a few secret ink messages from the Abwehr in Europe to Lüning. Then, after his detention, the Allies learned about several additional indirect (via Chilean agents) Abwehr cable messages to Lüning. The Allied counterespionage officials cooperated under a 1941 U.S. and British wartime intelligence agreement but needed time to track him down.[13]

Once the United States joined the war, this agreement was modified. The new form assigned the Western Hemisphere to U.S. intelligence and reduced British intelligence responsibility to British colonies and commonwealth partners. This agreement disturbed the British security agencies. Presumably, the withdrawal of British operations from most places in the Americas outside the commonwealth areas would seriously weaken supervision of Axis activities. The British were concerned because the U.S. government was not highly regarded in Latin America. It had few agents and little intelligence experience south of the border. Furthermore, the British officials feared that withdrawal in favor of U.S. counterintelligence would mark them as U.S. subordinates and seriously jeopardize postwar British efforts to return. Most important, British withdrawal would weaken efforts to counter Nazi propaganda and espionage activity in Latin America. Cuba was a case in point. British security was especially concerned about profascist and fifth-column activity there. Despite U.S. and Cuban claims of successful control of Nazis and fascists, British officials considered Cuban "handling of enemy aliens a farce; they are released on a standard payment."[14] British counterintelligence found the Cuban government weak, corrupt, and careless in controlling Axis aliens.

Even more disturbing, British officials distrusted the Batista government's moral commitment to the war effort. Batista had declared war "entirely on grounds of personal gain and prestige and is using war emergency measures to enrich himself and friends," according to one British official in Cuba. Other wealthy Cubans joined Batista in missing "the implications of the war except as a means of making money for themselves."[15] Many Cuban leaders, from a British perspective, seemed more interested in opening bank accounts than closing down Axis operations.

Nazi spies, of course, did their best to negate any Cuban, U.S., or

British efforts to uncover their work. During his stay in Cuba, Lüning tried, as we have seen, to build cover activities that offered an opportunity to earn a living as well. For example, he retained contact with his former Spanish tutor, Lola Ardela. Soon after the war began in Europe, Ardela had traveled to Buenos Aires, where she married a businessman from Bremen, Kurt Auerbach, who apparently had Jewish ties. During the war, the Auerbachs heard from Lüning twice, although they did not realize it. On February 24, 1941, Lüning congratulated them on their marriage. The second letter, dated May 6, 1942, puzzled them for a time. Someone named Enrique Luni inquired about entering into business with Kurt Auerbach. After Lüning's arrest in Havana and his cover name became public, the Auerbachs realized that the second letter had come from their friend.[16]

Then, apparently forgetting her advice to him several years earlier, Ardela and her husband could not figure out why Lüning, who had many close Jewish friends and seemed to despise the Nazis, would have joined the Abwehr. On reflection, she was "convinced that he did it only to leave Germany and avoid military service and thereafter had to produce [information and reports] for fear that members of his family would be harmed if he did not." The SIS agents valued the Auerbachs' view because they were reputedly anti-Nazi and Kurt had Jewish ties.[17] Most likely, Lüning had desired merely to retain an old friendship and to preserve a business option in the unlikely event he could get his family out of Germany.

While preparing Lüning for his mission in Havana, Hartmann had urged him to ask the Honduran diplomats in Havana for business contacts in Honduras because he was "a Honduran citizen [he had a Honduran passport]." Such contacts might provide Lüning with a livelihood and cover for any activity in the Caribbean region. In fact, Néstor Bermúdez, the Honduran consul general in Havana, introduced Lüning to several potential business partners. Bermúdez was an eager promoter but also a habitual drunkard. He looked to make a dollar any way he could in order to continue his drinking. He held an elevated post in Cuba only because of his prominent family.[18]

Lüning pursued various business ventures as cover activities. Several of his personal or business matters were related to the Wonder Bar. This bar was special only because it served dark bock beer and, hence, attracted Jews and other European immigrants. It also played a major role in Lüning's life in Havana. In his first days in the city, a bartender from the Wonder Bar, Emilio Pérez, had helped him find permanent, if small, accommodations in the building where he, Pérez, lived. Soon after his arrival, Lüning alleged that his girlfriend needed to contact him before he had his own living quarters, so Pérez allowed him to use his name and mailing address. Later, hoping to build a rewarding cover business, Lüning financed a women's clothing store in Havana, Estampa de Modas. He hired Pérez's wife, Claribel Stincer de Pérez (called Clarita), to manage the business. The store did poorly, and Lüning was unable to sell it. In general, he remained as unsuccessful in commerce in Havana as he had been in Hamburg. Still, he hoped that his business ventures might, ultimately, help him earn a living.[19]

Lüning explored other potential cover businesses. He contacted a ship broker, Alfred Morgan, in the Bay Islands of Honduras in search of ships he could sell in Cuba. Morgan was a second-generation resident of the Bay Islands. His father had succeeded in business and as a boat merchant, but Alfred encountered financial problems. Still, an SIS investigation concluded that he was essentially nonpolitical and known to favor the Allies. After inquiries, the SIS judged the Lüning-Morgan connection a legitimate business activity. Lüning's commission boat business reinforced his sham Honduran citizenship, promised to help him earn his living, and gave him reason to write shipping interests or ship brokers elsewhere in the Caribbean. These contacts might have supplied additional useful information for the Abwehr.[20] The German hoped the sales commissions would cover his living expenses and the costs of his espionage work.

The search for income-producing cover businesses continued. Lüning contacted various U.S. firms, mostly in the East and Midwest, about entering into import-export business arrangements, but without success.[21] Between his women's fashion store, his activity as a commission boat merchant, and his efforts to build an import-export business, he established a basis for writing to any place in the Americas. While a potential for information gathering existed, the U.S., British, and Cuban counterintelligence agents never uncovered Lüning correspondence that sought to use the business possibilities to do so. Thus, none of these ventures proved financially rewarding or produced valuable intelligence. This was consistent with his life experiences. During his thirty-one years, he stumbled through life, business, and the espionage worlds.

Lüning had confirmed his reputation as a ladies' man on his first night in Cuba. His diary recorded other romantic adventures. This intriguing aspect of his life in Havana unfortunately left hidden tracks and only a few revealing details. The SIS interrogated Lüning at great length and in detail regarding numerous entries in the fabricated notebook-diary. This diary described a year-and-a-half stay in Bremen and Hamburg as well as his first months in Havana. Some entries for Havana mentioned real encounters with bar women, prostitutes, and houses of prostitution, but the SIS censored the names. The agency compiled an "Explanation of notations in Notebooks of Lüning" (I did not see the diary) that is so heavily censored that it has limited value.[22] Thus, some information about the women in Lüning's Cuban life exists, but it is hidden behind a veil of secrecy.

In Havana, Lüning formed a relationship with a woman he called "Rebecca" (Enrique Rodríguez established that this was Olga López, the woman who requested to see Lüning on his last night before execution, according to the Castillo Príncipe Prison visitors' registry). A journalist, unfortunately of questionable reliability, claimed that Lüning met Rebecca in a bar; she became his mistress and loyal supporter. Although finding traces of Rebecca are not easy, she was apparently well-known in Havana. Some contemporary accounts of Lüning's last days mention her. An SIS report, based on interviews with Emilio Pérez and others in the building where Lüning lived, stated that Lüning had only one un-named woman guest (Rebecca, or Olga López?) in his room at Teniente Rey 366. Lüning told the SIS that he had a woman friend (the name is censored in the SIS copy sent to me) who worked in the Justice Ministry and lived "in the heights of Salón Cristal at Prado and Virtudes streets." This is the area where the elusive Rebecca was reputed to live.[23]

While pursuing women was Lüning's preferred activity, the Abwehr expected him to build a serviceable radio to communicate with Germany. Since radio communication was fundamental to his espionage service, Lüning dabbled in radio and electricity. He and Pérez visited electrical and radio stores to acquire the parts needed to assemble a radio. Yet building a radio challenged him. His major problems were poor soldering, an inability to read the design plan correctly, faulty connections, and an inability to locate a tube. His radio plan required a 6L6 tube and a "magnetic" 904, 904-wy, or 904REM (or, perhaps, a 906 or 903) tube. He and Emilio could not find the latter, new or used. So he experimented with alternative approaches, including the use of two 6L6 tubes. All his schemes proved unsuccessful. At one point in its investigation, the SIS thought that he had tried to get professional help to complete his radio. Over a six-month period, he had formed a friendship with an unnamed twenty-five-year-old Mexican electrician, a member of a radical Mexican political group. However, Lüning insisted that they merely visited houses of prostitution together. He denied asking for help with his radio because then the secrecy of his work would have been lost.[24] Lacking technical ability, Lüning was overmatched in his effort to get his radio to function.

Although Lüning could not build a functioning radio, he maintained secret ink contact with Germany roughly weekly. Yet his ability to communicate in secret ink was also flawed. The Abwehr complained of Lüning's tardy and indecipherable messages. The difficulties were not all his fault. He was responsible for any poor ink composition and faulty writing technique. However, he was not entirely responsible for the intervention of British Imperial Censorship (BIC). The BIC intentionally delayed forwarding the intercepted messages. The few surviving Hamburg Abwehr files not destroyed in bombing attacks indicate the receipt of only eight dispatches from agent A-3779. As a security measure, Abwehr headquarters stored information about agents in separate files for country, station, agent name, and agent number. Unfortunately, Lüning's name did not survive in the agent name card file index. The agent number card file did, however, indicate that agent A-3779 worked in Havana from October 1941 until August 1942. These files hold only the data on shipping extracted from Lüning's dispatches. These eight secret ink letters were delayed between eight and twelve weeks before their arrival in Germany. The earliest of these was written on January 5, 1942, but arrived only on March 5, 1942; the last was written on July 11 but arrived only on October 5.[25]

There were several possible explanations why Lüning's messages were illegible: the ink had been poorly prepared (an ingredient missing), it had been poorly applied to the paper, and the British process of exposing it might have weakened the writing, leaving it scarcely legible. In fact, in early 1943, Hoover informed the ONI director: "Some of Lüning's secret writing messages could not be twice examined for secret writing because the first test weakened the secret ink. This may have been one of the reasons why Lüning's secret writing messages could not be developed by his correspondent in Spain [the Abwehr recipient]."[26] Conceivably, the headache tablet paradinol—a common additive to German secret inks—might have strengthened the ink. He may have omitted this ingredient from his formulas because he was an inattentive or forgetful student. In any event, as we have seen, he never mentioned paradinol when discussing the secret inks with the SIS interrogators.[27]

The Abwehr leadership tried to animate their man in Havana. In March 1942, the British censors intercepted two notes from Germany to Lüning (one allegedly from Uncle Gustav and the other from an imaginary girlfriend, Isabel, in Gijón, Spain). The back side of the message from "Gustav" had a secret ink message from the Abwehr. It admonished Lüning to alter the secret ink composition and to write clearly. He interpreted the front side of this note from his superiors as open-language code. The writer described a long hard winter with time for reading. This could have meant that the Abwehr was not receiving his correspondence. The letter also declared his writing almost illegible. He was encouraged to buy a typewriter: "You see I have bought one, and have learned how to use it already." Since Lüning always wrote with a typewriter, he interpreted this letter to mean that he should get his radio up and that his secret ink was not being developed successfully. The letter called Lüning a lazy boy who was not working as hard as he should. Lüning considered the "gist of the letter . . . a subtle threat that he should get busy, write plainer and more often and get his radio into operation."

The writer inquired about the most popular book titles in the United States. During the interrogation covering this letter, Lüning replied that, if his uncle's return address had been on the envelope, he would have noted that *You Can't Do Business with Hitler* was a best seller. In fact, the Rhodes Scholar Douglas Miller's *You Can't Do Business with Hitler* was sixth on the nonfiction best-seller list for 1941. The book inspired a popular radio show that broadcast fifty-six programs in 1942 and early 1943.[28] Lüning took the implications of this letter seriously. He did his best to comply with the warnings he understood from this message.

The British censors intercepted a second message dated from Madrid on March 26, 1942. The cover letter, in Spanish, was signed by "Isabel" and addressed to her "dearest Enrique." She lamented receiving only one postcard from him since he left Europe. She complained about the lack of communications for the past six months (Lüning had been in Cuba for six months) despite his protestations of love when he departed. She could not stand the silence. She insisted that he respond to her letters and remove her uncertainty. The "Isabel" and "Uncle Gustav" letters were probably both from the Hamburg AST, which had grounds to complain.[29]

Between the lines of "Isabel's" letter, a secret ink message in English protested that just "seven letters [had been] received": "Letters 4 and 14 only were readable—in future please use liquid 1942. The other liquid, 19 [*sic;* 1941?], was useless if prepared without alcohol." The Abwehr admonished Lüning to paint the letters more carefully, equally, and with more moisture. The makeshift pen, it reminded him, consisted of two toothpicks held together with the second point about a quarter inch above the first. Between the separated points, swab cotton formed the inkwell. He was to soak up as much ink as the cotton would hold and then print letters. The writer also complained that Lüning's letters arrived so late that the news about merchant ships was worthless. The Abwehr announced plans to remit $1,000 at the end of March, probably from Buenos Aires, representing the funds as a partial payment of a legacy from a relative in Gijón. This proposal explains the two letters to the Honduran Consul, Bermúdez, inquiring about Lüning's location. Since Lüning never radioed, the Abwehr did not have his address.[30]

However, the Abwehr offered encouragement as well as criticism. It welcomed "the most interesting information on U.S. men-of-war. Reports about [illegible; ex-?] ports from Cuba. And bauxite from [illegible; British or Dutch Guyana?]." The writer inquired whether Lüning had found a microscope [for microdot communication]. His wife and son sent "love and greetings": "Sorry cousin Victor fell [reference to a relative who fell on the Russian front]. Confirm receipt of this letter in a cable to the firm Bienvenido—Alegría (Hijo) Gijón by stating your present address and bank." Confirming his lack of a radio, the Abwehr communicated with Lüning by open-language code or secret ink and expected him to reply by cable, not radio message.[31] In summary, his superiors warned that he was not operating as a satisfactory Abwehr agent.

Lüning's problems continued. In communications from Germany sent by way of Sweden, Spain, and Chile during the spring and summer of 1942, the spy's superiors admonished him repeatedly for his shortcomings. Later, in a summary of the SIS investigation into the Havana "master spy" dated December 1942, Hoover was advised, for the umpteenth time: "Luning, or Luni, as he was known to his unsuspecting associates, never was able to place a radio transmitter into operation because of his inability along technical lines and the scarcity of some of the necessary equipment." His radio never worked, and his secret ink communications were often illegible. The Abwehr and the SIS agreed about Lüning's failures.[32]

Even if Lüning worked ineffectively, the Abwehr needed to get him funds and hope his work improved. Tracing the funds that sustained him in Cuba proved difficult. One newspaper rumor had him living off his wife's inheritance. The *Washington Times Herald* alleged that a Boston bank sent him $1,500 monthly from his wife's inheritance. The FBI found no evidence of such transfers but noted a transfer to Lüning from Boston for $1,500. This was Abwehr money, however. The FBI also denied that Helga was an heiress, but, in fact, as we have seen, her great-grandfather and her grandfather had been rich. However, her grandmother, Emma Lassig Bartholomae, would have inherited first, then her mother, Olga, and her siblings, and Helga only after Olga's death. Some of the money may have gone directly to Olga and her siblings. While no sum is mentioned, Philip Bartholomae reportedly inherited a sizable fortune before 1914. On the eve of World War I, the theater press of New York referred to him as a millionaire producer-writer. Some FBI agents naturally wondered whether Philip had sent funds to Heinz, but they found absolutely no evidence that he did. How well the Lassig-Bartholomae fortunes, divided among the inheritors, survived the financial crisis of 1929 and the Great Depression is not clear. Also, whether Olga, residing in Germany, had received a share and was able to transfer the funds before the war began is unclear.[33]

The FBI-SIS investigation located three fund transfers for Lüning during his time in Havana. He received a $1,500 transfer in December 1941, $1,000 as an inheritance in March 1942, and another $1,500 on April 15, 1942, for a total of $4,000 (an SIS report concluded that Lüning had just over $7,000 ultimately, but that sum included the roughly $3,125 he had on departure from Barcelona). The Abwehr funds moved over complicated routes to avoid tracking. For example, the April 15, 1942, transfer of $1,500 began when Manuel Anibal Tapia of Santiago, Chile, sent funds to the First National Bank of Boston. This money then traveled to the Bank of London and South America in New York City and, finally, to the Banco de Boston in Havana. The FBI-SIS uncovered many scores of transfers made in the Western Hemisphere by Tapia, whom they suspected of financing various Nazi activities. The search ended when Tapia died of natural causes on December 16, 1942.[34] While Tapia passed beyond interrogation and justice, the other Abwehr agents operating in Chile could be tracked down.

SIS agents presumed that Lüning had a close association with Nazi agents in Chile, but they sought to uncover other contacts as well. In early 1942, Cuban censors intercepted two letters from Spain addressed to Lüning in care of the Honduran consul-general, Néstor Bermúdez. Cuban agents thought that they had found a Lüning contact with Spain. These letters from the Abwehr front firm Bienvenido Alegría (Hijo), Gijón, Spain, were directed to Bermúdez but meant for Lüning. The Cubans sent these letters to the FBI laboratory, expecting to uncover secret ink messages. That was not the case. The letters merely described the Bienvenido Alegría firm's attempt to notify Lüning about a forthcoming fund transfer that was part of an inheritance.[35] One sentence from a letter appeared to be open-language code: "Until you have proven your right to inherit, I do not consider myself in a position to give you any information as to the amount you are entitled to." Hoover thought that this sentence meant that Lüning would "not be reimbursed until he transmitted information." During questioning, Lüning denied repeatedly receiving correspondence through Bermúdez.[36] The Abwehr agents at Bienvenido Alegría needed his address and bank account number in order to transfer the "inheritance." Without a functioning radio, the Abwehr had no easy, convenient means of contacting Lüning or learning how to send him funds. A Honduran consulate was a logical place to inquire about a Honduran passport holder.

During an SIS interrogation, Lüning explained the meaning of the open-language code used in various cables and messages that inquired about his health and his travel plans. He and his Abwehr contacts used health to refer to the condition of his radio and travel to refer to his ability to broadcast. Once his radio was ready, Lüning had been instructed to cable "Sudameriat in Mexico City" the message: "Left hospital. Continue trip." This message would signal that the radio was ready to send and receive. If he had built a functioning radio and sent the requested cable to the Sudameriat address, he would have connected with Georg Nicolaus and a significant German spy group in Mexico. Lüning denied knowing who the contact was at the Sudameriat address. And the FBI knew that he had never cabled such a message.[37]

The Abwehr, through agents in the Americas, urged Lüning to get his radio working. An Abwehr agent in Chile, Carlos Robinson Hurley, inquired about the status of Lüning's radio in an open-language-coded cablegram of June 26, 1942: "Your letter February 13 received [by the Abwehr in Germany] third week in May. Worried about your health. Did you get out of the hospital sane [*sic*—; a false translation of the Spanish, *sano*, meaning "healthy"]? When will you continue your trip?" The message referred to Lüning's secret ink message to the Abwehr of February 13, 1942, in which he stated his hope to have his radio working soon. This message was in transit for thirteen weeks. Lüning interpreted Robinson's messages for the SIS. Robinson was worried about why there was no radio contact ("Worried about your health"), and he wondered whether the radio was ready to send ("Did you get out of the hospital healthy?"). "When will you continue your trip?" inquired about when Lüning would be able to broadcast.[38] While Lüning's radio never worked, the Hamburg AST naturally expected him to establish the ability to send radio messages.

The Hamburg Abwehr had strong reservations about the abilities of Lüning. He did not disappoint. His record is not that of a master spy. His communications were intercepted or seized when he was captured. His secret ink messages were intercepted and deciphered, but they never conveyed information that was clearly important. He relayed interesting financial or commercial information, but it was gleaned from published sources. Lüning had no contacts with key figures in Cuban society, and he lacked the education, desire, work ethic, and imagination to develop an effective plan for information gathering. His secret ink messages or brief cables reached Germany through Spanish or Portuguese drop boxes or via Chilean contacts. No Abwehr records indicated receipt of a radio message, and no Allied source mentioned an intercepted radio message. When the Abwehr needed a reply urgently, it always asked him to cable it to an intermediary.[39]

Still, Lüning labored to gather shipping and commercial information, and he sent secret ink messages to the Iberian Peninsula weekly. The topics of the messages encompassed common public political observations, popular technology, his problems building a radio, public knowledge about U.S. military activity in Cuba, and public information about shipping and commerce. One early secret ink message reported the movement of a British aircraft carrier in the direction of Puerto Rico. The British censors delayed this correspondence. The first intercepted message of October 13, 1941 (number 3), detailed Lüning's continuing effort, begun while working for B. Schoenfeld in earlier years, to establish a business relationship with the Asturr Trading Company in New York. Later, in late October 1941, he met with an Asturr agent in Havana. This projected business cover, which could have allowed Lüning to relocate to the United States, ended because the Asturr agent decided that Lüning was an unsuitable business partner.[40] As he had in the prewar years, Lüning wanted to settle in the United States or the Caribbean, yet, while awaiting better fortune, he continued to send secret ink messages.

In several of these messages, Lüning detailed his persistent effort to activate his radio. He worried most about a specific tube. Message number 18 stated: "Still searching one piece as other broke very scanty." Number 19 noted: "Everything ready but one piece [the 904 tube] still searching." Repeated visits to Havana radio shops failed to uncover the missing piece. After several unsuccessful attempts to get the radio working, in number 21 he lamented: "Delay because no No. 904-wy."[41] Even if he had encountered a 904 tube, his radio would have resisted use because its construction had, as we have seen, numerous faults.[42] Of course, without a 904 tube, he would never have been able to test his radio, thus exposing the flaws in its construction.

Lüning continually thought that he was close to completing his radio, and, thus, he contemplated the best conditions for sending and receiving. On February 9, 1942, he suggested: "Better between 4:00 and 5:00 P.M." Later, he explained to SIS agents that his original instructions had set the time for radio communications between 5:00 and 6:00 P.M. He wished to move the time for his potential radio contact forward one hour because many inhabitants of his rooming house returned from work between 5:00 and 6:00 P.M. At this earlier time, there would be fewer unexpected listeners.[43] The whole time in Havana he remained optimistic about completing the radio.

Lüning used the secret ink correspondence to request clarification of the two letters received from his Abwehr superiors in March 1942. Neither came from a source he clearly recognized as a German agent, so he wanted these messages repeated in a form he could comprehend. Despite his perplexed state, he continued his routine reporting. Message number 18 noted that seventeen U.S. and two British vessels were in Havana port. The British vessels (two and three thousand tons) were headed to Bermuda with sugar, alcohol, and meat. Lüning also reported that the United States was acquiring scrap metal in Cuba and shipping it to Florida every few days. The Abwehr welcomed the information about scrap metal shipments. However, while Lüning specified destination port and cargo, he did not specify the date of departure or the likely naval protection. In message number 46, for the week of July 25–30, 1942, he noted the gathering of a convoy with eighteen merchant and four coast guard vessels and U.S. airplanes to guard it. As was common, he did not mention the cargo, the destination, or the date of this convoy's departure.[44] In other messages about shipping, he left out one or more key items: the cargo, the destination, the departure date, or the type of convoy protection.

On several occasions, Lüning sought to patch up what he considered ruptured German relations. In message number 23, he used open-language code to declare that he was "fixing up new friendships lost by wardler [war declaration]."[45] On January 5, 1942, he mentioned trying to cultivate, as a future source, an "American friend," a sailor on an American vessel. Unfortunately, this sailor never returned to Havana.[46]

Some of his secret correspondence dealt with truly marginal information. On January 31, 1942, Lüning conveyed the navigational bearings of the meeting point of the east- and westbound passenger vessels sailing between Havana and Barcelona. Hartmann had requested these bearings before Lüning left Hamburg.[47] The message of April 18, 1942 (number 33), described the importance of gliders and indicated how to construct one. This "secret" information came from a recent copy of the widely distributed *Popular Mechanics Magazine,* not from Lüning's labors in Havana.[48] His messages held public, not confidential, information.

At times, Lüning's secret ink messages reported mere rumors. On June 13, 1942 (message number 38), he repeated a rumor that Batista was about to fall. On more solid ground, in late July 1942, he noted the street talk that Pan American Airways had purchased large tracts of land at San Ramón, Santa Fé, and San Julian. These sites were slated to become airports for U.S. and British anti-U-boat operations. The improvement of these air bases for U.S. use was public knowledge, however. Feeling isolated, Lüning complained that he had "not heard from you yet!! What shall I do?! Bye Bye Ev[ery]body."[49] He appeared to suffer from a lack of contact with his family, friends, even Abwehr officials.

Such espionage activity soon ended. In his last secret ink message, on August 24, 1942, Lüning reported on ships gathering in Havana, the allocation of scarce gasoline imports to the construction of airports (for antisubmarine patrolling), and the dissatisfaction of U.S. workers brought to Cuba for the high wage of $50 per week who then discovered they had to pay $30 per week for a room.[50] A week later he was detained.

Lüning's messages dealt primarily with Allied ships and commerce and, thus, could have served German U-boat operations. His references to the development of U.S. airfields in Cuba alerted the Abwehr and the German submarine service to the expectation of increased Allied antisubmarine operations. The U.S. government negotiated access for U.S. and British air force planes to several airports from which they sortied on anti-U-boat flights. While interesting news, this was not unusual. The Germans certainly expected aggressive Allied countermeasures to reduce the effectiveness of Nazi U-boats.[51] Cuba's size and location made it a central point for any successful anti-U-boat program.

Blackouts of coastal lighting were one effective means by which to curtail U-boat success. However, they were not easy to institute. In the first eleven months of 1942, the U-boats had free run of the Atlantic off the U.S. coast and of the Gulf of Mexico–Caribbean area. In the dark, U-boats waited a bit offshore and watched for silhouettes of passing freighters. The increased anti-U-boat activity altered Cuban life. In May 1942, the Cuban government ordered a blackout to avoid outlining freighters against the lights of Havana. It quickly rescinded the order, however, because the crime rate soared.[52]

The U.S. and local governments responded slowly to the U-boats operating near the U.S. coast. In mid-1942, the New Jersey state government issued the first blackout order, and other East Coast states soon followed suit. The coastal resort businesses in New Jersey and elsewhere protested the orders. The blackout was rescinded but then reinstated in late 1942.[53] Like the local politicians and businessmen in the film *Jaws*, these businessmen discounted the threat, even after they repeatedly saw vessels burning offshore in the evenings. Blackouts were effective antisubmarine policy but difficult to enforce.

Certainly, in the fall of 1942, with Nazi forces approaching Moscow and Stalingrad and in control of most of North Africa and the Japanese contending for control of the South Pacific at Guadalcanal, Port Moseby, and northern Australia, the Allies needed to act with energy and caution in the face of even small threats to security in the circum-Caribbean area. Throughout much of the war, U.S. fears of possible German threats often smothered U.S. trust in Latin American governments. U.S. leaders discounted the analysis of Latin American leaders (whether democratic, authoritarian, or militaristic) and frequently rejected Latin American input into anti-Axis programs in the Americas.[54] While U.S. officials welcomed the use of air bases and harbors in the circum-Caribbean, the antisubmarine campaign was essentially a U.S. and British operation.

The Allied intelligence and political leadership spun Lüning's capture into a significant event. This strategy undercut the propaganda value of an incredibly successful German U-boat campaign. In 1940, Admiral Karl Dönitz, the head of the German submarine fleet, and Admiral Erich Raeder, the chief of the German Naval High Command, had launched a tonnage campaign to sink as much Allied shipping as possible. When the war spread to include the United States, Dönitz and Raeder ordered Operation Paukenschlag [Drumroll] on December 12, 1941. This operation extended the U-boat tonnage strategy to Western Hemisphere waters. Early in the war, Dönitz had estimated (optimistically) that the Axis needed to sink at least 700,000 tons per month to choke Allied maritime activity (this should have been adjusted upward to at least 1 million tons, and probably 1.25 million tons, once the United States entered the war). This German strategy rested on a series of assumptions. After large shipping losses, presumably, the Allies would be unable to mount a meaningful campaign in Europe. Britain and the United States would face industrial-raw-material shortages that would impede gearing up for war production. In addition, Britain would face severe food shortages, if not starvation. And, finally, the dwindling Allied shipping might prevent the transfer of U.S. soldiers and supplies across the Atlantic to prepare for a European campaign. To initiate Operation Paukenschlag, Dönitz ordered six type IXb and IXc (about 1,050–1,200-ton) U-boats, each with twenty-two torpedoes, to operate off Cape Cod and Cape Hatteras. Paukenschlag U-boats fired the first torpedoes on January 12, 1942. They were incredibly successful.[55]

The initial success prompted Dönitz to expand the field of operations south. In January 1942, he sent five IXb's and IXc's to the Caribbean area. Once these U-boats were shifted to the Gulf of Mexico and the Caribbean, Germany's tonnage campaign achieved dramatically more spectacular results. In the ten months from February 1942 through November 1942, German submarines in the greater Gulf-Caribbean area saw their greatest success of the war. In the region from the South Atlantic nations into the Gulf-Caribbean and including the waters off Venezuela, Colombia, and Panama, Axis U-boats sank 609 ships (about two ships a day) with 3,122,456 tons—about 17.5 percent of Allied merchant tonnage lost between 1939 and 1945 on all seas (the Atlantic, the Pacific, the Mediterranean, the Arctic, the North Sea, and the Indian Ocean) to all forms of Axis attack (air, surface vessel, mine, land artillery, and U-boat). During these ten months, the Nazis lost only 22 U-boats. Thus, at a cost of about two U-boats per month, the U-boats sank a monthly average of 61 ships and 312,000 tons just in the Gulf-Caribbean waters and off the Southeastern U.S. coast.[56]

After November 1942, these horrendous losses declined slowly for several months before diminishing markedly in mid-1943. This enormous success came from, on average for 1942, five or six U-boats operating in the Gulf-Caribbean area. In November 1942, Allied losses to Axis submarines throughout the world rose to over 800,000 tons, the largest figure for any war month, despite Hitler's decision to withhold U-boats from the tonnage campaign. The November sinkings cost the Axis only two U-boats. Despite this spectacular success, Hitler continued to resist Dönitz and others who wished to shift more than a handful of U-boats to the North Atlantic and Caribbean regions.[57] Throughout 1942, the success, on a grand strategic level, of Nazi U-boats in the Caribbean area threatened the Panama Canal's ability to securely link the Atlantic and Pacific Oceans. In addition, the U-boat activity endangered U.S. access to petroleum and aviation gasoline, aluminum for airplane construction, and other vital raw materials. The stakes in the contest for control of the Gulf-Caribbean region were high in 1942.

The German U-boat campaign required a high level of planning and organization. Without forward naval bases, the U-boats confronted major logistic problems—chiefly refueling, replacing torpedoes and ammunition, and reprovisioning—if they were to operate efficiently in the Gulf-Caribbean. Scarce fuel supplies stunted German submarine activity. It was difficult to reach the area with enough fuel to allow ample patrolling. The figures are revealing. From submarine bases in western France, a one-way voyage to Bermuda was 3,000 nautical miles (the equivalent of 12.5 sailing days), to Trinidad 3,800 nautical miles (15.8 sailing days), to Aruba 4,000 nautical miles (16.6 sailing days), and to Galveston 4,600 nautical miles (19.2 sailing days). The smaller VII class submarines (about 500–700 tons) carried fuel for about 4,500–5,000 nautical miles at a typical mixture of efficient and top speeds; the larger IX class had fuel for about 9,000–9,500 nautical miles. Thus, type IX U-boats required 67 percent of their fuel supply for a round-trip to Bermuda, while type VII U-boats needed 67 percent of their fuel just to get to the Caribbean. The U-boats also had to manage their torpedo and artillery supplies carefully. The VIIb carried twelve to fourteen torpedoes, the VIIc and the IX class about twenty or twenty-two. The IX class could squeeze a few more torpedoes onto the ship if desired.[58] Fuel and torpedoes remained crucial supply problems for a highly efficient German U-boat campaign.

For a more successful Paukenschlag operation in the Caribbean, U-boat effectiveness required an improved fuel situation. At first, the German navy had used temporary solutions. Some U-boats had to return early in their trip out because of mechanical problems or damage from Allied air and sea attacks. These damaged boats or other available vessels heading to Europe were commonly sent to rendezvous points to transfer fuel before returning. For maximum effectiveness, refueling required a new, specialized U-boat type. The first type XIV U-tankers (1,700 tons), called *Milchkühe* [milk cows], proved invaluable for U-boat operations in the Caribbean. The U-tanker had no torpedo tubes and was armed only with flak guns. However, it carried 400–600 tons of extra fuel to transfer to attack U-boats, replacement torpedoes, extra ammunition, spare parts, and supplies. One refueling from a U-tanker added about 4,000 miles to a type VII submarine's range. The first XIV U-tanker entered service on April 22, 1942, some 500 sea miles northeast of Bermuda. In the first two weeks, it refueled and resupplied fourteen type

VII and two type IX U-boats. Ninety percent of the submarines in the Caribbean used the resupplying U-boats. The tankers greatly extended the duration of operations.[59]

Prior to the U-tankers, local refueling and resupplying reportedly came from Axis sympathizers in the Caribbean. U.S. officials suspected that German submarines had found local people who helped with refueling out of ideological or financial reasons. The principal suspects were the Gough brothers' network in British Honduras (now Belize) and several suspected sites in eastern Colombia and Venezuela. George Gough, his two brothers, and his son Alfred ran a local shipping service connecting Panama, the Central American coast to Belize, and Jamaica. U.S. surveillance planes noted modestly sized vessels carrying numerous fuel barrels on their decks. Some of these boats were thought to be from the Gough inter-Caribbean shipping service. Lüning's contact with Alfred Morgan of the Bay Islands, Honduras, raised a red flag—quickly put to rest—that Lüning used Morgan to contact the Gough brothers' espionage ring. The Gough family, however, had interacted with the Morgan family for decades. The SIS determined that the sporadic contact involved only ships for possible sale. British and U.S. security authorities arrested George Gough, Alfred Gough, and eighteen other suspects in July 1942. In April 1943, when the German U-boats had largely abandoned operations in the Caribbean, they were released for lack of evidence.[60] (Possibly there was no trial because the Allies did not wish to reveal their sources of information.) If the Gough brothers and a group of alleged Axis sympathizers on the Colombian-Venezuelan border had supplied U-boats, the strong U.S.-British countermeasures halted their activity. By mid-1942, the U-tankers made improvised, local refueling unnecessary.

Countless stories described German U-boat contact with residents along the U.S. Gulf-Caribbean coast. These are mostly tall tales. These stories told of German U-boats extracting fuel and provisions from local vessels in an effort to extend their patrolling. In the course of the war, there were almost ten thousand reported U-boat contacts or sightings. The FBI looked into about half. It could not verify any of the reports it investigated, although some could not be dismissed. Still, steps were taken to secure the U.S. coastal areas. In mid-1942, the U.S. Coast Guard, in close cooperation with the army, the navy, and the FBI, organized beach patrol units for all U.S. ocean beach areas. On foot and horseback, in small water craft, airplanes, and blimps, and manning fifty-foot watchtowers, the beach patrol units engaged twenty-four thousand officers and men for patrols and trained about thirty thousand volunteers to man the watchtowers. The beach patrols watched for enemy submarine activity, enemy invaders, or saboteurs and participated in the rescue of survivors of shipwrecked vessels and downed aircraft. After mid-1944, the beach patrols were phased out. Over a two-year period, no observer had ever seen a U-boat.[61] There is no persuasive evidence of the resupplying or refueling of German U-boats on the U.S. Gulf Coast.

The U-tankers, not locals in the Gulf-Caribbean, expanded U-boat successes. However, the destruction of Allied tonnage in the Atlantic and especially in the Gulf-Caribbean area suffered because Hitler insisted on holding large numbers of submarines in Norway and in the Mediterranean theaters. In early 1942, for example, of ninety-one German U-boats, thirty-six were in or designated for the Mediterranean or Norway, thirty-three were in repair, and only twenty-two were available for service in the Atlantic and Caribbean—and half of those twenty-two were in transit! Still worse, many in the Atlantic-Caribbean area were the smaller type VIIc, and only a few were the much larger type IX. Dönitz was mesmerized by a short-term policy. He was so possessed with quick success that he encouraged the building of the VIIs over the IXs because two VIIs could be built with the time and material needed for one IX. His project for a great Atlantic battle between U-boats and Allied shipping encountered difficulty from his own shortsightedness and from Raeder and Hitler. Hitler constantly reserved a large number of U-boats to serve geopolitical purposes rather than naval operations' objectives. For example, in late 1941, as Mussolini's troops in North Africa faced disaster, Hitler ordered Raeder to send twenty-five U-boats to the Mediterranean to disrupt British naval activity.[62] Hitler and Raeder were not nearly as committed to the U-boat strategy as Dönitz was.

Several U-boats in the Caribbean were brazen and, thus, attracted public attention. They sank vessels in broad daylight, in sight of the Tobago airport, for example, and boldly inside the harbors at Port of Spain, Trinidad, and at Castries on St. Lucia. The Caribbean was so unprotected in 1942 that six Italian submarines in the area sank thirty-four ships in six months. One German captain called the assault on U.S. shipping "the American Turkey Shoot." The U.S. naval historian Samuel E. Morison called it "the merry massacre." One Caribbeanist wrote: "In the Atlantic-Caribbean the U-boats came close to severing the vital lifeline to Great Britain as well as nearly crippling the U.S. war industry by cutting off the supply of raw materials."[63] From the Allied perspective, if Lüning's radio signals had guided part of the tonnage campaign, he could have been responsible for inflicting horrendous Allied losses. He would, thus, have represented a major threat to Allied survival. His radio never worked, however, and his efforts were inconsequential. Yet the Allies had no assured means of determining the ultimate value of this partial information. He might be sending additional information over other routes, or other German agents might be supplying some of the missing data. In fact, his mere presence—since he might build a radio—posed a danger that the Allies needed to end.

Unfortunately, in 1942, the success of German U-boats in the Caribbean boded ill for Lüning. Despite the lack of evidence, the Allies assigned him a significant role in supplying information to the U-boats. Naturally, the Cubans were gravely concerned with the U-boat war in the Caribbean. The large role assigned to Lüning stimulated their antipathy toward him. In particular, they blamed him for the sinking of two Cuban ships, the *Santiago de Cuba* and the *Manzanillo,* on August 12, 1942. In fact, Lüning played no role in sinking any vessel in the Caribbean.[64] Still, the horrendous Allied tonnage losses—for which someone had to be responsible—contributed to the decision to execute him. He paid with his life for the success of the German army in Europe and North America and of German submarines in the Atlantic and Gulf-Caribbean region.

German U-boat losses in the Gulf-Caribbean had been minimal early in 1942 and remained moderate even in late 1942. With few trained personnel or appropriate vessels and planes, the U.S. defense against Axis submarines was almost nonexistent until after mid-1942. From mid-

January to the end of April 1942, only one U-boat was lost in U.S. waters. For the whole of 1942, the ratio of ships sunk per U-boat lost in the Caribbean was 43.3. Worldwide in 1942, this ratio was 9.2. In the Caribbean in 1943, this ratio declined precipitously, to 2.3, because the Allied leaders recognized the need to secure this crucial area. Yet this region remained more favorable to U-boats than did the world as a whole. In the whole world, the ratio was 1.8 ships sunk per U-boat lost.[65] In early 1943, the wildly successful U-boat operations in the Gulf-Caribbean ended.

Between late 1942 and the spring of 1943, the combined efforts of the U.S. naval and air forces, the civilian watches, and the coast guard, in cooperation with Cuban and British forces, ultimately controlled the German U-boats in U.S. and Caribbean waters. The U.S. military slowly developed coastal defenses, a convoy system, and effective air patrolling. U.S. aircraft sank two U-boats off Newfoundland in March 1942 and one off Bermuda on June 30, 1942, but the first airplane sinking of a U-boat near the U.S. coast occurred only on July 7, 1942. Afterward, U.S. anti-U-boat defenses improved steadily. After November 1942, U-boat captains described mounting difficulties near the U.S. coast, so Dönitz shifted emphasis to North Atlantic convoys, the Caribbean region, and off Brazil. By the spring of 1943, submarine captains were reporting a level of countersubmarine activity in the Gulf-Caribbean region that forced the German submarines to remain underwater most of the time. This made the U-boats ineffective.[66] Thus, before mid-1943, the Axis had virtually abandoned U-boat missions in the Gulf-Caribbean. Later, on one or two occasions, small numbers of U-boats attempted to revive the glory of 1942. They failed badly.

The tonnage war failed. In the course of the war, the Axis coastal artillery, submarines, surface ships, mines, and airplanes sank about 17.5 million tons of Allied ships. Even Dönitz's low-side estimate that the Axis needed to sink 700,000 tons per month was well above the Axis capability to inflict losses. For only ten (February–November 1942) of the war's first forty-five months (September 1939–May 1943) were Allied losses near this low-side figure. Allied ship losses to Axis submarines in the last twenty-seven months of the war were comparatively light. The Axis never came very close to sinking a million tons in one month. Dönitz overlooked or inadequately estimated too many factors. For example, he miscalculated the U.S. ability to produce shipping, the determination of the Allies to acquire ships from neutral and occupied countries and to requisition interned enemy vessels, and the Allied capacity to salvage and repair sunk or damaged merchant vessels. His most serious oversight was his inability to evaluate Hitler and the German leadership critically. The Nazi leadership did not place a high value on the submarine strategy before the war, and it did not alter its point of view during the war.[67]

If Lüning posed no danger, there was no prestige to be gained from capturing him. So he had to be interpreted as dangerous. It was Lüning's misfortune that German success against Allied shipping peaked in the Gulf-Caribbean in the summer and fall of 1942. The Caribbean specialist Anthony Maingot concluded: "In the Caribbean [the U-boats] were successful beyond [Admiral Karl] Dönitz' most optimistic expectations. With only an average of five U-boats operational at any one time they controlled the whole Caribbean from 1941 to mid-1943. Especially relevant was the fact that over 50 per cent of the ships sunk were oil tankers, depriving the US of that vital resource."[68] Additionally, bauxite (aluminum ore), sugar, and coffee (both basic elements of U.S. military C and K rations) were vital wartime materials. These basic materials had to pass through the Gulf-Caribbean area. However, curtailing German U-boat devastation of Allied shipping did not require arresting Lüning. He never aided German U-boat operations.

Lüning did not meaningfully assist any branch of the German government. Reichschancellor Hitler, the Abwehr chief Admiral Canaris, the German submarine service, and the Abwehr got little of concrete utility from Lüning, and this seems consistent with Abwehr expectations after his training period. In late 1941, with most intelligent and capable Germans serving elsewhere, the Abwehr adopted the strategy of using numerous agents. It assumed that some would become effective spies and that the others, when caught, would reduce Allied surveillance of the competent agents.

The Abwehr had suspected Lüning would get caught. It sent him to Havana with no Caribbean contacts, few useful radio signals, no book code, and poor training in radio assembly and secret ink work. The Abwehr considered him a decoy. His capture, however, did, indeed, reduce the Allied surveillance of more competent agents. Lüning's greatest service to German intelligence operations was to divert extensive U.S., British, and Cuban counterintelligence resources and energy to tracking down his contacts and acquaintances. The FBI-SIS expended a large amount of manpower and time through May 1945 to examine, fruitlessly, scores of possible ties and to compile one of the largest files in the U.S. World War II counterintelligence service that deals with an individual. But reality intruded.

The SIS agents investigating Lüning could uncover only a modest amount of routine contact with the Abwehr drop boxes in Spain and Portugal, some few cable exchanges with Abwehr agents in Chile, and even fewer with people in Argentina, Honduras, and Mexico. These contacts allowed the Abwehr to get funds to and communicate with him. He gathered no special or secret information (what he did gather came from public observation and conversation and Havana's newspapers and magazines), and he did not undertake any special missions. He provided incomplete information on shipping activity, and the British even delayed those messages to make sure the faulty information was also outdated.

The SIS's extensive investigation of Lüning uncovered material that supported other investigations, but it produced little of importance because Lüning had not developed a means to obtain useful information and he had no significant contacts to uncover. U.S., British, and Cuban counterintelligence could link him only to a known Chilean spy group that served as an intermediary for cable exchanges and as an agent for transferring funds. In this sense, Lüning was an effective decoy. He diverted enormous resources to the pursuit of an unproductive and essentially harmless "spy." Initially, the SIS thought that they had captured a master spy. Ultimately, it concluded that he was a minor and ineffective agent. The rewards for his arrest were ample, however.

▶ 5 ◀

Failure and Fatality

To all appearances, the Germans operated an effective, dangerous spy network. The evidence was the catastrophically successful German U-boat campaign in the Gulf-Caribbean from February to November 1942. Presumably, terminating the German spy network in the Caribbean would involve hard work, intrigue, cunning, and humor. The end of Lüning's personal story had satiric and melodramatic twists. The British, U.S., and Cuban governments increased intelligence cooperation after the Japanese attack on Pearl Harbor. The newly established U.S. Office of Censorship under Director Byron Price joined the British Bermuda and Trinidad stations to monitor the airwaves, ship travel, and surface and airmail from the Americas to Europe in search of spies. Supplementing the British censors, the U.S. Office of Censorship grew quickly to 14,500 employees who examined letters, listened to telephone calls and radio signals, and scanned movies, magazines, and radio scripts.[1] The British, U.S., and Cuban counterintelligence agencies each played a role in the detection of Lüning and the destruction of the (phantom) Nazi spy network in the Caribbean.

Allied counterespionage had some moments of uncertainty as it began the search for Axis agents. The U.S., Cuban, British, and Mexican agents had to work out style and modes of coordination. Captain Mariano Faget y Díaz (the chief of the Cuban Bureau of Counterintelligence against Enemy Activities), Ambassador Spruille Braden, the SIS coordi-

93

nator in Cuba and legal attaché to the embassy, R. G. Leddy, and British MI6 agents in Cuba normally cooperated in counterintelligence. Still, monitoring, surveillance, and detention of suspected Axis agents tested their ability to work jointly.

Some early projects spun the wheels of the anti-Axis bandwagon. In the months prior to Lüning's arrest, Braden and his good friend Ernest Hemingway discussed a counterintelligence project. Hemingway wanted to organize a private information service based on the Spanish Republican refugees in Cuba. Ultimately, with Braden's blessing, he enlisted eighteen people.[2] He was convinced that Axis and Falangist agents in Cuba were numerous, active, and dangerous.

As Lüning was imprisoned, Hemingway's eighteen agents, in the pay of the U.S. government, began formal reports to the ambassador by way of the novelist. Although Hemingway was initially engaged to investigate the Spanish Falange in Cuba, he quickly branched out to all areas of intelligence gathering. He produced bizarre and comic reports. He developed a marked antipathy toward the Cuban chief of police, Benítez, and retained an old antipathy toward the FBI. He investigated Benítez and told stories about him publicly. This was potentially devastating to the U.S. embassy, which could not be involved in undermining and attacking principal officials of a host government. Hemingway acted with little thought but considerable vigor and emotion. He alleged that Benítez intended to overthrow Batista in December 1942 while the president and Braden were in Washington meeting with FDR (Batista's reward for having Lüning executed). His principal condemnatory evidence involved the regular rifle practice of the Cuban police. Leddy pointed out to the ambassador that the Cuban police force was part of the army and had for years taken rifle practice on a regular basis.[3]

In another incident, Hemingway charged that the Cubans allowed Prince Camilo Ruspoli, an interned Italian aristocratic fascist leader, to attend a public luncheon where he met with the Spanish chargé d'affaires, Pelayo García Olay. This alleged meeting provoked an image of fascist conspiracy in the novelist's mind. In response, the SIS interviewed hotel and waitstaff as well as several attendees at the luncheon. No one recalled seeing Ruspoli at the luncheon. Unfazed, Hemingway asked the ambassador to have the SIS not "grill" one of "his" waiters, who might otherwise no longer supply information. He also asked to see the SIS proof that Ruspoli was not in attendance, even after he had not supplied any substantiated evidence that he was. Naturally, the SIS did not intend to let a private, semiofficial intelligence agent see the official documents.[4]

Imagination remained the chief guide to Hemingway's espionage work. He viewed submarines as a major source for a variety of threats. Soon after he began his work, he accepted the rumors of a German oxygen-powered submarine. Almost axiomatically, he presumed that this new supersubmarine must be operating near Cuba. At a significant investment of man-hours, the SIS and Cuban officials did an inventory of all oxygen tanks on the island. All were accounted for. Nonplused, Hemingway reported that he had personally sighted a submarine make a transfer of people to the Spanish steamship *Marqués de Comillas* on December 9, 1942, off the Cuban coast. After the *Marqués de Comillas* docked in Havana, the SIS and Cuban police invested countless more man-hours in interviewing the forty crew members and fifty passengers—most of whom were antifascist repatriates. None of the interviewees knew anything about this meeting of a submarine with the vessel they were on. Always on the offensive, Hemingway angrily replied that, if the SIS rejected his report because it did not come from an FBI agent, it would regret the entrance of the saboteurs into the United States. Somehow, he decided that the German agents allegedly transferred were destined to operate in the United States. Furthermore, he insisted that the Germans planned to land thirty thousand agents from one thousand submarines (many times more than the German navy possessed) in Cuba to seize the island. Further investment of investigators' time found no remote corroboration of his story, so the SIS dismissed this report.[5]

Finally, in what should have deeply embarrassed him had he not been so self-absorbed and arrogant, Hemingway reported that his agents had witnessed a (their) suspect leave a tightly wrapped box at the Bar Basque in Havana. He claimed that it held vital espionage information. In response, Leddy and the first secretary of the embassy had the box brought immediately to the embassy and invited Hemingway to witness the event. In the novelist's presence, they opened the package and discovered a "cheap edition of the Life of St. Teresa." Angered rather than embarrassed, Hemingway later told third parties that the FBI had withdrawn the documents and left only the worthless book. The SIS confronted him before embassy staff, and he tried to laugh his comments off as joking but noted that it was a strange business. Thus, Leddy was unable, despite repeated use of numerous Cuban and SIS investigators, to substantiate any of the reported information. On April 1, 1943, Braden reluctantly terminated Hemingway's formal ties to the embassy, but the novelist quickly entered into an arrangement with the U.S. Navy, which supplied him funds and weapons to conduct antisubmarine patrols off Cuba's southern coast.[6] Hemingway was, at a minimum, Lüning's equal in espionage.

Cuba's importance lay in various factors, but its usefulness to supervise air, naval, and communications activity in the Gulf-Caribbean was extremely valuable. Cuba offered centrally located air and naval bases to counter highly successful German U-boat operation in the Gulf-Caribbean region. Its government cooperated with the U.S. and British counterintelligence work, initiating a separate, independent intelligence agency only in mid-1942. Almost immediately, Faget had complained to U.S. officials that he could not detain many suspects because his office was understaffed. In response to this problem, Braden urged an expansion in the Cuban counterintelligence police force and a bit of simultaneous empire building. He worked with the recently arrived SIS special agent W. Clair Spears, SIS agents John Little and Edwin Sweet, and Leddy and the embassy staff to win approval for the assignment of fifteen additional SIS personnel to the embassy. The Allies had legitimate concerns about possible Axis agents in Cuba radioing U-boats in the area. The new SIS agents would train Cuban radio technicians and join the Cuban police in monitoring local radio reports in the search for Axis activities in Cuba. Several SIS radio experts arrived on September 7, 1942, and installed special radio equipment for a direct link from the embassy in Havana to FBI headquarters in Washington. Then, two SIS radio operators arrived on September 15. The rest of the fifteen-person unit followed shortly.

These SIS agents may well have freed up Cuban officers to detain more suspected Axis agents.[7] Since the first of these SIS reinforcements arrived eight days after Lüning's arrest, they clearly had no role in stopping his activity.

Despite the buildup of the U.S. counterintelligence service in Cuba, the detection and arrest of Lüning resulted largely from the work of British censors in Bermuda. They intercepted and read Lüning's messages. After an appropriate delay to render the information harmless, the messages went to drop boxes in Portugal or Spain. The messages were released to continue on to Europe because SIS and British counterespionage experts judged the information in them essentially harmless.

The censors in Bermuda were highly efficient. They could sort through thousands of letters and packages, extract the suspicious letters, and open, expose, photograph, copy, and reseal the relevant materials, all within the normal stopover time of a Pan American plane. The volume of work was impressive (see table 1). However, Lüning's modest language skills and general unsuitability for espionage rewarded the censors' work. His careless use of German words in his Spanish cover letters—*residenz* for *residencia* and *blatt* for *papel* [paper]—alerted them to examine the letters more closely.[8] The apprentice spy was learning his trade through trial and many errors.

The Bermuda station intercepted its first Lüning message on October 14, 1941, and shared this and other relevant materials with the State Department on a near daily basis. The State Department then distributed the British intercepts to the FBI-SIS, the Military Intelligence Division (MID), the Office of Naval Intelligence (ONI), and the U.S. Office of Censorship. Determining how many agents operated in Cuba

Correspondence Sorting at the Princess and Bermudiana Hotels

	1940	1941	1942	1943
Letters sorted	a	13,072,700	6,830,000	1,717,000
Ships processed	53	113	33	1
Aircraft processed	94	223	166	166

[a] Not available

required vigilance and careful analysis. The names and addresses of the Mutz agent's cover letters changed continually and were imaginary anyway (although the Allied counterintelligence agents would know this only after Lüning had been captured). Yet an analysis of the messages indicated that this agent (or agents) was operating in or near Havana. Initial efforts did not locate him (them). In a coincidence, a British official actually visited "Luni" at his apartment in January 1942. The British, however, were suspicious because he had German roots, wrote to foreign countries, and possessed a Honduran passport, not because of any specific evidence that he was a German agent.[9] Most likely, the British agents in Cuba were interested in any person of German origin.

A big break occurred in mid-1942 when a British mail sorter encountered a letter with a careless secret ink message. The enemy agent requested that instructions be sent to what appeared to be the actual home address of the sender, specifically, to Enrique Augusto Luni in care of Emilio Pérez at Teniente Rey 366 II, Havana. A well-trained agent would have used a drop box address in Havana. Shortly, a letter from Europe, with Uncle Gustav Lüning's name as sender and containing coded language instructions, arrived for Luni. Apparently, the "Havana secret writing" agent was Enrique Augusto Luni.[10] Caution was called for because the Havana Abwehr agent had used numerous false identities.

J. Edgar Hoover, the Cuban president, Batista, and his police chief, Benítez, all recognized the value of doing something against this spy. They needed to defend Allied shipping and support the U.S. war effort. In this specific situation, because there was a presumption of a spy network, Hoover, the SIS, Braden, U.S. embassy officials, and even the chief of Cuba's counterintelligence bureau, Captain Faget (who ten years later would earn a reputation for brutality and harshness during Batista's second period as president [and this time also as dictator] in Cuba), argued to observe, rather than arrest, the suspected German agent.[11]

The U.S. and British officials hoped that Luni might lead them to more of the spy network. The U-boats' devastation of Allied shipping in the Gulf-Caribbean seemed way beyond the capacity of a lone German agent. To disrupt a network of agents, the U.S. and Cuban counterintelligence agents needed to observe Luni. Ultimately, they would learn about his mode of work and his network of agents and informants. Seizing Luni immediately would make it less rewarding, and, perhaps, impossible, to follow his contacts. However, Benítez ignored the objections.[12] Even in this ominous situation, the Cuban general weighed his personal political ambition to become president of Cuba against the war effort. His ambition won. He wanted media attention with photographs, press conferences, and public praise. More important, he knew that Batista urgently wanted a major success to impress U.S. officials in the forthcoming negotiations over financial aid and the price and quota of sugar for the 1943 Cuban sugar crop. In fact, U.S. officials were not happy with the spy's arrest.

Various Allied organizations had collaborated to detect and arrest Lüning. First, the British censors had shared the intercepted address and the new cover name with the SIS. Then Cuban intelligence officials and an SIS agent brought copies of the messages provided by the British to the Cuban postal authorities, who confirmed that an Enrique Augusto Luni received mail at the Teniente Rey address. Still, the Allied agents needed to act circumspectly since this Abwehr agent operated under more than thirty aliases and false addresses. It was necessary to verify his identity before intervening. Cuban postal workers concocted a scheme. Early on August 31, 1942, they called Luni downstairs to sign for a dummy registered letter. The suspect signed with the name Luni and was arrested immediately. His room was searched at once. SIS agent 253 (probably Sweet) and a British agent participated in the arrest and search. The SIS agent notified FBI headquarters at once.[13] While the British censors, SIS agents, and Cuban police and postal officials shared in the arrest, the U.S. agents played the smallest role. Presumably, they had arrested one of the principal Axis agents in the Western Hemisphere.

Captain Faget led the search of Luni's room. (In a twist befitting this story, Faget's son was arrested in Florida in February 2000, accused of spying for Fidel Castro's Cuba.) The police demanded his passport and papers. At some point, he gave his legal name as Heinz August Lüning. In his room, the police seized a radio transmitter and receiver, the plans for building such an apparatus, and materials (such as a soldering iron and batteries) needed to construct a radio. The room also contained the chemicals and other materials for secret ink writing, an inexpensive Bosch-Lomb microscope for reading microdots, and a large file with drafts or copies of his correspondence. Lüning confessed immediately.[14]

Once Lüning was arrested over U.S. objections, the SIS urged Benítez and the Cuban government not to make the arrest public. The SIS did not want Lüning's confederates alerted. In addition, the SIS intended to use Luni's identity to contact his fellow Nazi agents in the Americas. The Cuban police willingly masked Lüning's capture. They simply arrested fifteen other spy suspects from lists with over a thousand names of Axis aliens or suspected spies. These detentions were reported in the Cuban newspapers on September 1 and 3, 1942, but without names or even an indication of where the arrests had taken place.[15]

On the day of Lüning's arrest, Benítez arrived at the scene with other high-ranking army and navy officials. Lüning cooperated. He offered information about all other agents or contacts he knew in the Western Hemisphere. To underscore the value of cooperation, Benítez told the German agent, when U.S., British, and Cuban agents were present, that he might avoid execution if he cooperated fully. Benítez also agreed that SIS 253 (Sweet) and Captain Faget would be in charge of the interrogation of the prisoner.[16] The SIS and Faget were disheartened because Benítez brought a huge entourage (publicity) to the scene, thereby frightening away any possible contacts who might have come to see Lüning.

Before mid-1944, Benítez published his version of the Lüning case in the popular *True Detective*. Perhaps he sold his distorted story because Batista had just deported him. In this popular magazine, Benítez dramatized his role in the case. He claimed, for example, that he, Faget, and a policeman climbed the stairs to surprise and arrest Lüning. His fantasy greatly increased his own labor for the Allied cause. He alleged that the interrogation of Lüning led to the breaking up of a principal Nazi network and of subnetworks of Nazi spies in Chile and Argentina and the capture of a Japanese spy, Amano, in Panama, where, of course, he threatened the canal. There is no record of this Japanese agent in any document or newspaper, although all the other arrests of single spies or groups of spies as the result of Lüning's case were boldly reported to assure the people in the Americas that the Allied governments were taking their enemies off the streets. There is not even an oblique reference to any Japanese agent linked to Lüning in any SIS, MI6, or Cuban document, and there are thousands of documents that mention numerous spies or spy suspects.[17]

Lüning's premature arrest was not the only fly in the SIS's ointment. Benítez's self-promotion continued to undermine good counterintelligence work. From the beginning, the SIS had intended to complete the construction of Lüning's radio and to initiate contact with Abwehr agents in Chile and Germany in an effort to extract additional information about German activity in the Americas. Several days after the arrest, they contacted Carlos Robinson in Chile. The Cuban police chief, however, nullified their efforts. Benítez, eagerly pursuing personal glory, considered five days as sufficient time to unravel the German spy network in the Americas. On September 5, again in an attempt to maximize his reputation and enhance his public image, he unilaterally announced the capture of Lüning to the press. To seize the press's attention, he repeated the image of this Abwehr agent as the master German spy in the Americas. To draw even more attention to himself, he allowed Lüning to speak briefly to the reporters. The spy praised Cuban society and described his work as merely supplying commercial information. Of course, Benítez also elevated his nonexistent role in the capture of the Nazi master spy to a central spot. The SIS complained: "In view of the widespread publicity given this case by the Cuban authorities, the possibility of utilizing the radio in possession of the subject to communicate with the enemy by us has been eliminated."[18] The premature publicity of Lüning's arrest killed any response from the SIS telegram to Robinson. Benítez was far more helpful to the Germans than the Allies.

The SIS described Benítez "unfavorably as a vain and publicity-hungry individual." Clearly, he pursued his selfish political ambition without regard to the Allied counterespionage activity in Cuba.[19] Other intelligence agencies agreed with the SIS assessment of Benítez. The MID noted: "9-9-42. The arrest of Lüning most unfortunate because it will increase the difficulty of locating other enemy agents in Cuba, and impede to some extent what seemed like fair progress lately made in their detection. The cause of this publicity can be laid to one thing, the inordinate love of publicity Chief of Police, General Benítez possesses."[20] The MID thought that the Allies were on the verge of an even greater success until Benítez spoiled the operation. The Abwehr card index of prominent foreign personalities described Benítez as "self-selected to become commander of the Cuban forces which will operate with U.S. forces." A British Foreign Office report called him "a shady character."[21] All the intelligence agencies recognized him as ambitious, egotistical, and self-serving.

On September 6, Braden was "livid with rage" over Benítez's actions. In the following days, he repeatedly brought up the matter with the Cuban prime minister, Ramón Zaydín, and Batista.[22] Braden's dissatisfaction with the premature exposure of Lüning's arrest did not subside. Two weeks later, he had compiled a memorandum of points for further discussion with Batista. For example, Braden stressed, it was imperative to "keep *all* intelligence information absolutely secret." He compared Benítez's action with "giving the opposing general one's plan of attack." Moreover, he was upset with the incredibly thoughtless permission granted to the Cuban press to interview Lüning, who then presented himself in a sympathetic manner. Such interviews hindered further investigation. Unfortunately, Braden's emotions weakened his memorandum because he incorporated false charges. He suggested, on the basis of unsubstantiated (and bad) information from Ernest Hemingway, that a large subversive organization existed in Cuba that furnished information and supplies to German submarines. This enemy organization might seize Cuba. He projected that those Germans on the island would be strengthened by Hemingway's thirty thousand agents from one thousand submarines. This threat was unproved, unrealistic, and patently false.[23]

Braden offered pointed suggestions for the Batista regime. All reports of enemy activity should go directly to Faget, who should have sole investigative authority. To preserve secrecy, no superior officers should appear at any arrest scene. Benítez's entourage had created such a disturbance at Lüning's arrest that any enemy agents would have been scared away. There should be no publicity until all leads had been investigated to the satisfaction of both the Cuban and the U.S. officials. Furthermore, Faget should be given at least the temporary rank of lieutenant colonel, all necessary instructions should be issued to implement the memorandum's suggestions, and effort should be made, in the future, to avert unwanted publicity. Finally, U.S. officials assured Batista that Faget was unaware of any of the material in this memorandum.[24]

At least initially, U.S. officials presumed that they had hit the mother lode with Lüning's arrest. This accorded with their operating principle: the greater the spy, the greater the prestige. Lüning was treated as one of the principal Abwehr agents in the Americas. Yet, over the next seventy days, the information that he offered had modest value at best. The SIS already knew or suspected much that he revealed. His information confirmed suspicions, filled in gaps, and supplied details, sidelights, and perspective on Nazi activity in the Americas. But there was little new. For example, his information helped close down some known German spy activity in Chile. In search of more, the SIS relentlessly pursued his contacts in Latin America.[25] Even as the investigation failed to uncover significant actual espionage, Benítez, Braden, Hoover, and Batista inflated Lüning's importance in the search for recognition, praise, and approval. They all connected Lüning to the immensely successful Axis U-boat campaign.

Once Benítez inappropriately made Lüning's capture public, the U.S. and Cuban counterintelligence officials made the most of the situation. They converted the capture into personal prestige, recognition, and expanded power for their agencies. They broadcast the allegation that the Nazi master spy led a network of espionage in the Americas. U.S. and Cuban newspapers and magazines labeled him a significant agent. His capture unleashed a starburst—bright, spectacular, but short-lived. His espionage activity, trials, appeals, and execution were frequently front-page news items. His case was reported regularly in the *New York Times*, the *Washington Post*, the *Diario de la marina*, and *El mundo* and occasionally in other major U.S. and Cuban newspapers, at times with photographs. Even the *Times* of London carried several brief items about Lüning despite the wartime paper scarcity limiting the newspaper to eight pages at most. Photographs of Lüning, his trial courtroom, his radio, and other people involved in the process appeared frequently in the weeklies *Carteles* and *La Bohemia* and in *True Detective*. Naturally, newspapers throughout Latin America followed the story. Although U.S. officials were bitterly dissatisfied with the early arrest, they ultimately approved rewards for Benítez and Batista because that position simultaneously reflected approval and praise for Hoover, the FBI-SIS, and the U.S. embassy.[26] Thus, in late 1942, Lüning's case received considerable attention and celebrity.

Cuban officials described the arrested thirty-one-year-old German as "one of the most important spies yet captured in America": "The authorities indicated he would escape the firing squad by becoming a government witness." Cuban and U.S. newspapers adopted this position, calling Lüning variously a "master" spy, a "key German spy," a "leading German spy," or, in Nelson Rockefeller's words, the "key figure in a vast espionage ring operating in the hemisphere."[27] Benítez, who lacked understanding of the Lüning case or of intelligence work in general, inappropriately and erroneously alleged that Lüning confessed to "participating in widespread espionage activities," including sending "by shortwave radio and by code letters information concerning the arrival and departure in Cuba of ships of Allied and neutral nations." He retained this false and uninformed viewpoint at least into mid-1944.[28]

Ambassador Braden, one high-ranking official at the U.S. Office of Censorship, and several historians of World War II espionage twisted Lüning's story in ways that have continued to obscure the nature and quality of Lüning's spy work. Braden's self-serving fairy tale of the arrest and execution gravely distorted the whole Lüning story. The ambassador ignored the central role of the British Bermuda station censors and implied that Lüning was found through the hard work of tracing nonexistent radio messages. His version mocked the truth but served his personal ambition. Not surprisingly, his tale confirmed the decision to establish additional SIS agents at the U.S. embassy in Havana two weeks after Lüning's capture.

Lüning facilitated tracing his work as a spy. After his arrest, and hoping to avoid execution, he revealed essentially everything to the SIS. He even revealed some contact information that he never used because it was conditioned on the use of a radio. The information from his interrogations seems quite reliable. The FBI-SIS confirmed parts of his story in the course of interviews with people throughout the Americas who had had a relationship with him.

In a long series of interviews, Lüning told his story to Captain Faget, other Cuban officials, SIS and FCC agents (Edwin L. Sweet, John B. Little, Charles Hogg, and probably others), and British agents (Harold T. Riddle and perhaps others) in Cuba. In fact, he claimed that he gathered and transmitted economic information to Europe only by secret ink or cable messages.[29] Others asserted different conduct.

Cuban, U.S., and British agents interrogated Lüning frequently during his ten weeks in prison. Cuban interrogators conducted the first interview on September 1, in Spanish, and without an SIS agent present. The Cubans made the most of their time alone with Lüning. On the basis of this interview only, they alleged at Lüning's trial that he admitted to sending radio messages to German submarines off Cuba's coast. Cuban officials interpreted Lüning's statements that he communicated information to Germany by way of Spain and Portugal to mean that he had used the poorly constructed apparatus in his room to radio information about Allied shipping to German submarines in the Caribbean. This was the first time, according to SIS officials, that the Cubans had interrogated anyone with a transcriber present. Confidentially, the SIS agents considered the transcript of the Cuban Spanish-language interrogation almost worthless. Later, the Cubans, with one or two SIS agents (and sometimes a British agent) present, interviewed Lüning further. At the second interrogation with U.S. agents present, Lüning repeatedly denied that he had ever used the radio. In later interrogations, he always denied using the radio. Soon after the trial, Little and a second agent (probably Sweet) questioned Lüning extensively eight times from September 21 to September 29, sometimes with a Cuban or British agent present. In the midst of these interrogations, the Cuban courts ordered the seizure of Lüning's property.[30] Numerous additional interviews followed between the death sentence and the execution.

At the first interview, Cuban interrogators had clearly misunderstood Lüning. He meant that he had communicated with drop boxes in Portugal and Spain using secret ink or telegrams, and the Cuban police chose to understand that he communicated via radio. He had no reason to mislead the Cubans. He desired to save his life. The FBI-SIS checked his interrogations against captured correspondence and interviews with dozens of acquaintances in Cuba, the United States, Santo Domingo, Argentina, Honduras, Mexico, and Chile. None of the seized copies or drafts of correspondence was a radio message. The FBI-SIS and British agents had intercepted cables and secret messages that corroborated parts of Lüning's information. Keeping in mind that he wanted to protect his family in Hamburg, the large body of evidence indicated that Lüning was, essentially, an open, credible, and truthful witness.[31] He tried to hide something important on only one occasion. During the interrogations, he described two secret inks, the technique to develop the inks, his radio code, and the use of microscopic dots. For an unknown reason, he withheld information about the third, rarely used, secret ink until ten days before his execution.[32] While Lüning withheld this one piece of information, he volunteered several contacts in the United States and Latin America who might be Abwehr agents.

Despite Cuban implications and Braden's false story, radio-locating work played no role in uncovering Lüning. The sole SIS radio specialist in Havana in early 1942, Edwin Sweet, had initiated the surveillance of enemy radio work in Cuba early in 1942. He was not involved in uncovering Lüning. In his various reports, he never mentioned intercepting a radio message from a German agent. Charles Hogg, an FCC official in Havana who encouraged the training of Cubans to monitor radio messages, never alluded to intercepting a radio signal from Lüning.[33] Hogg, Sweet, and other U.S. agents and officials closely associated with operations against the Axis radios did not accuse Lüning of radio contact with anyone.

During the arrest, Faget noted the canaries flying loose in Lüning's room and the solid metal shutters on the windows. Both items could have shielded his radio operations. Cuba's principal newspaper, the *Diario de la marina,* pursued this idea. It suggested that Lüning used his radio to communicate with contacts in Lisbon, Portugal, and Gijón, Spain.

However, his antenna was placed for north-south communication. The Hamburg Abwehr school taught that direct east-west Cuban-German radio contact was difficult most of the year. SIS and U.S. radio experts confirmed that east-west radio contact was difficult, in particular for a radio of moderate power such as Lüning's apparatus. They agreed that the more reliable radio communications route was south to Chile or Argentina and then relayed, north again, to Western Europe. Lüning had been advised to contact Argentina or Chile by radio, but, as he told the SIS, Hartmann never explained to him which wavelengths to use or how to contact Argentina.[34] Lüning would not receive a fair evaluation of his radio use. Cubans were so angered over the U-boat sinkings of two Cuban vessels with considerable loss of life just before the spy's detention that most accepted the worst interpretation of Lüning's words. Benítez and other Cuban police officials seized public favor when they suggested that they had captured the Nazi spy who contacted submarines.

Lüning emphatically and repeatedly denied ever sending or receiving a radio signal. On September 16, 1942, two days before his trial, J. Edgar Hoover alleged that Lüning had a "powerful short wave transmitter and was ready to put the same into use at the time of his apprehension." The second clause implied that the shortwave radio was not operable, merely "ready to put . . . into use." A week later, after a thorough examination of the radio, and after Lüning's death sentence, Hoover concluded: "To the best of our knowledge, Lüning never used his short wave equipment and had never attempted to make contact with it up to the time of his arrest."[35] An SIS final summary report from mid-December 1942 concluded: "Lüning, or Luni, as he was known to his unsuspecting associates, never was able to place a radio transmitter into operation because of his inability along technical lines and the scarcity of some of the necessary equipment."[36]

The Cubans initially thought the radio worked, but that view was unsustainable. Prior to the trial, two Cuban radio experts spent days examining the radio. They concluded that the radio had never functioned. At trial, the prosecution willfully distorted their testimony and report. The Cuban prosecutor underscored the opening lines of their report. He emphasized the spy's intention to build a radio and transmit. This view twisted the detailed and lengthy examination of and report about Lüning's radio. The experts recounted seven major errors at the terminals, several improperly soldered or broken parts, improper wiring, an improper tuning system, and batteries too weak to send for long. In their detailed analysis, they noted that two terminals absolutely essential for this radio to send a signal had never been used for anything. They did not find even a tiny scratch or a drop of grease or flux on either terminal. Their conclusion read: "There was the intention of building a radio transmitter, but . . . this was not carried out due to the evident incompetence of the builder." Further, they went on: "The seized apparatus never transmitted and we also believe that it cannot operate in any fashion due to the material incapacities mentioned in the report."[37] The evidence was conclusive; Lüning never got his radio to operate.

In a sense, the Abwehr confirmed that the radio never worked. Soon after Lüning's arrest, the SIS and Cuban agents intercepted two cables from the Abwehr agent Carlos Robinson in Chile to Lüning. The first dated September 4, 1942, stated an expectation that Lüning would be able to radio Chile about September 15 or 16. A day later, not having heard from Lüning, Robinson asked him to "commence" radio broadcasts as suggested. These brief messages indicate that the Abwehr agents in Chile still awaited Lüning's initiation of radio work.[38] These cables underscore the evidence that the radio never worked.

The surviving Abwehr files mention only secret ink messages, never the receipt, or even the immediate expectation of receipt, of a radio signal. The two Abwehr instructions to Lüning in March 1942, another Abwehr message of June 26, 1942, and the two Robinson telegrams of early September 1942 asked him to telegraph replies to urgent matters. It seems quite clear. Those demands for telegrams made sense only if he did not have a functioning radio.[39] Until several days before his arrest, Lüning sent secret ink messages containing only a small fraction of the information that could have been transmitted in a few minutes of radio time. Despite the absence of evidence, the allegations of radio signals would not go away. They thrived because U.S. and Cuban officials benefited from distorting Lüning's espionage work. In particular, they left room to make him responsible for Nazi submarines sinking Cuban and Allied vessels.

The FCC attempted to monitor all radio communications in the Americas. When the Radio Intelligence Division of the FCC learned of alleged Lüning radio messages, it requested details, such as the sending frequencies, because "there is nothing in our files which can be connected with the reported transmissions made by this German agent."[40] The evidence, except some interrogators' willful misunderstanding of the term *communicate* at the initial interview, indicated that the transmitter had not been used.

Lüning admitted to "communicating" directly with Germany, via Spain and Portugal, through secret ink messages, and indirectly through cable messages to Chile or Argentina, but never with a radio. No one, not the FBI-SIS, not the British Bermuda station, not British security agencies, not the U.S. Office of Censorship, not the radio surveillance of the FCC, not German Abwehr records, and not the Cuban intelligence, ever produced or described a single radio signal from Lüning. The British Bermuda station and the U.S. Office of Censorship intercepted only letters, secret ink messages, and various telegrams and cables to and from Lüning. Finally, the two cables from Chile for Lüning, arriving shortly after he was arrested, inquired whether he was ready to begin radio broadcasting.[41] After Lüning's detention, the Germans were still waiting for his first radio contact.

Nevertheless, at the trial, the prosecution cleverly manipulated and twisted the evidence. Innuendo and clever partial truths allowed for the worst interpretation. The radio was admitted as evidence to show that the Abwehr agent had made "a bona fide effort to comply" with his instructions from Germany. Several witnesses testified to the existence of a powerful transmitter, which, however, "was incapable of being used to transmit messages in its present condition." This language allowed speculation about prior use of the radio to contact German submarines. Although the Cuban experts determined that the radio never had worked, the prosecution distorted their report to allow for possible radio use. The Cuban court chose to leave open whether the radio had worked at one time but was not functioning at the time of his arrest. Hoover's SIS refused to correct the erroneous evaluation of Lüning's radio activity. To sway the Cuban courts, Cuban prosecutors underscored that Lüning intended to radio German U-boats (an allegation that was, in itself, untrue, nothing in his instructions or correspondence even implying contact with U-boats), and, in any event, his conduct contributed to the loss of Cuban and Allied lives and ships.[42] These allegations about contact with German U-boats were fictitious and self-serving.

In fact, there does not seem to be any documented case (as opposed to rumors) in the Americas of land-based radio contact with a U-boat. If there were any, most likely, they were seldom and would have involved the Gough brothers or the operatives on the Colombian and Venezuelan coasts. Even here, the most likely scenario would be for a U-boat in need of fuel or provisions to radio the German navy. The navy would then contact operatives to arrange a rendezvous point. Once a meeting spot was set, navy headquarters would recontact the U-boat.

There was method to the madness of alluding to Lüning's radio contact with German U-boats. The unsubstantiated and erroneous charge that Lüning's contact with U-boats took Cuban lives formed the basis on which the death penalty was demanded. Lüning's condemnation was based on the most unfavorable interpretation of his efforts to supply maritime information to Germany, the hypothetical assumption that his radio might have worked earlier, and his alleged desire to contribute to the loss of Allied lives and vessels.

Historically, punishment for espionage, especially the death penalty, has been used for public effect. A death sentence shows the determination of the existing government to persevere at a time when a war flounders. The executions of Mata Hari in 1917, the six (of eight) Germans captured in mid-1942 after landing in Florida and on Long Island to conduct sabotage, and Lüning all occurred during periods of disturbing military failures and heightened insecurity. Even the execution of Julius and Ethel Rosenberg in 1953 occurred when U.S. officials and the public feared that the West was losing the cold war. The six Germans executed in the United States in 1942 were tried in secrecy before military tribunals, just like Lüning, despite grave constitutional reservations. However, the depressed military situation around the world in 1942 encouraged the use of military tribunals because they had increased secrecy and allowed for harsher penalties. Espionage trials have commonly

dispensed prison terms, especially when evidence indicated no significant loss of information.

The governments of Roosevelt and Batista both wanted Lüning's
blood to demonstrate their determined resistance to the Axis. However,
all the information that Lüning gathered and transmitted in written form
came from the public media and barrooms. Therefore, the death penalty
made little sense unless he sent radio signals to submarines. Unfortunately for Lüning, German U-boat 508 (Captain Staats) had sunk two
Cuban vessels—the *Santiago de Cuba* (1,685 tons) and the *Manzanillo*
(1,025 tons)—off the Cuban coast on August 12, 1942, nineteen days
before he was arrested. To demonstrate a more vigorous Allied conduct
in the war, the Cubans needed to believe that he contacted the U-boats
that sank these vessels. Then executing him would extract a rough justice
and demonstrate Cuba's valuable contribution to the war effort.[43] Ultimately, Lüning paid the highest price to satisfy the need of Cuba and the
United States to appear as heroes in breaking up a network of U-boats.

Some U.S. sources exaggerated Lüning's cleverness, radio skills,
and successes and inappropriately labeled him "the Bird Man of Morro
Castle." In another instance of self-serving misinformation, Braden and
the others initially alleged that he kept canaries in his room to muffle the
noises of his radio. In 1945, the writer Kurt Singer detailed a distorted
story of Lüning's life, capture, trial, and execution. Allegedly, the canaries in his room represented a clever trick to allow him time to hide the
radio (claiming a bird was loose) before opening the door. The birds
also justified closing the metal shutters on the windows to shield the alleged radio activity from sight and sound. Unfortunately, Singer's story
negated his own dramatic hypothesis. Several pages later, he contended
that the Cuban police found the radio in the basement of Lüning's business, Estampa de Modas, many blocks away from his apartment. In fact,
the Cubans (with an SIS and a British MI6 agent participating) found
the radio in his room, and it did not work. Other writers and journalists
uncritically accepted the canary story. It adds a marvelous, if untrue,
twist to the story. In any event, Lüning insisted that the canaries were
not part of his training.[44] The simplest explanation is the most feasible.
He worked on his radio, mixed secret ink, or wrote secret ink messages

in his room. An alleged loose canary allowed him time to hide materials before opening the door.

While in custody, Lüning was talkative. He offered up whatever information he had on any subject broached. He divulged his background and training information. He volunteered that the Honduran Consul in Hamburg, Majín Herrera A., had sold the Abwehr his Honduran passport but that he received it only a few days before his departure.[45] His interrogations aided to a small degree the pursuit of the suppliers of illegal Abwehr passports. Long after his death, the SIS and other U.S. agencies pursued these suppliers.

The SIS also questioned Lüning repeatedly and intensively about his classmates at the Hamburg Abwehr school. He denied knowing his classmates by their legal names, but he willingly revealed their code names and detailed physical descriptions of both them and three instructors. He shared his assessment of their abilities and characteristics. The SIS agents showed him scores of photographs of suspected agents in the hope that he might identify some. He positively identified only one, that of Herman Otto Neubauer—one of the eight saboteurs who landed in the United States in mid-1942. (And Neubauer had already been executed.) In addition, Lüning found several other people familiar. His uncertainty was not necessarily withholding cooperation. One has to remember that he was trained separately from the other agents in training during his six-week class. He saw them only briefly and infrequently. There were multiple classes in Hamburg and various Abwehr training schools in Germany.[46] It is highly unlikely that he ever saw the hundreds of earlier or later trainees.

On several occasions, Lüning was reminded that his cooperation might influence the Cubans not to request the death penalty. Reportedly, Lüning replied: "If there was anything within his power to assist in any way to identify any of the other Germans operating in the Western Hemisphere he would willingly do so, particularly in view of the fact that such assistance on his part might result in some clemency from the Cuban President." In the end, he claimed to have "furnished full, complete, and truthful information concerning his connection and activities with the German espionage system."[47] Nevertheless, circumstances—the ongoing Allied defeats in Europe and Asia—undermined his situation.

A background story to the court proceedings actually and ironically reinforced a central theme of U.S. counterintelligence interest in the case. On September 9, 1942, the Cuban minister of justice had appointed Gustavo Schumann-Poveda the translator of English and German documents as well as the stenographer at Lüning's trial. This appointment produced a touch of controversy. Schumann-Poveda had served as Cuban consul in Bremen until the post was closed in early 1942. After the trial, the Cuban foreign minister inquired about the blank passports of the Bremen consulate. U.S. officials were deeply concerned about Latin American consuls loosely issuing passports to Abwehr agents. The ex-consul claimed that he left those blank passports in the consular safe when he closed the office. The Lüning file does not hold the conclusion of Schumann-Poveda's passport story.[48]

The biased sentiment in Cuban society continued to deal Lüning a bad hand. Misfortune haunted him. On September 12, 1942, German U-boats sank a vessel in sight of the Cuban coast a few days before five judges of the Fifth Court of the Urgency Tribunal (Tribunal de Urgencia, Quinta Sala) tried him. Case number 1366 for 1942 occurred in secret proceedings from 9:45 A.M. until 4:15 P.M. on September 18. While the court proceedings were secret, the press was informed generally about the case, including the trial testimony. Cuba's civil code did not allow the death penalty. To circumvent this obstacle, the chief prosecutor, Dr. Mauricio Monteagudo, used a civil court but charged Lüning under Cuba's military code, the only judicial code in Cuba that allowed capital punishment. Specifically, the justice officials alleged that Lüning was responsible for the loss of Cuban lives on the *Santiago de Cuba* and the *Manzanillo*.[49] This was a questionable procedure.

Although the prosecutor urged the death penalty, Lüning's principal lawyer, Dr. Armando Rabell y Duque, insisted that the civil statutes, in particular article 3 of the Law of Security and Public Order, allowed only a maximum sixteen-year sentence. He challenged the civil Urgency Court's use of military law on powerful constitutional grounds. The German was a civilian, not a uniformed soldier, and, hence, not readily subject to military law. Domestic civil peace reigned in Cuba, Rabell added, and, hence, there was no need to resort to emergency or special procedures. It was unconstitutional, he argued, for a civil court to try a civilian under military law when Cuban courts functioned without problem and Cuban society was not in disarray.[50] Rabell saw no legal or constitutional basis for trying Lüning for a capital offense.

Before the trial, both the SIS and the Cuban experts knew that this radio "was incapable of being used to transmit messages in its present condition." Nevertheless, the Cuban minister of justice approved the charge that Lüning's radio contact with U-boats led to the loss of Allied lives. Since the secret trial records were not available, how Rabell attempted to refute this charge is unknown. On September 19, 1942, the court condemned Lüning to die by firing squad. Certainly, many Cubans held Lüning responsible for killing Cuban and Allied sailors, so the public supported a denial of his appeal.[51] Condemning Lüning to death had strong, widespread approval in Cuba.

An SIS agent attended Lüning's secret trial. He reported: "The subject reiterated, and experts verified, that the radio apparatus found in possession of the subject at the time of his arrest was incapable of being used to transmit messages. . . . However, it was allowed in evidence to show that Lüning made a bona fide effort to comply with the instructions he had received in Germany." In fact, the court testimony left open the possibility that the radio had functioned earlier. The court's death sentence sent the SIS agent rushing to notify Braden. The agent, unaware that Cuban law automatically appealed death sentences to the supreme court, had urged the U.S. ambassador to request a thirty-day postponement of the execution to allow a thorough interrogation of the Abwehr agent. The SIS needed time to gather photographs of suspected German agents for him to identify. Fearing that the Cubans might conduct a speedy execution, Braden asked Batista to delay the process while the FBI-SIS hurried photographs from Washington. Indeed, the agent noted, Lüning "may think that by further cooperation in identifying other spies, he may entertain some hope of having his sentence lessened by the Supreme Tribunal or by the President of the Republic."[52] The FBI-SIS wanted to extract every conceivable value from Lüning before he died. The death threat might make him even more cooperative.

Circumstances from the war fueled the Cuban public sentiment against Lüning. On October 17, 1942, a German U-boat sank a vessel in sight of the Cuban coast just before the Cuban supreme court heard the appeal of Lüning's death sentence. On October 31, it confirmed the death penalty, releasing its written decision on November 2. Only Supreme Court Justice Miguel Angel Rodríguez Morejón had rejected the maximum penalty, deciding for a prison sentence. Customarily, when the court's decision was not unanimous, the judicial system produced a reduced sentence. Not for the ill-fated Lüning, however. In early November 1942, only a presidential pardon could save his life.[53]

The misrepresentation of Lüning's role in the U-boat attacks on Cuban vessels that took Cuban lives poisoned public opinion toward him. An emotional belief in his contact with U-boats clouded popular sentiment. The Cuban public so vociferously and angrily condemned Lüning that he was brought to trial under heavy guard. Soon after the trial, several workers' meetings urged his immediate execution. Various Cuban cabinet ministers, in a rush to judgment and to popularity, criticized the delay caused by the appeals and the constitutional challenges. These ministers publicly proclaimed their willingness to see him shot quickly.[54] Cuban opinion at all levels welcomed the death sentence for the Abwehr agent.

Unfortunately for Lüning, in late 1942 the Allies urgently needed a scapegoat. The war was going badly in Europe, North Africa, and the Pacific. In addition, Axis submarine activity in the Atlantic, and more spectacularly in the Gulf-Caribbean, was devastating Allied shipping. In this bleak situation, and to curry U.S. favor, the Cuban civilian courts used military law to sentence the German spy to death. According to Ambassador Braden's self-serving and unlikely story, Batista, unwilling to order the execution, allowed the ambassador to make the final decision on Lüning's fate—sixteen years in prison or execution. Braden, in his own unsubstantiated version, opted for the firing squad. Later, he admitted to faint second thoughts when he saw Lüning's photograph in a magazine: "I had no particular qualms about [the sentence], though I do confess, I found his pictures in the paper a bit disturbing."[55] Braden was the self-selected hero in locating and destroying a dangerous Nazi spy.

It is interesting to recall that, after the death sentence was pronounced, Braden asked Batista to delay the execution out of fear that the Cuban president would sign the order at once. The Cuban media also expected a quick execution. There is neither collaboration nor reason to accept Braden's version. In fact, a later SIS inquiry found no evidence that Batista was reluctant to order Lüning's death.[56] Batista was not soft, and he knew the value of executing Lüning for his own goals of an invitation to the White House, increased U.S. commercial and military assistance, and improvement in the price and quota for Cuban sugar in the U.S. market. In fact, the U.S.-Cuban negotiations on the sugar price for the 1943 crop were scheduled to begin about the time Batista signed Lüning's death warrant. Of course, Batista may have tested Braden about the execution. He may well have wanted to check the resolve of Braden and the U.S. government. After all, only two months earlier, Braden had complained bitterly about the public announcement of Lüning's arrest. Certainly, Batista had no desire to annoy the U.S. ambassador again. In addition, Batista knew that Cuban workers and members of his cabinet publicly urged Lüning's execution. So killing him brought popularity and would maximize the outcome of the U.S.-Cuban sugar agreement. Batista would have spared Lüning only had the U.S. government objected to his execution.[57]

Since the Cuban justice minister quickly found no reason to grant clemency, Batista rejected a pardon. After the confirmation of the death penalty and the rejection of a pardon, Lüning faced death. Once the spy was heading to an execution, a U.S. naval intelligence officer questioned the wisdom of shooting someone who had cooperated and confessed everything he knew. The naval officer saw a downside. The spy's execution might persuade other captured Abwehr agents to withhold information since they would be shot anyway.[58] The ongoing, precarious circumstances in which the Allied war effort found itself, however, were inhospitable for clemency despite Lüning's cooperation.

By tradition, Cuban officials notified a condemned prisoner at least twenty-four hours prior to the execution. Again, Lüning was given unusual treatment. He only received sixteen hours' notice. He entered death row at 4:00 P.M. on November 9. He slept little and played checkers and Parcheesi with his lawyer Rabell and one guard, Modesto García Tuñón, most of the night. He won eight checker games with Rabell but lost two Parcheesi matches to García Tuñón. About 5:00 A.M. on November 10, he wrote a letter to his wife in Hamburg. As a last wish, he asked permission to wear a pendant with a photograph of his wife around his neck during the execution and to have that pendant buried with him. This wish was granted. The end surprised him. He reportedly told the firing squad officer: "I did not sleep all night long in expectation of a pardon. I did not expect to be shot, but I am at your disposition." Just before leaving for the execution, he handed Rabell a note: "In spite of the sentence from the Cubans, I continue to believe that my activities did not cause any direct injury to Cuba. I am of Latin origins."[59] If these were Lüning's last words, his mother's Latin ancestry and his own desire not to injure anyone were on his mind as he faced the firing squad. Lüning met a harsh end. He was anti-Nazi and served in the Abwehr only to avoid military service. Even his efforts, severely criticized by his Abwehr handlers, were apparently primarily motivated to prevent his wife, child, and parents from suffering from Nazi retribution.

During his last days, it seems probable that Lüning was also denied personal comfort. Several sources, including General Benítez and one contemporary newspaper, contended that Lüning's Cuban girlfriend, commonly known as Rebecca (Olga López, according to the Castillo Príncipe Prison visitors' registry), repeatedly tried to see him in prison. She was always refused permission. Likewise, Lüning's requests to see her were always denied. According to one story, on the evening of November 9, she waited outside the prison all night. Then, on the morning of November 10, she followed his coffin to Potter's Field at the Colón Cemetery. In 1952, Olga Lüning went to Havana to return Heinz's body to Hamburg.[60]

Prior to his execution, Lüning requested permission to confess to two Spanish Catholic priests from the Dominican Republic, the Reverend Angel Rey and the Reverend José Romero—both pro–Francisco Franco soldiers in the Spanish Civil War and opposed to the Allies. Lüning, Lutheran at birth, apparently converted to Catholicism to marry his American wife. Some acquaintances in Cuba doubted that conversion. Nevertheless, Lüning specifically asked to have Father Romero hear his last confession. One informer thoughtlessly suspected that Lüning wanted to see a priest in order to contact the German government.[61] But Lüning had been in prison for ten weeks, and one should remember that he had failed to gather useful information when he was free.

Lüning's execution exhibited macabre characteristics. About 7:55 A.M., he was taken from his cell, accompanied by the execution party of an officer and eight soldiers and Father Romero to the southern moat of the Castillo Príncipe Prison. Four of the eight soldiers were under orders to shoot for the head, the other four to shoot for the heart. When asked for his last words, Lüning reportedly addressed the priest: "Father, the only thing I ask is that peace and liberty may reign on earth. I have fulfilled my duty to my country." Lüning refused a blindfold. It was two minutes before 8:00. Then the macabre unrolled. The officer had the firing squad face Lüning at about twenty paces. The officer lowered his sword, the signal to fire, only between the fourth and the fifth chimes as the prison's tower clock struck eight. Lüning was executed at 8:00 A.M. on November 10, 1942 (in an odd coincidence, his father had committed suicide on November 10, 1929). He fell backward when shot. From the rush of blood, it appeared that he had been hit in the head and chest and that no coup de grâce was needed. Although the judicial order forbade newspaper and other unofficial observers, a few local and foreign journalists, various Cuban authorities, at least two U.S. embassy or SIS officials, and, perhaps, a British agent witnessed the execution. A photographer, also a witness, published a series of photographs in the popular Havana photomagazine *Bohemia* soon after the execution. The Cuban government, however, tried to confiscate all copies of that issue.[62]

The final SIS summary report erroneously presumed that the appeals and execution were delayed to allow the SIS to extract all the information Lüning possessed about espionage in the Western Hemisphere. Yet a lapse of only ten weeks from capture to trial, constitutionally mandated appeal, presidential review, and execution did not incorporate much delay.[63]

Despite the numerous participants in and witnesses to Lüning's execution, a rumor started immediately. Supposedly, Lüning had bribed Cuban officials to help him escape by plane. The Catholic priests who saw him in his last weeks may have been involved. Of course, the SIS rejected such wild allegations since several U.S. agents were present at the execution. Two Cuban doctors examined the corpse and declared Lüning dead. The death certificate cited internal hemorrhaging from the action of a firing squad as the cause of death. After various formalities, the body was buried in Colón Cemetery at 11:30 A.M.[64]

After the execution, the head of the Hamburg AST (the naval captain Herbert Wichmann) agreed to arrange the delivery of Lüning's letter to his wife.[65] Lüning's letter read as follows:

Mammy [Helga] Darling:

I was so very happy, when I received your nice letter. I was arrested already, when your lines were given me, like a wonderful surprise from heaven, in those dark and terrible days I spent during the last time, and you can't imagine how I felt morally thinking of you, the boy and the parents, and I still do not know, if there will be a possibility to join the family someday. Hope you, Hunky [his son, Adolf Bartholomae], Dad [his uncle Gustav Adolf] & Mussy [his aunt Olga] & the whole family and Arabella [illegible; a pet?] and Enso [illegible; a pet?] etc, are alright and will be safe until the end of this war.

Your people [the U.S. interrogators and officials] and the Cubans treat me very nice, and I shall never forget what they have done for me during these hard weeks.

I like to tell you by this opportunity that I am a victim of a bad preparation and a very bad organization [the Abwehr] Dr. K[oelln?] is so proud of, and I have the wish I always had; that he and his bandits might go to hell this time, so that everybody can breath [sic] fresh air again. I never liked this job, pardner [sic], you know that quite well, and that's exactly what makes my feeling awfully mad.—I guess the Chicago [his wife's aunt, Ella Bartholomae, and uncle, Philip Bartholomae, residing in Los Angeles] and Milwaukee

[his uncle Julius Lüning] families are informed, since I gave their
addresses to somebody.

That's all for this time, Mammy dear, hold your head high and
give many, many kisses to Hunky, Mussy, and Dad, and a lot of love
to yourself. In the firm hope and trusting that God will help me.
I am always

Bunny [Heinz August Lüning][66]

The Transocean news service, confidentially linked to the German
government, forwarded a report from the United Press service in Havana that Lüning was "the first German spy ever executed." That was not
correct, although he was the only German spy executed in Latin America
during World War II. The report repeated the baseless allegation that he
was executed "because of radio contacts with German submarines which
led to the sinking of allied ship tonnage."[67] This rumor followed Lüning
to the grave and beyond.

Benítez and Batista pointed to Cuba's role in breaking up Lüning's
(phantom) spy ring as a major step in reducing the effectiveness of German U-boats. Their action helped secure all Allied interests in the greater Caribbean area from Axis attack. Benítez expressed his view to the
Washington press on October 26, 1942. A month after Lüning's execution, during a talk in the United States, Bastista asserted that breaking
the Lüning operation went a long way toward ending the highly successful German U-boat campaign in the Gulf of Mexico–Caribbean area.[68]
Batista's self-congratulatory interpretation was all smoke and mirrors.
The chief Cuban contribution to curtailing German U-boats involved
making air and naval bases available for U.S. and British antisubmarine
activity. More airplane patrols, airports, convoy escort vessels, an effective and widespread communications system, and better-trained naval
and air force personnel made the Caribbean too costly for the German
U-boats by mid-1943.

Executing Lüning contributed nothing to reducing German U-boat
activity or successes. It did, however, greatly increase the public perception that Cuba and the United States were turning around an important
part of the war against the Axis. Thus, Allied leaders hyped and dis-

torted the significance of Lüning's capture and execution as a major step toward ending Nazi U-boat activity in the Gulf-Caribbean. His death would help alter the flow of negative reports about the war and suggest a brighter tomorrow.

The question remains, why did Lüning join the Abwehr and place himself in danger for a regime he disliked? The most plausible interpretation of his activity comes from his Guatemalan friend and tutor Lola Ardela. In 1943, the SIS interviewed her in Buenos Aires, where she was then living. Aware of Lüning's anti-Nazi sentiments, his many Jewish friends in Hamburg, and his various thwarted attempts to leave Germany with his family, she gave it as her opinion that he had pursued the Abwehr assignment to escape military service. He then, she surmised, produced information to keep his family and loved ones safe from retaliatory action by the Nazis. During his interview with Cuban reporters, Lüning claimed: "Once here, I could do nothing but go ahead with what I was told to do. My family lives in Germany. If I had been a very enthusiastic Nazi, I would feel very badly for having failed in the completion of my mission—for having been detained. As it is, I don't feel at all badly about it."[69] Moreover, Lüning had gathered little important information.

British, U.S., and Cuban counterespionage cooperation led to Lüning's capture. Despite the buildup of the U.S. counterintelligence service in Cuba beginning in early 1942, British censors at the Bermuda station detected the activity of a German secret agent. While U.S. and Cuban officials inflated and distorted their roles in Lüning's demise, the British were reserved. In fact, it was the British censors who detected his secret ink messages and located his home address in Havana. A British MI6 agent in Cuba was present at his detention, but was reserved about his role. British intelligence, cheerfully guarding its secrecy, received almost no publicity for its role. The British followed the practice that, in a secret agency, everything should be kept as secret as possible.

Since FBI-SIS officials from the top to the bottom had grossly exaggerated Lüning's importance, it was necessary to find some evidence to sustain the allegations against him. (It was also necessary to keep the file closed for as long as possible.) In the end, a Cuban firing squad ended the life of Lüning, perhaps the only German agent in Latin America who opposed Hitler's plans for war and conquest. Still convinced after his death that Lüning was a master spy, the FBI-SIS followed scores of leads, even as late as May 1945. But no meaningful contacts in the Americas were found, nothing to suggest that anyone else was a part of his espionage activity.[70]

Lüning was a reluctant Abwehr agent whose career served to achieve personal goals for others. His execution in late 1942 responded more to the political needs and the personal ambitions of key figures in Cuba and the United States than to any damage this bumbling German had inflicted on the Allies. Rather than a master spy or a male Mata Hari, Lüning was revealed by the FBI-SIS investigations to be a naive agent with no ability to gather useful information and few relations with Abwehr personnel elsewhere in the Americas. The U.S. and Cuban officials advanced his story as a sign of the reversal of the string of Axis successes. His execution ruptured what was presented as a significant source of Axis intelligence about Caribbean shipping and the use of the Panama Canal and a threat to the strategic link between the Atlantic and Pacific theaters.

Graham Greene in Noel Coward's swimming pool, Jamaica. The British novelist and MI6 agent during World War II wrote *Our Man in Havana,* which probably borrowed a lot from the Heinz August Lüning case. Courtesy Catherine Walton/Graham Greene Papers, Georgetown University, Research Archive.

(Above) Schwachhauser Heerstrasse 98, Bremen, Lüning's residence in Bremen. The left side of this building was where Lüning lived as a child in the 1920s until he moved to Hamburg in 1931. Photograph by Ebba Schoonover.

(Right) Philip Bartholomae as a senior at Rensselaer Polytechnic Institute in Troy, New York, when he was about twenty-one years of age. Courtesy Rensselaer Polytechnic Institute Library.

(Above) The residence of Gustav Lüning at Alte Landstrasse 62 in Hamburg Altona, where he and his family lived from 1931 until his death in 1942. Photo by Ebba Schoonover.

(Left) Maria-Louisa Strasse 61, Hamburg, the Abwehr safe residence for Lüning in 1941–1942. This was a cover address for Abwehr agents, including Heinz. He used this address (and the associated telephone number) as his residence in the notebook-diary in which he constructed the story of his work as a language tutor. Photo by Ebba Schoonover.

(Above) Klopstockstrasse 2–8, Hamburg Altona, the Abwehr training building. The far-right-hand entrance served an Abwehr bureau and pension; Lüning received some of his training there. Photo by Ebba Schoonover.

(Right) Estampa de Modas, the women's clothing store that Lüning ran as a cover in Havana. The manager was Clarita Pérez, the wife of Emilio Pérez. Courtesy *True Detective* magazine.

Bar Puerto Chico, which Lüning visited often to try to get information on shipping or economic activity for his Abwehr reports. Courtesy *True Detective* magazine.

Emilio Pérez (Lüning's friend and Wonder Bar bartender), his wife Clarita (manager of Lüning's Estampa de Modas clothing shop), and their child Enrique Augusto (named after Heinz), 1945 photograph.

(Right) Mariano Faget, the Cuban counterespionage chief in 1942. At the time, he had no reputation for brutality, and U.S. officials considered him quite competent. He returned with Batista in the 1950s, when he became known as a brutal, cruel police officer. Courtesy *True Detective* magazine.

(Left) Manuel Benítez, the vain, self-absorbed Cuban chief of police from 1941 to 1944, when Batista dismissed him and sent him out of the country. Courtesy *True Detective* magazine.

(Right) Lüning at his arrest on August 31, 1942 (a photograph attached to the MID report of the arrest). Courtesy FBI headquarters, Washington, D.C.

Heinz Lüning in a circular image in the Cuban police files. Courtesy *Carteles* and *True Detective* magazines.

Lüning in the door to his jail cell. Courtesy *Carteles* and *True Detective* magazines.

Lüning sitting by his radio, which never functioned. Courtesy *Carteles* and *True Detective* magazines.

Lüning on the day of his trial. Courtesy *Carteles* and *True Detective* magazines.

Lüning waiting at his trial under guard. Besides preventing his escape, the two Cuban policeman were also protecting him from attack, there being widespread popular anger in Cuba directed at him. Courtesy *Carteles* and *True Detective* magazines.

Lüning under heavy Cuban police guard. There were some threats made against him as well as a lot of bitter, aggressive talk and newspaper material. Courtesy *Carteles* and *True Detective* magazines.

Lüning before the tribunal on the day of his trial. His lawyer, Rabell, is behind him. Courtesy *Carteles* and *True Detective* magazines.

The hearse carrying Lüning's body to Colón Cemetery in Havana. Lüning was buried in the pauper's corner. His Aunt Olga removed his body and brought it back to Hamburg in mid-1952. Courtesy *Carteles* and *True Detective* magazines.

J. Edgar Hoover and Benítez look at map in the Washington, D.C., FBI Headquarters during Benítez's October 1942 visit. Courtesy *True Detective* magazine.

REPÚBLICA DE HONDURAS

PASAPORTE

Nombre del portador

Enrique Augusto Luni

No.: 3 2 .

Registro: 8 7

Front cover of Lüning's Republic of Honduras passport, no. 32, registry 87. Courtesy FBI headquarters, Washington, D.C.

INDENTIDAD

Nacionalidad *hondureña.*

Edad *29 años*

Lugar de nacimiento *Utila,.*

Estado civil *soltero.*

Profesión u oficio *Comerciante*

Estatura *alta.*

Cabellos *negros.*

Ojos *oscuros.*

Nariz *aguileña.*

Barba *redonda.*

Color *blanco*

Señas particulares *ninguna*

Válido por *5 años.*

Identity information for Lüning's passport noting, for example, that he was born in Utila, Honduras. Courtesy FBI headquarters, Washington, D.C.

Benítez observes trainees in pistol practice at the FBI firearms, Quantico, Va., during the October 1942 visit. Courtesy *True Detective* magazine.

6

Their Man in Havana

On October 25, 1942, Washington, D.C., police motorcycles escorted a vain Cuban chief of police, General Manuel Benítez, through the capital, for a meeting with J. Edgar Hoover. Benítez and Hoover basked in the light of photographers' flashbulbs as they shared the glory of capturing Germany's master spy in the Americas. They also shared a cover-up. Hoover knew, and Benítez should have known, that Lüning was not a master spy. He had never radioed German submarines, and British censors in Bermuda had done most of the work to catch him. Just over a month later, President Franklin D. Roosevelt would wine and dine Cuban president Fulgencio Batista, who was given the honor of spending a night in the White House as these two chief executives expanded the charade of the destruction of a major German spy network.

In September 1942, Lüning was packaged as a key spy because the Allies needed to show aggressive, successful counteraction to the threat of defeat from the Nazi submarine campaign. His operational location in Havana, Cuba, near where more than six hundred Allied vessels were sunk in ten months of 1942, allowed the U.S., British, and Cuban counterintelligence agencies to shift much responsibility for these disastrous losses to Lüning. The counterintelligence agencies boasted of their imagined roles in Lüning's arrest to garner credit for ending this bleeding of Allied shipping.[1]

Likewise, Allied counterintelligence expected recognition for its

123

(pretended) termination of this danger. Batista, Benítez, Braden, Hoover, and the SIS benefited from the capture of a faux major German spy. Hyping the arrest made it appear that Cuban intelligence and the SIS were curtailing the frequent U-boat sinkings of Allied vessels. Crushing the "most important" Nazi spy ring in the Americas might mitigate Allied reverses, which continued through 1942. Such news comforted the U.S. citizenry after a year of bad news from the Pacific, East Asian, European, North African, Atlantic, and Caribbean theaters. In reality, the Allied development of effective antisubmarine air patrols, better-trained flight and ship crews, and more antisubmarine surface vessels drove the U-boats away.

Using Lüning's capture as a starting point, Benítez and Batista obtained invitations to Washington, D.C., to reap rewards and gain prestige. The ambitious Benítez, who sought to succeed Batista, had prematurely arrested the spy and then released his identity to bolster his reputation and political position. To further enhance his standing, he claimed that several Cuban intelligence agents would undergo training in the FBI school in Virginia. Hoover tried to quash that brazen step. He announced that the FBI courses were only for FBI trainees and a few domestic policemen. For good measure, he added that the few courses scheduled were full. The FBI chief was placed in an awkward spot, however. Lüning's arrest made Benítez appear as a diligent and loyal U.S. ally. There was no suitable way to avoid a visit from him. Ultimately, Hoover even allowed a few Cubans to attend the school.[2]

In late October 1942, Hoover salved Benítez's ego. In addition to providing the motorcycle escort and the publicity photographs, Hoover praised the general's role (nonexistent) in capturing Lüning. Hoover labeled the arrest of Lüning a "magnificent" piece of work; he judged it a case with positive ramifications throughout the hemisphere. The *New York Times* summarized Hoover's praise: the Lüning case "probably would prove to be the outstanding spy case in the hemisphere." Benítez was, actually, ineffective in counterespionage. He had, however, political sense. While in Washington, he praised the SIS's work with Cuban officials. He boasted that the two nations had worked together on the Lüning case and had unraveled espionage connections to other parts of

Latin America also. In public, he emphasized the broad-based Cuban support of the Allied war effort. He suggested that U.S.-Cuban cooperation would, ultimately, eliminate Axis espionage in the Americas. Benítez needed pampering because he was "inordinately vain, love[d] display, [and] Pomp and Circumstance." To gratify his vanity, the FBI hosted a banquet in his honor, arranged a visit to the FBI academy, and set up a courtesy visit with General George C. Marshall. Nevertheless, FBI officials resented his appearance, which they privately considered an undesired self-invitation. According to SIS agents in Cuba, Benítez had an "increasing and somewhat sinister stature in Cuba." Although Hoover disliked Benítez's brazen conduct, once the trip became unavoidable, he promoted the general's visit as a shared celebration of U.S.-Cuban success against German submarines. Moreover, their meeting might promote even closer coordination in the future.[3]

Batista also exploited Lüning's capture. The judgment to execute Lüning suited him. Since he had come to power in 1940, he had repeatedly sought an invitation to Washington to legitimize his authority. He had redoubled his effort once Cuba declared war on Germany. However, the U.S. government politely turned aside all his requests. Throughout 1942, Batista let the U.S. government know that he still wished an invitation. Lüning's death changed his fate. Lüning was shot at 8:00 A.M. on November 10 and officially declared dead several hours later. Once the U.S. embassy in Havana received official notification of his death, it informed the State Department of his execution. The State Department, rewarded Batista. It announced his forthcoming state visit that same afternoon. Four weeks after Lüning's execution, Batista was banqueted in Washington and allowed the honor of a night in the White House.[4] In an ironic sense, Lüning arranged Batista's invitation to Washington.

Batista used his visit to gain support from Americans. On December 6, 1942, he awarded Edwin L. Sweet, the first FBI-SIS agent to train Cuban radio technicians, the Cuban Order of Police Merit in Washington, D.C. The implication that these Cuban radio specialists aided in the capture of Lüning was misleading. Lüning, as we have seen, never sent a radio signal.[5]

Batista desperately wanted to strengthen Cuba's ties to the United

States. To that end, he linked Lüning's arrest and death sentence to a major reduction of German U-boat action in the Gulf-Caribbean area. The *Washington Post* agreed and underscored Batista's valuable contribution to the anti-U-boat campaign. Batista, the *Post* noted, had proved his friendship in other ways. He had declared war on Japan and Germany on December 9, 1941, immediately after the U.S. declaration of war, and had placed Cuban ports and airports at the disposal of U.S. forces. And he had captured and executed the head of a major spy ring in the Americas. Given this record of support, the Cubans expected economic assistance, a larger sugar quota at a higher price, and enhanced military aid from the U.S. government.[6]

The arrest of Lüning energized the FBI's efforts to trace and disrupt the issuing and use of false passports. U.S. officials suspected that most passports came from Latin American consular and diplomatic officials in Europe. Lüning had entered Cuba with an improperly issued Honduran passport. He guessed that the Honduran consul in Hamburg, Majín Herrera A., and the Honduran consul general, Lucas Paredes (in Berlin), had sold about three hundred passports. He had some bad information. Paredes could have been involved in the sale of passports only until mid-1935, at which point he had been recalled at the German government's request after he objected strenuously to the Gestapo's treatment of his Jewish wife. Of course, Paredes could have sold false passports before mid-1935, and his successor could have sold illegal passports afterward. Majín Herrera, in Lüning's view, was not part of an Abwehr spy system but merely an opportunist who enriched himself by selling passports to the Abwehr, to Jews, and to others trying to flee Europe. In fact, Lüning had tried to acquire a Honduran passport privately in 1939 and 1940 but could not afford Herrera's price of thirty thousand reichsmarks for three passports. Once Lüning entered the Abwehr academy, the price became friendlier. The Abwehr received a 50 percent discount.[7]

U.S. officials, curious about how many improper passports went to German intelligence agents, expected Honduran cooperation to track down those with false passports. At times, the U.S. government's requests displayed unintentional humor. For example, in September 1942, the U.S. minister in Honduras asked the foreign minister for a list of all passports issued by Majín Herrera in Hamburg. The foreign minister, stunned by the naïveté of the proposal, expressed doubt that Herrera had supplied the Foreign Ministry with the names and personal data for improperly issued passports for which he had pocketed the fees. Then the U.S. minister brazenly suggested that, if Honduras exchanged all its passports, it would invalidate all improperly issued ones. The U.S. minister did not offer to pay for this laborious and expensive exchange of passports or to take steps to lessen the burden on Honduras.[8]

The Honduran foreign minister had, in fact, tried to recall Herrera in 1938, but the consul's connections to people close to President Tiburcio Carías Andino led to the withdrawal of the request. In early 1941, however, the German government canceled Herrera's exequatur—the authorization to function as a consul. It did not expel him, or even object to him personally; it was simply retaliating for the expulsion of a German official from Honduras. Although Herrera was no longer a consul, he continued to use the Honduran passport forms, seals, and stamps to issue "authentic" passports to Abwehr agents at a large discount from the street price. Not surprisingly, he held favor with the German government. Later, when Germany interned the other Latin American diplomatic and consular officials, it did not intern him.[9]

The foreign minister saw no obvious way to help the U.S. government. Still, he understood the problem of illegal passports for U.S. counterespionage activity and promised to discuss the matter with President Carías. Meanwhile, he suggested a simple, inexpensive alternative. Since Herrera allegedly drew $300 monthly from a Boston bank, the U.S. government could easily determine which bank and stop the transfers. This suggestion transferred a vastly reduced cost and effort to the U.S. government in the search for the records of the improper passports. Before long, the U.S. government learned that Herrera maintained a sizable account at a New York City bank. It did not block the funds, however. Rather, it tracked their route to Barcelona and waited until after Lüning's death. Then the FBI interviewed Herrera in Barcelona. Unfortunately, the FBI file on Lüning does not contain the report of the interview. Conceivably, Herrera, with his country at war with Germany and his funds in U.S. banks, might wish to cooperate. Ultimately, after a review of the costs and difficulties, President Carías ordered new passports. When the process was completed, all old Honduran passports, such as those Herrera had sold Lüning, would be invalid.[10]

Between 1933 and 1942, many thousands of illegal passports were issued in Europe. Apparently, Latin American consular and diplomatic officials and former officials issued many of these illegal documents. Beyond the scope of this investigation were the numerous *promesas* [documents that seemed to promise entrance into a Latin American country] that various agents of Latin American governments issued in the United States. The *promesas* seldom served to bring someone to the Western Hemisphere, but they might offer some protection to the holder in Europe. However, the illegal passports were often used to gain entrance to a country in the Western Hemisphere. Probably some Latin American officials issued *promesas* or passports out of a sense of humanity and compassion. Many adopted this course for material gain. As illegal documents, these passports remain largely untraceable. There is no verifiable way to determine how many were issued or to describe who the recipients were.

Apparently, thousands of Jewish refugees acquired passports. Numerous other passport recipients belonged to other groups persecuted by the Nazis. Since various Nazi agencies—principally the Abwehr, the Gestapo, the AO (the Nazi Party Foreign Bureau), the Foreign Ministry, and the SD (the German Security Service)—wanted to send clandestine agents to the New World, those Latin Americans selling false passports or travel documents in Nazi-controlled areas had to sell some to Nazi agents at a reduced price to remain in business. Obviously, the sellers kept few records of their transactions. Without information about the recipients, there was no way to sort the deserving from the undeserving. The apparently humane course to allow anyone with legal or illegal documents to enter the Americas carried an unknown price. Some with illegal passports would be Nazi agents, and, if they were successful in their espionage and sabotage work, the war would be prolonged, and the Nazi extermination camps might have extracted a higher toll than the number saved by accepting all passports. In the last years of the war, the Nazi extermination camps killed three to five thousand Jews daily. If the Nazi agents allowed to enter the Western Hemisphere with false documents were able to cause disruptions that lengthened the war for a week, the Jewish death toll would have risen another twenty to thirty-five thousand. It was an impossible calculus.

Of course, the U.S. government was interested in the issuance of illegal passports in Europe. It vigorously pursued any information that might help expose German agents in the Americas. Assuming that numerous German intelligence agents traveled on false passports, it examined Lüning's case in the hope of shedding light on the sources and recipients of improperly issued passports. It hoped to uncover the names, numbers, and issuers of illegal documents.[11]

Efforts to reveal German spies with Latin American passports occupied the FBI-SIS and the State Department for years. In October 1942, soon after Lüning's arrest, U.S. officials asked all Latin American governments about the passports their officials had issued in Germany (and in Europe) since late 1940. It learned a lot generally but little of use to determine specifically who held the illicit passports. For example, Guatemala had issued thirty-five passports in Germany, Peru had issued twenty-six in Europe (but only four in Germany), and Uruguay had issued twenty-two in Germany, all in Hamburg. El Salvador reported that it had not kept records of the few passports issued in Europe before war broke out. Another FBI interviewee who had spent considerable time in Europe claimed that it was common knowledge that the consuls of smaller South and Central American countries sold passports. He recalled that the Peruvian consul in Berne "made a great fortune out of questionable transactions with reference to passports and visas for Peru."[12] Of course, these governments could report only about legal passports, not about improperly issued ones.

After over two months of determined investigations and inquiries by SIS and State Department officials in each Latin American country, in January 1943 the FBI compiled an eighty-three-page summary report describing the status in half the countries of Latin America. The composite image of false passports was startling. The report revealed how commonly illegal or uncontrolled passports were available for sale. The prospect that large numbers of Nazi agents might be operating throughout Latin America and the Caribbean was discomforting.

Some Latin American governments were cooperative, and others were not. Yet the resistance was not always out of opposition to the United States. Several Latin American countries—Bolivia, El Salvador, Haiti, Nicaragua, and Peru—had few records even for official passports. For various reasons, the report did not present information on official passports for Brazil, Venezuela, Paraguay, Colombia, Mexico, Cuba, Panama, Ecuador, Argentina, or Chile. Brazil and Mexico were unwilling to supply blanket information on all passports but agreed to consider each case where U.S. officials had reasonable suspicion. State Department officials in some countries with pro-Axis sympathies—Argentina and Chile, for example—were unwilling even to request information formally because any such request would generate ill will and no response.

Still, the numerous opportunities for Nazi agents to acquire passports could have allowed a flood of Abwehr agents. For example, there were migration agents in Vichy France who regularly advertised their services in the newspapers, offering to obtain passports to the Americas for a hefty fee. The longevity of these businesses and their extensive publicity suggested close cooperation between the migration agents and Latin American and Caribbean countries. One credible observer in France thought that consuls from Brazil, Venezuela, Paraguay, and Uruguay were the principal suppliers for these agents. Of course, U.S. officials worried that some who obtained these false papers would try to enter the United States. While the number of passports sold was unknown, the fact that migration agents advertised over a long period of time in various news media suggested a healthy business.[13]

The U.S. government's search for improper passports uncovered alarming situations. Evidently, Abwehr agents had numerous opportunities for illegal entry into the Americas. The Costa Rican government had sent 1,202 passports to its consuls in Lisbon, Portugal, and Stockholm in July 1940. The consular agents were supposed to submit a form to San José for each passport issued, but not a single form had come back. However, Costa Rica had no records for the years before 1940 either. The Nicaraguan government had no records for passports, but it had authorized only fifty for the whole world in the previous few years. Still, the Nicaraguan Foreign Ministry estimated that a former official in

Germany had retained the consular seal and issued over two thousand passports. A second former Nicaraguan official in Spain had also issued an unspecified large number of passports. The Peruvian consular official in Warsaw issued a number of authorized passports, but he was not forwarding records. The Peruvian government suspected unauthorized passports also. The Bolivian government received reports that several honorary consuls in Europe who were authorized to issue passports sold them, but it had few records.[14] The Latin American countries issued modest numbers of legal passports and kept poor records of even these.

Clearly, a larger number of passports were issued illegally in Europe in the name of Latin American countries. Haiti, for example, offered a fountain of opportunities for German agents or people fleeing Europe. Haitian policies presented several routes for Europeans to gain access to the Americas. Between 1937 and 1942, it was possible to obtain Haitian citizenship, and, hence, a passport, without visiting the country. A simple commitment to invest and live in Haiti in the near future was sufficient. Since the Haitian government had not supervised these open commitments, the program was a source of deception and corruption. Many Europeans received Haitian citizenship between 1937 and 1942 without moving or investing there. The outbreak of war changed this. On February 4, 1942, a decree cautioned all those enjoying special Haitian citizenship to follow all conditions—investment and residency—or lose their citizenship on August 5, 1942. Other disturbing information surfaced about Haiti. A Swiss banker named Ditisheim of Leuscher and Company had facilitated a loan deal for Haiti. The Haitian government had rewarded him with one hundred blank, signed passports. Rumor circulated that a Haitian passport cost $3,000 in 1942. One person the FBI was watching for other reasons, Juan Enrique Emden, stated that, early in the war, he had purchased a Haitian passport in Switzerland for $3,500. He also held a Chilean passport.[15] In a few cases, it seems possible to track an illegal passport from Latin American officials, but generally it is impossible.

Friederich Wilhelm Engelhorn, an immigrant on the SS *Magallenes*, also perceived a European "passport racket" that centered on the consular representatives of the small Central and South American countries.

Several of these agents, in his view, sold passports to whoever had the cash.[16] During interviews following Lüning's arrest, SIS investigators discovered that several of Lüning's acquaintances from the *Villa de Madrid* and from Havana had purchased naturalization papers and passports from Western Hemisphere nations.[17]

Only in late May 1944 did the U.S. government decide to recognize the European passports issued under unusual circumstances. This was less a reversal of policy than a calculation that the Axis powers, especially their submarine activity, had declined so much that a few Nazi agents posed little threat. By mid-1944, Nazi forces were defeated in Africa, Sicily, and southern and central Italy, and Italy had surrendered and changed sides. Soviet forces were preparing to launch a major attack to clear the German forces from their homeland. Large U.S., British, Canadian, and French forces were ready to invade Europe. In the Pacific, the Japanese were being pushed back toward their homeland. The dreaded German U-boat and Luftwaffe forces were essentially legends with minuscule actual fighting capacity. The possible danger from spies in the Caribbean was approaching zero. There were no U-boats to contact.[18]

One Abwehr holder of an illegal passport was known: Lüning. He was captured in Cuba, and the Cubans intended to make something of that fortuitous opportunity. U.S. and Cuban officials were able to track down Lüning's network of German intelligence subagents in the Americas. Thus, while Graham Greene's fictional spy, James Wormold, created imaginary agents, the SIS created an imaginary circle of spies and subagents tied to Lüning. He had no agents working under him. Still, Lüning suspected that two people in Havana might be Abwehr agents. His suspicions of other possible agents were unreliable because he was poorly trained and not particularly bright. In fact, he had little verifiable information about other German agents in the Americas. After investigating leads for two and a half years, the SIS became convinced that Lüning had no important contacts.[19]

Lüning played a role in one significant SIS campaign against a major Nazi intelligence ring in the Americas. He contributed in a small way to the breakup of a well-known ring of German agents in Chile. U.S. officials notified the Chilean government about some Lüning–Carlos Robinson Hurley espionage correspondence. On September 18, the Chileans arrested Robinson and two others. Ten days later, the U.S. embassy in Santiago, Chile, at the request of senior Chilean officials, called the U.S. embassy in Havana to inquire about testimony in the Lüning case that related to German spies in Chile. The SIS outlined the case. Lüning then copied in longhand the SIS draft statement of his relationship to Carlos Robinson in Chile. This statement arrived at the U.S. embassy on October 8, 1942. Meanwhile, on September 29, Benítez had cabled the police chief in Santiago that Lüning's confession proved conclusively (but, alas, mistakenly) that Robinson was Lüning's superior. On October 4, the Chilean minister in Havana inquired whether the case against Lüning "was really serious." The Cubans were insulted. After Robinson and two associates were arrested, the Chilean ring remained free for three weeks. There were other Nazi agents in Chile. Then Undersecretary of State Sumner Welles, impatient, sharply criticized Chilean conduct in a tough speech on the evening of October 9 in Boston. Soon afterward, the Chileans arrested a number of suspected agents. This Chilean Abwehr ring included Luis Russ Benzinger, Sebastian Krunckel, Carlos Feuerbacher, Osvaldo Schlegel, Alfredo Klaiber Maier (the manager of Banco Germánico in Santiago), Carlos Robinson, Guillermo Dorbach Burg, Hans Borchers, and Francisco Muller. However, Chile closed down a powerful, German-operated radio only in early November.[20] The Chileans responded only to prodding.

Lüning described in detail his telegraph contact with Robinson and Klaiber Maier. Since the text of most of these cables is not available, it is evident only that there were various communications over several routes in Chile. Robinson had exchanged cables with Lüning on behalf of Dorbach Burg, the owner of a lubricating oil factory near Santiago. Robinson maintained that he did so because he and Dorbach had married sisters. Although Robinson and Dorbach were German agents, the nature of the information exchanged with Lüning was not clear.[21] Klaiber Maier first contacted Lüning in June 1942 at the request of his friend Francisco Muller, who was in Barcelona at the time. In two instances, Muller's correspondence for Lüning included paid replies that Klaiber had forwarded to Muller.[22] These German Chileans served as intermediaries for Abwehr correspondence. As Lüning's radio did not work, he occasionally contacted Europe via Chile as an alternative to the secret ink messages. The Abwehr also used this route to inquire about his work.

In the search for network agents, the SIS inquired about several passengers from Europe who established relationships with Lüning. Georges Herschon Beilin and Lüning met on the *Villa de Madrid*. Beilin, a Russian émigré, grew up near Leipzig but moved to France before World War I. He lived there until he decided to flee Europe. For some reason, when the SIS appeared, he hid his relationship to Lüning. When the relationship became known, the Cuban police arrested him.[23] His fate is not revealed in these SIS records.

The SIS also investigated Friederich Engelhorn, who soon left for Honduras. The Honduran consul in Havana had introduced Engelhorn and Lüning because he thought that these "Honduran citizens" might do business together. In Lüning's mind, Engelhorn was also a German agent with a fraudulent Honduran passport. Despite his departure for Honduras, Lüning believed that Engelhorn lived in Mexico City. Later, to SIS interviewers, Engelhorn claimed that Lüning spoke English without a German accent and was dark and that he had therefore presumed that Lüning was not German. The SIS watched Engelhorn and his mail closely for some time but found no evidence of espionage activity.[24]

Another acquaintance of Lüning's, Annie Lehmann, a widow and former resident of Berlin, had arrived on the SS *Magallenes* along with Engelhorn. She fell under suspicion because she had corresponded with Engelhorn as a favor for a fellow female passenger who lacked Cuban authorization to receive mail at her hotel. Her situation attracted interest because she had purchased naturalization papers and a passport from Haitian officials in Brussels. Of further interest, she vainly pursued entrance into the United States, where, she claimed, she had inherited property from her late husband.[25] In fact, various U.S.-bound immigrants were stuck in Cuba because of heightened security and lack of passenger space between Havana and the United States. After extensive investigation, the SIS could not establish any espionage link between Lüning and a passenger.

The SIS labored diligently for years to uncover an espionage association between Lüning and the people he contacted about business. However, his correspondence with them involved only his efforts to earn a living and create cover activity. In one instance, SIS agents investigated a merchant, Antonio López, in Buenos Aires, Argentina. Lüning had used this old acquaintance, a business associate of Uncle Gustav's, as an intermediary to communicate with the Abwehr in Hamburg. Lüning, who had not informed López about the objective of his correspondence, doubted that López was willingly involved in Abwehr work. In early 1943, the Argentine police and the SIS agent in Buenos Aires agreed with that assessment.[26]

The FBI-SIS examined all of Lüning's contacts in the Americas, whether from efforts to gather information, to create cover businesses, or to pursue social or leisure activity. A few days after his death, Hoover observed that none of the U.S. firms with which he had had contact had "knowledge of Lüning and his activities . . . and investigation has shown that these firms are old, reliable, well-established concerns and are in no way connected with espionage activities. No information has been developed suggesting Lüning had any espionage contacts in the United States."[27] Lüning's contact with U.S. firms was, as the spy portrayed them, an effort to establish legitimate business ties that might allow him to earn a living.

Batista was determined to use the crisis of the war to establish warmer personal and national ties to the United States. In December 1942, he twisted the capture and execution of Lüning into a heroic act. He emphasized Cuba's role in Lüning's arrest and claimed that German U-boat activity shrank after Lüning's (phantom) network was destroyed. Not Cuban and U.S. counterespionage labor but vastly increased airplane patrolling and ship antisubmarine activity with better-trained air force and naval personnel and larger, better-trained and equipped convoys reduced U-boat effectiveness.

Batista even risked diplomatic capital to win U.S. support. During his visit to New York City in mid-December 1942, he consciously strained relations with Spain. At an interview, he emphasized that an Allied invasion of Spain, where the Falangist government was especially friendly to Nazi Germany, would receive "a total ovation throughout the Americas." "Only a few Falangists might disapprove, and they don't count," he added. He justified an invasion of the Iberian Peninsula if necessary to shut down Nazi and fascist intelligence and economic activity unfriendly to the Allied cause. Spanish officials, conveyors of the cultural roots of many Cubans, were incensed. However, Batista's stance bolstered Cuba's relations with the United States at a time when the price and quota for sugar and a general economic aid package were under discussion.[28] In his view, contemporary relations with the United States superseded traditional ties with Spain.

In Cuba, Spanish diplomats carried a special burden that left them vulnerable to public criticism. They represented the despised Germans and their interests after Cuban-German relations were severed at the end of 1941. They obtained the most capable defense for Lüning. The Spanish chargé kept Germany informed of the Lüning situation. On November 11, 1942, he reported Lüning's execution. He and Lüning's lawyer had exhausted all alternatives to save the Abwehr agent. A second report, dated December 9, 1942, described Lüning's death and enclosed Lüning's letter to Helga dated November 9, 1942.[29] Summaries of these reports remain, but the actual dispatches were destroyed when the train of the Nazi foreign minister, Ribbentrop, was bombed in 1945. Spanish diplomats pursued an unpopular task in representing German interests.

Lüning was almost unknown in Germany. The general public knew nothing of him. His family's notification of his death underscored the Abwehr's lack of interest in an unproductive agent. The German Foreign Ministry asked the Abwehr to present the letter to Helga Lüning. In the interchange between the Foreign Ministry and the Abwehr, the Abwehr's distance from Lüning became clear. Lüning was dead. The Foreign Ministry wrote: "Lüning war—so weit hier bekannt—für die Abwehr tätig" [Lüning was—so far as known here—active for the Abwehr]. The Abwehr corrected this sentence in its reply: "Lüning ist beim Amt Ausland/Abwehr bekannt" [Lüning is known to the Amt Ausland/Abwehr]. Even in death, Lüning was not acknowledged by the Abwehr as an agent. Perhaps it did not consider him a "real" member of the intelligence service, merely a decoy. Or perhaps the refusal to name even a dead agent was standard security policy.[30] Postwar German studies of World War II espionage scarcely mention Lüning (the Hamburg Abwehr records were largely destroyed, and the FBI-SIS records were classified).

The FBI-SIS and Cuban construction of a Lüning legend survived the war in Theodore F. Koop's melodramatic memoir *Weapon of Silence* (1946) and in the popular, prolific journalist Kurt Singer's 1945 *Spies and Traitors during World War II*. Koop, the special assistant to the director of the U.S. Office of Censorship, depicted Lüning as a central figure in Germany's espionage in the Americas during World War II. Singer's story of a talented, romantic, deceptive agent bordered on fiction; it only marginally represented the reality of Lüning's life.

A critical reading of Koop's book exposed the manipulated image of Lüning as a master spy. Koop, aware that Lüning's radio never worked, nevertheless painted him as a threat to shipping in the Gulf-Caribbean area and to the U.S. invasion of North Africa. However, Koop, who had access to all intercepts, could not reproduce a single piece of vital information from any Lüning message. To the contrary, his summaries of secret messages—presumably he selected Lüning's more telling and damaging work—revealed essentially harmless information. Nevertheless, after Koop made Lüning the center of the Office of Censorship's counterespionage success in chapter 1, Lüning's central role resurfaced in many of the next twenty chapters, at least on the periphery. In effect, Koop treats Lüning as the head of German espionage in North America and the Caribbean. It was widely known in U.S. intelligence circles that this was a false image. Apparently, the Office of Censorship needed to inflate its meager counterespionage role. Without important evidence, Koop constructed the image of Lüning as a master spy. Mary Knight, the secretary to Byron Price, the director of the Office of Censorship, spun a tale similar to Koop's. Her story also elevated Lüning's case—in which the Office of Censorship was barely involved—to a major event and then linked it to many other cases.[31] Koop and Knight fabricated the Office of Censorship's role in capturing Lüning and breaking up a significant Nazi spy network.

Lüning's service was used to pursue various objectives, some of which had little to do with World War II. Honduran politics in 1944 exploited the Nazi spy story. Opponents of President Carías Andino accused the dictator's government of Nazi ties largely on the basis of Lüning's Abwehr service. The Carías opposition argued that the Honduran consul in Hamburg sold the passport and that the Honduran consul general in Havana worked with Lüning. These Carías appointees demonstrated his government's ties to the Nazis and, hence, made him unfit to govern Honduras. The charges were weakened because they commonly included charges against the Honduran consul general in Berlin, Lucas Paredes, in the conspiracy to aid Hitler. Parades, however, had left Germany in mid-1935 because the Gestapo mistreated his Jewish wife. Paredes had no known contact with Lüning and a hostile relationship with the Nazis in the weeks before he was forced to leave.[32]

Lüning's story, often in overdrawn form, surfaced in other popular versions at the war's end or after. In mid-1944, as we have seen, the widely popular *True Detective* published Manuel Benítez's version of the Lüning case, "On Radio Berlin." This story was full of distortions, half truths, and untruths. It was, nevertheless, translated and serialized in *Mañana* (Havana) in 1947. The German journalist Klaus-Peter Bochow wrote a sketch of Lüning's espionage activity that is so confused, inventive, and erroneous that it can be viewed only as fiction. Bochow fit Lüning's story into a book about the FBI's thrilling cases (ignoring that the SIS was legally and technically separate during the war) to entice German readers.[33]

The Allied counterintelligence leaders enhanced their careers, seized the spotlight, and gained prestige through claims of destroying a major Nazi spy ring that they deceptively linked to a threat from German U-boat operations in the Caribbean basin. If the Abwehr intentionally sent Lüning out to distract the Allied counterintelligence, he was, in fact, a masterstroke of someone's conception, but not a master spy. The FBI-SIS initially considered Lüning a dangerous spy. Therefore, for two and a half years, it used scores of agents across the United States and throughout Latin America to interview hundreds of people. The file grew between 1942 and 1945. The various reports for each investigating region concluded that Lüning had no espionage contacts in the United States, Cuba, the Caribbean, or South America except for only a few specific links in Chile and Argentina for occasional communications. Still, the FBI and Hoover had continued to exaggerate his importance long after his limitations were evident. Since the FBI-SIS had few success stories to exploit during World War II, Hoover was reluctant to give up on Lüning. The SIS agents continued to pursue leads, conduct interviews, and generate further leads until May 31, 1945, when the SIS agent John N. Speakes finally announced that the case was being closed.[34] In the end, the German was an isolated and ineffective agent whose pinnacle of usefulness was as a decoy and a scapegoat.

Hoover, other U.S. and Cuban officials, and the Cuban and U.S. newspapers repeatedly designated Lüning a "grave threat" and labeled him a "Key German Spy."[35] Braden, the FBI-SIS, the Office of Censorship, Cuban intelligence, Batista, the *Diario de la marina,* the *New York Times,* the *Washington Post,* the Associated Press, and Benítez in *True Detective* treated Lüning as if he were the chief German espionage agent in the Americas. The media generally accepted the official Allied version because it attracted attention, won praise, and sold newspapers. These characterizations reveal the irony of reality and overdramatized Lüning's espionage activity.

The British avoided self-congratulatory publicity with regard to this secret work, but they were significant participants in Lüning's demise. The British censors at the Bermuda station had first intercepted a Lüning secret ink message. Then they captured and deciphered most of Lüning's subsequent secret ink messages. After they intercepted the spy's real address in Havana, U.S., British, and Cuban officials captured him on August 31, 1942. While the U.S. and Cuban officials characterized Lüning as a master spy of the Americas, the British Secret Intelligence Service (MI6) and Imperial Censorship were more realistic in evaluating his espionage labor. The flood of self-praise from the publicity-seeking officials of Cuba and the United States obscured the effective British labor.

German, British, U.S., and Cuban agents dealt with Lüning and his espionage career. His selection, training, service, and death as an Abwehr agent engaged four governments that valued him chiefly for their ability to manipulate his service and image. The Abwehr saw him as a decoy, contributing to the security of the other Nazi agents. The managed public relations image of Lüning reflected well on various agencies and leaders—the Office of Censorship, Batista, Benítez, Braden, the FBI-SIS, and Hoover—who exploited the situation. Still, Lüning's story endured best in *Our Man in Havana*, Graham Greene's marvelous satiric novel of counterespionage.

If the SIS and Cuban officials did not present Lüning as dangerous, there would be neither prestige nor reward for capturing him. So the Allied intelligence version of Lüning's story is revealing. His radio did not work. He had poor skills in writing in secret ink and little sense for useful information. He repeatedly misnumbered his secret ink messages. Nevertheless, some U.S. and Cuban observers designated him a "grave threat" and compared him with Mata Hari. This spy's activity was twisted to suit U.S. and Cuban needs. Cuban intelligence officials implied that he radioed German submarines even though their own radio experts insisted that the radio had never functioned. SIS and FCC agents also knew that his radio never worked.

Why this duality—publicly projecting the image of a dangerous spy yet privately aware that he was ineffective? The appearance of breaking up a major Axis intelligence and U-boat network in the Americas offered the Cuban government and U.S. counterintelligence an opportunity to gain institutional power and public favor. Vital raw materials and supplies would move from South America and the Caribbean area to the war industries and training facilities in North America and Europe. The resultant transit of men and war materials would win the wars in Europe and the Pacific by using the Panama Canal regularly. U.S. and Cuban officials alleged that the capture of Lüning and the rupture of his spy network was instrumental in winning the war. They were pushing the Allies back from the edge of defeat.

7

Graham Greene's Man in Havana

Lüning was reincarnated fifteen years later in the guise of James Wormold, Great Britain's and Graham Greene's "man in Havana." Graham Greene, who served in MI6 and shared responsibility for oversight of British counterespionage in the Caribbean in 1943 and 1944, apparently drew on the importance assigned to Lüning and the large volume of material about him when he wrote the 1958 *Our Man in Havana*.

A brief sketch of Greene's novel should allow the reader to discern similarities between Heinz August Lüning and Wormold, Greene's fictional Anglican British resident in Havana and MI6 spy. The novel is set in the 1950s. Wormold, a quiet and inactive resident of the city, owns a vacuum cleaner agency. Although his wife has left him, he had promised to raise their teenage daughter as a Catholic. The girl is expensive to manage. Wormold is faced with an ominous financial burden—she wants a horse, and that entails a sizable monthly stable bill, at the Havana Country Club, no less.

Suddenly, and despite the fact that he apparently has no background in intelligence work, Wormold is offered the opportunity to supplement his income with a handsome salary and expenses as MI6's man in Havana. Even more amazingly, he is expected to recruit subagents, who will naturally get salaries and expenses. Wormold stands before a gold mine.

A string of nonexistent agents and their varied fictional expenses and real bonuses for good work (the good work leaps from the inventive mind of Wormold only) could solve his financial woes. Soon under pressure to do something beyond routine reports, he traces an outline of vacuum cleaner parts that he reports as the product of dangerous work, undertaken in the eastern mountains of Cuba, by one of his subagents. His stock and that of his subagents ratchets up when these drawings are interpreted as exposing an ominous enemy-secret-weapon site. The bonuses for such excellent work shoot into the stratosphere.

This cheery and cheeky story has a downside. This success induces Britain's (unspecified) enemies to eliminate Wormold's agents. The inexperienced Wormold had borrowed the names of real people. These poor souls begin to die or suffer attacks under mysterious circumstances. Ultimately, the agents of the unnamed evil power are eliminated. Wormold's deception is exposed, however, and he is recalled to London. MI6's director is unable to discipline Wormold because that would demonstrate the incompetence and gullibility of the leadership. The only way out is to present Wormold with the Order of the British Empire and make him an instructor in the MI6 training school. He will teach new agents how to run a station abroad.

Both the SIS's investigation and Greene's story describe supposedly master spies who ultimately wavered between disinterest and incompetence. Lüning's spy experience served in some way as a model for Wormold. The large, varied body of evidence to support this contention is essentially circumstantial. There are numerous similarities in the two characters and their stories. There is little direct evidence because Greene wrote little specifically about his MI6 service. He did acknowledge, however, that *Our Man in Havana* drew on his experience with MI6. In this light, the variety of circumstances, plot and character similarities, and numerous details that Wormold and Lüning shared have additional force in convincing the reader.

Greene should have known a great deal about Lüning's adventure. He claimed that his three years of MI6 experience, especially the fifteen months' service in London at the Portugal desk (which oversaw the New World), involved reading file, after file, after file. One of the larger files, mostly from FBI-SIS's counterspies, but also from MI6's Havana agent, would have dealt with Lüning's case. These files supplied Greene with material for *Our Man in Havana:* "So it was that experiences in my little shack in Freetown [in 1942 and early 1943] recalled in a more comfortable room off St. James's [at the Portugal desk] gave me the idea of what twelve years later became *Our Man in Havana.*"[1] Thus, Greene's work at the Portugal desk helped him write about Wormold.

There is no reason why any scholar who has analyzed Greene or *Our Man in Havana* should have even known about Lüning's service and death in Havana. Lüning's espionage activity was media news in late 1942 and again, to a lesser extent, from 1945 to 1947. This information circulated in the area of international politics, not literature. (The huge document collection at FBI headquarters was guarded under secret classification until I requested most of it in 2001 and 2002.) In my case, I started with the espionage and political aspects of Lüning and, after a year's research, realized that I had met this German agent somewhere earlier under different circumstances. Lüning's spy persona survived in a disguised form.

Like many spies, both Lüning and Wormold lived in constructed imaginary worlds. In Greene's novel, the British top spies interpreted the world of James Wormold's imaginary agents—drawings of vacuum cleaner parts—as a threat to world peace. Lüning's ties to imaginary sub-agents endangered the world. In the real world, the Cuban police chief, Benítez, insisted that Lüning had contacts throughout the region and radioed German U-boats regularly. Benítez had no substantiation; it just fit the self-image he needed for his political aspirations. The FBI-SIS investigation used smoke and mirrors to connect Lüning to just about every spy or spy ring in the Americas. It imagined a threat to world peace—Lüning's nonexistent spy ring guiding an immensely successful U-boat warfare—every bit as dangerous as Wormold's drawings of vacuum cleaner parts.[2]

Both Wormold and Lüning revealed fundamental incompetence as far as the basics of their jobs were concerned. Consider Greene's comic Wormold, who owned a vacuum cleaner shop but, early in the novel, could not disconnect a common cleaning attachment from the vacuum hose. In an interesting comparison, Lüning, a radio and secret ink spy, could not build a radio, mix the ink, or write with it properly.[3]

Reading the Lüning file and *Our Man in Havana* produces considerable evidence to link the real Abwehr agent to the fictional British spy. First, there are many similarities in the personalities and characteristics of Lüning and Wormold. For example, both were largely failures in commercial ventures. They also shared a bumbling approach to espionage, due in part to their lack of training: Lüning received six weeks training at the Hamburg Abwehr academy and Wormold only a few hours in a Havana hotel one night. The reputation of both derived from nonexistent subagents. One scholar commented: "Wormold has no idea how to recruit his own local spy ring nor what he would do with it if he had one, but his newfound affluence soon encourages him to invent what he cannot find, including plans for some gigantically mysterious installations in the mountains." In a parallel light, the German spy who could not mix ink also did not know how to complete his radio or what to do with it if completed.[4] Both faced huge challenges with the fundamentals of their espionage service.

Both Lüning and Wormold sparkled because of nonexistent subagents. While Wormold created imaginary subagents and an imaginary secret location for a secret weapon in the Cuban mountains, SIS intelligence officials created Lüning's imaginary subagent network and imaginary contacts with German U-boats that allegedly threatened the existence of a free Western Hemisphere and Europe. Both Wormold and Lüning were interpreted as key elements in stories that gravely endangered the Western world. Their reputations rested on contacts with nonexistent agents. Wormold supplied no meaningful information to his handlers and Lüning only modest amounts. For both the FBI and Wormold, image trumped substance.

Wormold and Lüning were reluctant secret agents with little training, interest in the job, or skill. Neither knew how to gather information or build a network. The U.S. and Cuban counterintelligence agencies, however, described Lüning as an apparent master spy. Wormold's drawings of vacuum cleaner parts made him a master spy. Despite the self-serving, congratulatory puff of U.S. and Cuban reports (for capturing

Lüning), Lüning's bungling nature closely resembled Greene's reluctant British MI6 spy and vacuum cleaner salesman Wormold. These reluctant agents accepted their positions not from conviction or duty but as a way to escape personal dilemmas. Scores of interrogations of Lüning revealed many details that recur in Wormold's life. Lüning wanted most to be left alone with his family and friends in Hamburg, just as Wormold preferred to be left alone with his daughter and a few friends in Havana. Strong family ties—especially to a beloved single child—motivated both agents. Wormold was an Anglican who brought up his daughter as a Catholic; Lüning was a Lutheran who apparently converted to Catholicism for his wife and child.[5] Wormold needed funds to support his daughter's lifestyle, and Lüning needed to escape military service in a manner that would not injure his family.

Further similarities in details link the novel's spy and Lüning's real-life adventure. Both lived a few minutes from and frequented the Wonder Bar—a nondescript establishment that attracted Jews and other Eastern Europeans because it served dark bock beer. Greene's novel, in fact, opens in the Wonder Bar, an important site that is revisited often in *Our Man in Havana*. Soon after Lüning arrived in Havana, he discovered the Wonder Bar. One of its bartenders, Emilio Pérez (who named his son, born in 1943, Enrique Augusto Pérez after Lüning), became his close friend. Emilio recommended that Lüning take living quarters near the Wonder Bar. Lüning visited the bar to see Emilio. In the novel, Wormold visited the bar regularly with his close friend Dr. Hasselbacher, an old Austrian doctor. Both spies had talented Cuban police captains as opponents. Lüning's chief opponent in Cuba was Captain Mariano Faget y Díaz, a capable and intelligent agent, while Wormold confronted a Captain Segura who possessed similar qualities.[6] Both Lüning and Wormold had contact with Havana's strippers, prostitutes, and bar girls. Both specifically and emphatically condemned war or conflict rooted in nationalism, capitalism, or other isms. Lüning rejected Nazi ideology and military expansionism, while Wormold denied the British and Western rhetoric of idealism or nationalism behind the cold war.[7]

Other evidence linking the real Abwehr agent to the fictional British spy comes from Greene's service in MI6. First, he served as a field agent in Sierra Leone from the end of 1941 until early 1943. There, he monitored the French forces in North Africa until the American and British forces drove the Germans out and the Vichy French surrendered. Once North Africa was in Allied hands, Greene returned to Great Britain. His friend Kim Philby headed Section V of MI6. In mid-1943, Philby named Greene to head the Portugal desk of Section V. This intelligence station oversaw the work of the Abwehr agents in Portugal and of German agents in the Americas who used drop boxes in that country.[8]

Greene used bits and pieces of his MI6 experience dredged up from his memory and subconscious when writing. While his mind drew on many people, moral situations, and events that he had experienced, often he could not reconstruct the thought line to the sources. The busy writer found: "The British agent Wormold in *Our Man in Havana* has no origin that I can recognize, but the elegant Hawthorne owes a little, in his more imaginative flights, to an officer in the same service who was at one time my chief [Kim Philby?]."[9] Despite this self-analysis, the novel does draw on the past. Greene borrowed the name of the fictional Havana agent from an engineer named Wormwold he knew in Freetown, Sierra Leone. He gave his own agent number, 59200, from his Freetown service to the fictional Wormwold, an insider spoof. Since an agent's code number reflected the country where he served, an MI6 agent in Cuba could not have had the number 59200. Thus, bits of Wormold came from Greene's Freetown past.[10]

There is one direct link, if only routine rather than a smoking gun, between Greene and the Lüning story. Greene's service at the Portugal desk gave him access to, and, in fact, an obligation to read, the voluminous documents of Lüning's file. Of course, Lüning's story was no longer secret after September 5, 1942. Dozens of Cuban and U.S. newspapers and magazines published hundreds of stories and photo-essays on Lüning's capture, trial, and execution from early September to mid-November 1942. Even the *Times* of London, a mere four- or eight-page newspaper during the war, published several items on Lüning. In mid-1944, *True Detective* published Benítez's long story about the Lüning case. And Greene was a voracious newspaper reader. Later, in the immediate post–World War II era, Koop, Singer, and Bochow and periodicals like *Mañana* (Havana), *Ecos* (Havana), and *Diario latino* (San Salvador) published thrilling public versions of Lüning's spy career. Whether Greene read any of these journalistic works on Lüning is not clear, but, since they touched on a spy in an area under his supervision, they might have refreshed his memory. Additionally, MI6 maintained at least one agent in Havana during World War II. Thus, from his duty reading or from the public press, Greene encountered the Lüning episode. Another strange coincidence rests in the Graham Greene Papers at Boston College. Greene traveled to Cuba repeatedly beginning in the mid-1950s. Not surprisingly, he owned several maps related to Havana and Cuba in the 1950s, but he also had a high-quality, large, detailed map of Havana for 1942, the year Lüning was active there. It is a mystery why (or how) he acquired and preserved such a map, one more than ten years out of date at the time of his visit.[11]

The FBI-SIS continued to pursue leads intended to tie Lüning to a Western Hemisphere spy network long after his execution. The numerous FBI-SIS reports from this persistent investigation became part of the SIS-MI6 information exchanges and should have passed over Greene's desk in 1943 and 1944. This U.S. material supplemented the MI6 agent reports from Havana. Thus, Greene had material on Lüning, potentially relative to the future *Our Man in Havana,* on his desk regularly. He recognized this potential. In his words, the Portugal desk assignment was the stuff of "a Secret Service comedy" and a "spectacular source of good, satiric material."[12] Lüning's case was certainly not the only unusual story, but it oozed with irony, satire, and humorous material.

Greene's writing method allows for some insight into the link between Lüning and Wormold. Greene insisted that his novels and stories came from his conscious labor, strongly refined and altered by his subconscious. His writing regime and belief in his subconscious are well-known. They are described in his autobiographies, in various interviews, by his friends, and through characters in his novels. He wrote a set number of words per day (five to eight hundred words initially, but fewer as he aged), reread them in the evening, and then reworked them the next day after his subconscious had sifted through the text overnight.

Early in his career, Greene had a character—a fictional novelist,

Maurice Bendix—explain their shared writing technique: "When young one builds up habits of work that one believes will last a lifetime and withstand any catastrophe. Over twenty years I have probably averaged five hundred words a day for five days a week. I can produce a novel in a year, and that allows time for revision and correction of the typescript. I have always been very methodical and when my quota of work is done, I break off even in the middle of a scene. Every now and then during the morning's work I count what I have done and mark off the hundreds on my manuscript. . . . There on the front page of my typescript is marked the figure—83,764 [words]. When I was young not even a love affair would alter my schedule. A love affair had to begin after lunch, and however late I might be in getting to bed—so long as I slept in my own bed—I would read the morning's work over and sleep on it."[13] In Greene's style, the role of the subconscious was key. Thus, things from his past surfaced to enter or refine his writing.

A friend late in Greene's life, Yvonne Cloetta, described the role of the subconscious precisely: "It is well known that Graham was always very interested in dreams, and that he relied a great deal on the role played by the subconscious in writing. He would sit down to work straightway after breakfast, writing until he had five hundred words. He was in the habit of then rereading, every evening before going to bed, the section of the novel or story he had written in the morning, leaving his subconscious to work during the night."[14] The subconscious played a significant role in organizing and polishing his texts.

Greene once described the central role of the subconscious in his methodology in a simple form: "So a book is put together little by little, in a painstaking fashion while the unconscious is simultaneously at work. . . . I re-read my morning's work just before bedtime, to stimulate my unconscious—or my subconscious if you prefer—in the hope that it will sort out the problems."[15] His heavy reliance on characters, places, events, and stories from his subconscious to inhabit, revise, and polish his novels increases the likelihood that pieces of Lüning's character, personality, conduct, and story line embedded in the writer's subconscious influenced the formation of Wormold in Havana.

Greene's work was both a collaboration and a struggle between his conscious and his subconscious: "I work closely with my unconscious, but I still don't understand how it functions—what is the origin of my writing, the manner in which it comes to me—even though I know more or less what's going to happen." Greene critiqued writing: "So one shouldn't speak too much of technique or craftsmanship. I place great reliance on what I take to be the unconscious. . . . This isn't to say that writing is magic; magic does take a hand, though, in little touches—the right element to make the various parts cohere drops into place at the proper time without my realizing it. One has to be borne up by a sort of faith in one's unconscious."[16] The collaboration of Greene's conscious and subconscious could explain the numerous similarities in plot, character, and location shared between Wormold (the conscious narrative story) and Lüning (the subconscious baggage from hundreds of pages of SIS and MI6 files).

Not only did the subconscious produce parts of characters, scenes, dialogue, details, and story lines, but it often led Greene to a subject. Thus, the idea of an author selecting a topic for a story amused him: "I couldn't help smiling when I thought of all the readers who have asked me why I sometimes write thrillers, as though a writer chooses his subject instead of the subject choosing him."[17] So the subconscious guided a writer to a topic as well as editing the treatment of the topic. The wit, irony, and absurdity of the Lüning story would have been a powerful subconscious guide.

Greene's subconscious produced parts of characters, details, and story lines in forms he did not understand clearly. For example, the character Pyle in Greene's *The Quiet American* worked for the U.S. economic mission in Vietnam. Greene always maintained that there was no specific model for Pyle. Then a major source emerged from his subconscious twenty-five years after the novel was written. During an interview, Greene recalled the spouse of a female secretary at the U.S. embassy in Saigon in the 1950s. He had taken the wife to lunch on occasion but scarcely knew the husband. This woman's husband, he remembered, shared some of Pyle's characteristics—baseless ideological zeal and a largely closed mind—and he also worked at the U.S. economic mission in Vietnam.[18] Greene's subconscious held information well but worked slowly at times. A mere fourteen years separated Lüning from Wormold.

From his subconscious, Greene decided: "My experiences in M.I.6. in My Own World [Greene's designation for his dream world, the subconscious] were far more interesting than the desk work which I performed during three years in the Common World [Greene's real world, the conscious]. Curiously enough, of the dozen or so characters I knew then only a couple found their way into the world I am writing of now."[19] Clearly, this is a careless, false assertion. The manifestations of the subconscious are not transparent or rational. For example, Greene needed to be prodded twenty-five years later to recognize a principal source of Pyle's character. By definition, he was not conscious of the things his subconscious held.

In another instance of the emergence of the subconscious in a conscious literary endeavor, Greene recalled working for MGM in 1944 and 1945. At that time, he developed the film script for *The Tenth Man* and only later realized that the characters and plot came from a story he had sketched in 1937.[20] After *The Tenth Man,* Greene drew on his service at the Portugal desk to develop a story about British intelligence in the Baltic area before World War II. This story, called "Nobody to Blame," written for the Brazilian film director Alberto Cavalcanti, had similarities to *Our Man in Havana* and the Lüning case. The film project was not pursued because, Cavalcanti claimed, the British Board of Film Censors would not grant a certificate. The roadblock, however, was not censorship but Britain's MI5, the domestic security agency (similar to the FBI). It had warned Cavalcanti that MI6 might sue for breach of the Official Secrets Act. The MI6 film project resurfaced in the late 1950s in altered form as *Our Man in Havana.*[21]

The story line of "Nobody to Blame" exhibits important similarities with, but also several differences from, *Our Man in Havana.* This earlier story's hero was younger than Wormold, and the secretary-typist sent to aid the agent was an all-business spinster. This hero, an MI6 operative, somehow discovers the day and hour of the German attack on Poland. However, the operative, who had created imaginary agents in order to obtain their salary and expenses to keep his wife in a style beyond what he earned as an agent for Singer Sewing Machines, was exposed as a fraud. Thus, when his report on the forthcoming German attack on Poland arrived in London, no one paid attention to the information.[22]

Did Greene borrow from Lüning's spy career to create James Wormold? He addressed this matter indirectly in his autobiography, *Ways of Escape*. In it, he claimed that the revised version of "Nobody to Blame" found general inspiration in his work for MI6, especially at the Portugal desk.[23] Since he often could not recall the precise sources for the specific details of his stories, the similarity of the real Lüning case and the Wormold invention suggests that his subconscious connected the real and the fictional spies.

Our Man in Havana used specific details from Greene's MI6 experience. Both Greene and Lüning had female companions. Greene's secretary at Freetown, a young, vivacious woman, Doris Temple, apparently served as playmate and femme fatale. In *Our Man in Havana,* Beatrice was Wormold's lively secretary and, later, lover. Lüning found a loyal companion and information source in Rebecca (Olga López), a government employee and occasional bar girl.[24]

Norman Sherry, Greene's authorized biographer (in the sense of Greene's willingness to cooperate, not in any editorial sense), ventured a guess about what inspired the character Wormold. He thought that the inspiration was "an agent named Paul Fidrmuc, alias *Ostro.* Fidrmuc, a Czech businessman, . . . became a German citizen, worked for the Abwehr for a number of years in Denmark and Rome, and then settled in Portugal. His reports to the Abwehr originated in Lisbon and . . . first came to the S.I.S. [MI6] notice . . . in the decrypts from Bletchley Park. . . . *Ostro's* reports on Britain were recognized by British intelligence as fraudulent, but they were well written, carefully structured to give the impression that the reports came from various agents in the field."[25] These well-crafted, false reports are similar to the reports Wormold created for his imaginary agents. However, Greene's work required him to read a great deal about Lüning as well as about Fidrmuc. Since *Our Man in Havana* was written fourteen years after Greene worked with these case files, and given his entrenched writing style, he could have subconsciously drawn on both. However, other than false reports, Fidrmuc shared little with Lüning or Wormold. As far as we know, he was not a bumbling type, his family and religion were not central to his life, he apparently wanted to be a spy (he served in several posts), he had espionage skills, he was not in Havana and so did not know the Wonder Bar, and his best friend and girlfriend seem irrelevant. Almost the only similarity with Wormold was that he used invented material.

The sources for *Our Man in Havana* seem varied. Greene claimed that, while tracing German Abwehr activity in Portugal, he had come across many cases of officers who "spent much of their time sending home completely erroneous reports based on information received from imaginary agents": "It was a paying game, especially when expenses and bonuses were added to the cypher's salary."[26] Thus, Fidrmuc was not a unique source of false reports. While the specific cases that Greene read at the Portugal desk shaped the ideas and characters in *Our Man in Havana*, the practice of an agent falsifying reports, creating imaginary people, and engaging in other Wormoldian or Lunian activities did not originate in World War II. Greene had used these ideas already in "Nobody to Blame" in 1944, but this sort of espionage conduct had been recurring for millennia.

The quality of Greene's MI6 satire impressed Malcolm Muggeridge, a friend, a fellow Oxonian, a writer, and also an MI6 agent. He judged Greene to be an acceptable field agent but a superb head of section at headquarters: "I mean he was tremendously good at dealing with agents and working out cover plans and things like that and justifiably was very highly thought of. He understood what he was about as his novel *Our Man in Havana* shows. It's the most brilliant book on intelligence that's ever been written because it gets inside the whole fantasy of the thing. He gives you the whole feeling of it, the ludicrousness of it and yet the way people get caught up in it. You have to take it seriously and yet it's all based on fantasy."[27] Greene's exceptional qualities as section head also meant that he read the MI6 and FBI-SIS field reports and summaries, including those about Lüning.

The selection of Cuba as the setting for a satiric work on MI6 occurred during one of Greene's visits to Havana in the 1950s. He enjoyed Havana's famous Florida Restaurant's daiquiris and Morro crabs, its brothel life, its slot machines, and the Shanghai Theater's nude acts and blue movies. He realized that "fantastic Havana" offered a marvelous setting for a novel about MI6. The pre–World War II Baltic setting of "Nobody to Blame" made the story "too dark for comedy." *Our Man in Havana*, written in 1957 and early 1958, Greene emphasized, was not about Cuba; it was about MI6. Until the late 1950s, he was not aware of the torture and imprisonment rampant in Cuba. He first traveled around Cuba (outside Havana) in late 1957 when he brought warm sweaters and socks to Santiago de Cuba for Fidel Castro's 26 July movement—the revolutionary anti-Batista movement that ultimately gained power on January 1, 1959. Thus, before he wrote the novel, he had not known Cuba or any Cubans well.[28]

During the filming of *Our Man in Havana*, the centrality of comedy and satire was reinforced. Planning to film on the island began in 1958. When Greene and the director, Carol Reed, started to film in 1959, the new Cuban government wanted a more critical view of Batista's rule, especially the cruel police leader Colonel Esteban Ventura Novo. Greene and Reed, however, could not make a light comedy with a heavy, dark central character. Greene's "real subject was the absurdity of the British agent and not the justice of a revolution." During another interview, he insisted that "*Our Man in Havana* is a good comic novel": "The object was not to talk about Cuba but to make fun of the Secret Service. Havana was merely the background, an accident—it had nothing to do with my sympathy for Fidel."[29]

Greene was aware that many associated Captain Segura with the "unsavory character" Colonel Ventura Novo, but Ventura Novo was not a conscious source of Segura. Greene learned about him only after the novel had been written. Lüning's chief opponent in Cuba was the clever, capable, and intelligent Captain Mariano Faget.[30] In the SIS reports, Greene would have read much about Faget, whom U.S. embassy and SIS officials valued highly. Faget was not depicted as cruel and harsh in the early 1940s, although his reputation changed markedly for the worse after he returned to police work to serve Batista in the 1950s. Faget in the 1940s seems a better model for Segura. The fictional Segura was a capable, professional, informed, and determined official; he was not portrayed as wantonly cruel.

Both Lüning and Wormold were reluctant, maladroit, nonviolent, ineffective, uninformed, and inexperienced people who got in over their heads when they became involved in espionage. Both had conflicting Catholic-Protestant threads in their lives, operated in Havana, had close ties to the Wonder Bar, lived within a hundred yards of the Wonder Bar, had contact with the bars, strip joints, and prostitutes and others of the shady side of life, had loyal, loving women in Havana, used common technology to "inform" their bosses, rejected their side's ideological arguments for war (hot or cold), gave little importance to the nationalism of their country, and both had one adored child. The stories of Lüning and Wormwold had other similarities. Both Wormold and Lüning operated in a constructed environment and obtained reputations from contacts with nonexistent agents. Yet, there were two concrete differences: the fictional Wormwold got the girl and was promoted; the real Lüning was denied a visit from the girl and was shot.

Lüning achieved some of his goals—he avoided Nazi military service, and he preserved the life and the freedom from retribution of the parents who adopted him and his wife and child. He did not achieve the Abwehr goals (and, I suspect, at least partially intentionally) of supplying the Nazi government with useful, valuable information about Allied shipping in the Caribbean, and he unwittingly provided the inspiration for Graham Greene's marvelous novel of espionage and love in Havana.

CONCLUSION

A Story More Familiar Than Expected

Lüning's brief career served others more effectively than it served him. He was, in fact, first Hitler's, then Canaris's, Benítez's, Batista's, Braden's, and Hoover's man in Havana. After the war, Lüning became Theodore Koop's, Kurt Singer's, Klaus-Peter Bochow's, and Graham Greene's man in Havana. Two politicians, one politician-bureaucrat, three secret service heads, one censorship bureaucrat, two journalists, and one serious novelist with an impish sense of humor were the public beneficiaries of Lüning's Abwehr service. It seems that he was everybody's man in Havana but his own.

Hitler's regime, Batista, Benítez, Braden, Hoover, Koop, Singer, Bochow, and Greene all achieved some personal success or advancement from Lüning's career and death. Hitler's Abwehr received a little information and a significant decoy. Batista's counterespionage service captured a master spy and paved the way for Cuba's ambitious chief of police, Benítez, to visit Washington, D.C., already in late October 1942. Batista followed in early December 1942. The Cubans used Lüning's capture to obtain political acknowledgment of Batista's government, a better sugar agreement, economic development funds, and more military aid. Braden expanded his influence through the increased intelligence work of the SIS staff at his embassy. Hoover boosted his image and expected to gain in bureaucratic politics. Koop, Singer, and Bochow published books and articles. Greene's successful *Our Man in Havana*, quickly turned into an entertaining film, drew on Lüning's career. Lüning received a firing squad. All his luck was bad.[1]

Hoover's SIS used the intercepts of the British censors at the Bermuda station to inform the Cuban intelligence officials and, reluctantly, to celebrate when the Cubans prematurely took Lüning into custody. Within a few weeks, U.S. and Cuban radio experts knew the German agent's radio had never worked. Nevertheless, the Americans and Cubans accepted his conviction for allegedly radioing U-boats off Cuba's coasts and, thus, contributing to the deaths of Cubans. Lüning's death sentence signaled the apex of the Cuban-SIS campaign against the deadly German submarines. In the public view, the SIS and Cuban police shut down the devastating Nazi U-boat tonnage campaign. The U.S.-Cuban counter-espionage operations had safeguarded the vital commerce in industrial war materials and the route for commerce and movement of men and supplies to conduct war in the Atlantic and Pacific theaters. They pulled the Allies back from the edge of defeat and projected an image of victory. They preserved a major element of the Allied capacity to make war.

The summary report of the FBI-SIS extended the ironic tragedy of this person: "Lüning's execution for acting as an espionage agent is the first occasion in Cuban history as a republic that an individual has been executed for espionage activities."[2] Of the hundreds of Nazi agents in Latin America during World War II, Lüning was the only one executed. He was probably the least harmful German agent in the Western Hemisphere. He certainly was a rare type since he despised Hitler and the Nazis and had long opposed the war he saw coming. He was an ineffective agent. He left no great personal legacy. Nothing in his activity in Cuba indicated a master spy at work.

All the FBI-SIS work in Latin America from 1941 to 1945 led to only one death sentence, that of a bumbling Abwehr agent with a long anti-Nazi record. Perhaps Lüning's greatest success, although it proved deadly, was that he escaped military service in Germany in a manner that avoided repercussions for his family. Only in this sense was he his own man in Havana. And he apparently stimulated Greene to create a brother in Havana—James Wormold.

In the longer view, Lüning's story had other consequences. It allowed

Batista to regain the good graces of U.S. politicians and national security officials after several years beyond the pale. It initiated the close cooperation between FBI-SIS officials and Cuba's brutal secret police that continued until the fall of Batista's second government on New Year's Day in 1959. This informal alliance of U.S. officials with Batista's secret police contributed to the hatred and distrust of many Cubans toward the United States and encouraged support for Fidel Castro's revolution in the late 1950s.

And, finally, one might consider a more contemporary observation. In the early twenty-first century, across the island of Cuba from Havana (near where Britain's top espionage officials believed Wormold's subagent had found those deadly enemy secret weapons in the early cold war), the U.S. government is holding hundreds of "subversives" as dangerous enemies of the United States. Yet the lack of concrete charges or reliable information about the detainees' deeds or threatening conduct suggests that a number of Lünings and Wormolds may be interspersed among some hard-core Al-Qaeda agents. In many cases in the early twenty-first century, U.S. officials acted as if the United States and its allies were on the edge of defeat.

Just as the United States and Cuba extracted the ultimate penalty from Lüning in order to show how determined and successful the U.S. and Cuban governments were in resisting the onslaught of Nazi submarines, some contemporary prisoners from the Middle East are paying a very high price because the U.S. government wants to project determination and the expectation of success. It struts as an aggressive antiterrorist force even though it often does not know who might be an Al-Qaeda member. It wants to demonstrate its determined resistance to terrorism, but it frequently has trouble identifying terrorists. Some of these alleged master terrorists at Guantánamo are the brothers of the master spies Lüning and Wormold. The U.S. role in these current events seems, all too often, almost a tragicomedic sequel to its role in the earlier episodes. Perhaps the spirits of Lüning and Wormold will emerge from the past to free the U.S. government from this impending danger of punishing the innocent and fearing remote Wormoldian (imaginary) weapons sites and Lunian (imaginary) spy networks.

Lüning had gone to Cuba, not to serve the Nazi state, but because he did not want to serve in the Nazi military. His life had been restless, aimless, and self-indulgent. He pursued good times, a good drink, and girls, girls, and girls. At some point in the early 1930s, the prospect of war concerned him because he disliked the racist, militaristic, and belligerent conduct of the Nazi leaders. By 1937, he wanted desperately to avoid fighting in the war he foresaw engulfing Europe.

How did this anti-Nazi come to join the Abwehr and serve in Cuba? Although Lüning opposed war and despised the Nazis, tight government control of departures and of the export or conversion of hard currency meant that he was unable to escape Nazi Germany with his family. When he opted to join the Abwehr rather than do military service in Hitler's army, he embarked on a course that led to his becoming the only German spy executed in Latin America during World War II. A reluctant espionage agent who was simple, bumbling, poorly educated and trained, and technically ineffective and awkward in his work, he stumbled and faltered toward a firing squad. At the time and later, many participants or observers of the drama of the 1940s saw an opportunity to profit from Lüning's life, labor, and death. Hoover, Batista, and others twisted and distorted his Abwehr service into a threat that brought the Allied nations to the edge of defeat so that his death heaped honor and prestige on them. To an outside observer, Lüning's life appeared comic and humorous—until it found a tragic and brutal end.

Notes

Preface

1. Koop, *Weapon of Silence*, 4.
2. Knight, "Secret War"; *Washington Post,* October 8, 1946, 14.

Introduction

1. Herring, *Aid to Russia,* 43–50; Kimball, *Forged in War,* 159–63.

1. A Troubled Life

1. Friederike van der Linde (Standesamt, Bremen-Mitte, Germany), telephone conversations with the author, June 17, 2002, July 29, 2004, and e-mail to the author, May 18, 2004; Adressbücher and Einwohner-Kartei, Staatsarchiv, Bremen; Lars Worgull (Staatsarchiv, Bremen, Germany), e-mails to the author, August 17, 23, 2006.
2. J. Edgar Hoover to Adolf A. Berle Jr., September 11, 1942, MID 201 Lüning, file x8536413, box 131E, RG 319, NARA; memo on Lüning, December 3, 1942, file 65-44610-384, sec. 10, FBI HQ Archive.
3. Hoover to Berle, November 24, 1942, and James W. Pumpelly, U.S. military attaché, to D. R. Kerr, military attaché, February 1, 1943, MID 201 Lüning, file x8536413, box 131E, RG 319, NARA; certificate of marriage, H. A. Lüning and Helga Barbara Lüning, May 8, 1936, Department of Records and Information Service, City of New York.
4. SIS 253, FBI summary report, October 6, 1942 [censored], pp. 2–3, file 65-44610-164, sec. 5, SIS 491, report on Heinz August Lüning, August 9, 1943, pp. 1, 3, file 65-44610-630x, sec. 17, and Hoover to Berle, November 13, 1942, p. 3, file 65-44610-381, sec. 10, FBI HQ Archive.
5. Charles Goodwin, report, February 15, 1943, file 65-44610-513, sec. 17, FBI HQ Archive.
6. Hoover to Berle, November 24, 1942, and Pumpelly to Kerr, February 1, 1943, MID 201 Lüning, file x8536413, box 131E, RG 319, NARA; SIS 253, FBI

summary report, October 6, 1942 [censored], pp. 2–3, file 65-44610-164, sec. 5, SIS 491, report on Lüning, August 9, 1943, pp. 1, 3, file 65-44610-630x, sec. 17, and Hoover to Berle, November 13, 1942, p. 3, file 65-44610-381, sec. 10, FBI HQ Archive.

7. A. M. Warren to Secretary of State, October 13, 1942, 800.20237/202, box 3220, December File (1940–44), RG 59, NARA; Pumpelly to Kerr, February 16, 1943, MID 201 Lüning, 2-1-43, file x8536413, box 131E, RG 319, NARA.

8. Hoover to Berle, November 24, 1942, MID 201 Lüning, file x8536413, box 131E, RG 319, NARA; Warren to Secretary of State, November 10, 1942, and State Department to Consul in Curacao, West Indies, November 10, 1942, 800.20237/202, box 3220, December File (1940–44), RG 59, NARA.

9. Pumpelly to Kerr, February 16, 1943, MID 201 Lüning, file x8536413, box 131E, RG 319, NARA.

10. Ibid.

11. SIS 491, report on Lüning, August 9, 1943, p. 2, file 65-44610-630x, sec. 17, FBI HQ Archive.

12. Marriage license no. 31059 (1876–1878) for George Bartholomae and Emma Lassig, Cook County Clerk of Court, Chicago; *Chicago Tribune,* June 17, 1900, 39; Moritz Lassig obituary, *Chicago Daily Tribune,* January 8, 1902, 4; Maura Rogan (Winnetka Historical Society, Winnetka, IL), e-mail to the author, December 13, 2005; memo FBI, October 10, 1942, file 65-44610-140, sec. 5, and Charles Goodwin, report, February 15, 1943, file 65-44610-513, sec. 15, FBI HQ Archive.

13. Death certificates for Philip Henry Bartholomae and Ella Bartholomae, Cook County Clerk of Court, Chicago; www.ancestry.com for census, passenger ship registries, and military draft registration documents for the Bartholomaes and Julius Luening; memo FBI, October 10, 1942, file 65-44610-140, sec. 5, and Charles Goodwin, report, February 15, 1943, file 65-44610-513, sec. 15, FBI HQ Archive.

14. Amy Rupert (Rensselaer Polytechnic Institute, Troy, NY), e-mail to the author, September 27, 2005; Rensselaer Polytechnic Institute, *Transit,* 35; SIS 253, FBI summary report, October 6, 1942 [censored], p. 4, file 65-44610-164, sec. 5, FBI HQ Archive.

15. Los Angeles field report, October 1, 1942, Foxworth to Hoover, October 7, 1942, files 65-44610-148 and -151, sec. 5, FBI HQ Archive.

16. Boardman, *American Musical Theater,* 333, 345, 357–58, 376, 388, 410–11, 460–61; Bloom, *Broadway,* 35, 74, 276, 425; Norton, *Chronology of American Musical Theater,* 2:32, 37, 87, 134, 138–39, 182–84, 256–57, 376–78, 3:322; Mantle and Sherwood, eds., *Best Plays,* 435, 474; Mantle, ed., *Best Plays,* 541; Mordden, *Make Believe,* 94; Jones, *Our Musicals, Ourselves,* 46; *New York Times,* September 7, 1913, X3.

17. Gänzl, *Encyclopedia of the Musical Theatre,* 1:119–20, 219–30, and *British Musical Theatre,* 2:93, 103–7, 1008; Grant, *Broadway Musical,* 139; Boardman, *American Musical Theater,* 333, 345, 357–58, 376, 388, 410–11, 460–61; Rodgers, *Musical Stages,* 20; Ewen, *Richard Rodgers,* 52.

18. Los Angeles field report, October 1, 1942, and Foxworth to Hoover, October 7, 1942, files 65-44610-148 and -151, sec. 5, and FBI summary reports, December 30, 1942, February 15, 1943, files 65-44610-450 and -513, sec. 12, FBI HQ Archive.

19. Los Angeles field report, October 1, 1942, and Foxworth to Hoover, October 7, 1942, files 65-44610-148 and -151, sec. 5, and FBI summary reports, December 30, 1942, February 15, 1943, files 65-44610-450 and -513, sec. 12, FBI HQ Archive.

20. Memo, September 14, 1942, pp. 2–3, file 65-44610-12, sec. 2, J. Walter Yaegley, FBI report, September 25, 1942, p. 1, file 65-44610-98, sec. 4, Los Angeles field report, October 1, 1942, Foxworth to Hoover, October 7, 1942, and Hoover to [censored], October 9, 1942, files 65-44610-148, -151, and -162, sec. 5, and FBI summary report, February 15, 1943, file 65-44610-513, sec. 12, FBI HQ Archive; Julius Luening draft registration card, 1917–1918, www. ancestry.com.

21. Transcription of the first Spanish-language interrogation, September 1, 1942, file 65-44610-130, sec. 4, and SIS 253, FBI summary report, October 6, 1942 [censored], p. 4, file 65-44610-164, sec. 5, FBI HQ Archive. Friederike Scholz (Hamburger Sportverein, Hamburg), e-mail to the author, June 16, 2004, reported that the Hamburger Sportverein archive has suffered losses. Her search revealed nothing to either confirm or refute Lüning's story. On the relation between sport clubs and the Nazis, see Havemann, *Fußball unterm Hakenkreuz,* 130–35.

22. SIS 253, FBI summary report, October 6, 1942 [censored], pp. 3–4, file 65-44610-164, sec. 5, FBI HQ Archive.

23. SIS 491 to U.S. Embassy, Lola Ardela de Tejar [?] interview, August 9, 1943, file 65-44610-630, sec. 17, and A. George Haner report, August 4, 1944, file 65-44610-677, sec. 19, FBI HQ Archive.

24. Hoover to Berle, September 11, 1942, enclosing a memo, September 11, 1942, MID 201 Lüning, 9-11-42, file x8536413, box 131E, RG 319, NARA; Hoover to Berle, November 24, 1942, enclosing a memo, November 24, 1942, Dec F 1940–44, box 3220, RG 59, NARA; Hoover, "Memorandum for the Attorney General," September 16, 1942, case file 146-7-0, "Lüning," RG 65, NARA.

25. Re: Heinz August Lüning, September 16, 1943, MID memo re: Lüning, September 16, 1942, and Hoover to Berle, September 16, 1942, enclosing a memo "from a reliable and confidential source," MID 201 Lüning, file x8536413, box 131E, RG 319, NARA; Koop, *Weapon of Silence,* 3–15, 77, 90–99; SIS 491, re-

port on Lüning, August 9, 1943, pp. 1, 3, file 65-44610-630x, sec. 17, FBI HQ Archive.

26. SIS 491 to U.S. Embassy, Ardela interview, August 9, 1943, file 65-44610-630, sec. 17, FBI HQ Archive; Pumpelly, February 16, 1943, enclosing a memo, September 11, 1942, 33 MID 201 Lüning, 16-Feb-43, file x8536413, box 131E, RG 319, NARA. On Lüning's life and career in the Abwehr, see Koop, *Weapon of Silence*, 3–15, 77, 90–91; Farago, *Game of the Foxes*, 505; and Kahn, *The Codebreakers*, 514–15. Both Braden (*Diplomats and Demagogues*, 287–88) and Singer (*Spies and Traitors*, 109–14) need to be treated with suspicion and caution.

27. SIS 253, FBI summary report, October 6, 1942 [censored], pp. 4–5, file 65-44610-164, sec. 5, and SIS 253, memo, September 17, 1942, p. 1, file 65-44610-15, sec. 2, FBI HQ Archive (copy also in file 65-44610-250X1, sec. 7).

2. The World He Scarcely Knew

1. Langley, "Theodore Roosevelt," 607; Newfarmer, *From Gunboats to Diplomacy*, 23 (quote).

2. Maingot, *The United States and the Caribbean*, 53–54; Dallek, *Franklin D. Roosevelt*, 265–67; Goda, *Tomorrow the World*, xiii–xxvi, 12, 16–17, 194–202.

3. Maingot, *The United States and the Caribbean*, 51–53.

4. Baptiste, *War, Cooperation and Conflict*; Kelshall, *U-Boat War*; Maingot, *The United States and the Caribbean*.

5. Pérez, *Cuba and the United States*, 179–207; Dosal, *Cuba Libre*, 42–62.

6. Parry and Sherlock, *Short History of the West Indies*, 254; Rogozinski, *Brief History of the Caribbean*, 230; Mecham, *United States–Latin American Relations*, 302.

7. Pérez, *Cuba and the United States*, 179–207.

8. O'Brien, *Revolutionary Mission*, 55, 231–23; Mazarr, *Semper Fidel*, 209; Dallek, *Franklin D. Roosevelt*, 62–63.

9. Aguilar, *Cuba 1933*, ix.

10. Pérez, *Cuba and the United States*, 179–207; Dur and Gilcrease, "Downfall of a Cuban Dictator," 255, 271–76; Gellman, *Good Neighbor Diplomacy*, 37–38; Mecham, *United States–Latin American Relations*, 304; Zeuske, *Kleine Geschichte Kubas*, 171.

11. Pérez, *Cuba and the United States*, 179–207; Dallek, *Franklin D. Roosevelt*, 234.

12. Newfarmer, *From Gunboats to Diplomacy*, 25–26.

13. Friedman, *Nazis and Good Neighbors*, 4–5, 84–88; Gellman, *Good Neighbor Diplomacy*, 106 (quote); Clayton and Conniff, *History of Modern Latin America*, 366; Dallek, *Franklin D. Roosevelt*, 175.

14. Gellman, *Good Neighbor Diplomacy*, 105; Friedman, *Nazis and Good Neighbors*, 2.

15. Maingot, *The United States and the Caribbean,* 48–49; Berger, "Crisis Diplomacy," 295–97; Friedman, *Nazis and Good Neighbors,* 2; Masterson with Funada-Classen, *The Japanese in Latin America,* 112–13; Lübken, *Bedrohliche Nähe,* 72–76.

16. Compton, *The Swastika and the Eagle,* 87.

17. Snell, *Illusion and Necessity,* 104.

18. Gellman, *Good Neighbor Diplomacy,* 112 (quote); Dallek, *Franklin D. Roosevelt,* 266; Maney, "Franklin D. Roosevelt," 606; Lübken, *Bedrohliche Nähe,* 10–11.

19. Maingot, *The United States and the Caribbean,* 49; Kossok, "Sonderauftrag Südamerika," 246–47; Gellman, *Good Neighbor Diplomacy,* 78 (Burchard reference, Thomas quote); Kahn, *Hitler's Spies,* 523–43.

20. Gellman, *Good Neighbor Diplomacy,* 115; Lübken, *Bedrohliche Nähe,* 22, 48–53, 72–76.

21. Kahn, *Hitler's Spies,* 523–43.

22. Kossok, "Sonderauftrag Südamerika," 254.

23. Smith, *American Diplomacy,* 27–28.

24. Maingot, *The United States and the Caribbean,* 62–63; Humphreys, *Latin America and the Second World War,* 2:17; Lübken, *Bedrohliche Nähe,* 187–235.

25. Maingot, *The United States and the Caribbean,* 62–63; Humphreys, *Latin America and the Second World War,* 2:17; Lübken, *Bedrohliche Nähe,* 187–235.

26. Gellman, *Good Neighbor Diplomacy,* 108–9.

27. Ibid., 38; Mecham, *United States–Latin American Relations,* 306.

28. Mecham, *United States–Latin American Relations,* 306; Dosal, *Cuba Libre,* 64–67; "S.O.E. in Latin America," n.d. [March 1942?], p. 6, HS 8/61, and "Memorandum by S.O.E. on Axis Penetration in South and Central America," April 1, 1942, app. A, p. 2 (quote), HS 8/24, PRO, London.

29. Stuart and Tigner, *Latin America and the United States,* 356–57; Benítez, "On Radio Berlin," 73.

30. Kahn, *Hitler's Spies,* 226–36. On Canaris, see Abhagen, *Canaris;* Bassett, *Hitler's Spy Chief;* Brissard, *Canaris,* 12–13, 16–23, 50–51, 247–51; Calic, *Reinhard Heydrich,* 37–39, 45–46, 48, 182; Höhne, *Canaris,* 85–87, 162–65, 176–79, 182–83, 197–98; MacDonald, *Killing of Reinhard Heydrich,* 12–13, 33–35, 163–64; Mueller, *Canaris;* and Paine, *German Military Intelligence.*

31. Rout and Bratzel, *Shadow War,* 18 (quote); Hilton, *Hitler's Secret War,* 1–3, 18–19; Friedman, *Nazis and Good Neighbors,* 78, 113, 148; Schramm, *Der Geheimdienst im Zweiten Weltkrieg,* 399; Reile, *Geheime Westfront,* 317ff.; memo, September 14, 1942, p. 3, file 65-44610-12, sec. 2, FBI HQ Archive.

32. Brammer, *Spionageabwehr Hamburg,* 11–13, 19, 27.

33. Leverkuehn, *German Military Intelligence,* 27–39, and *Der geheime Nach-*

richtendienst, 9–11, 16–17; Rout and Bratzel, *Shadow War,* 1–24; Hilton, *Hitler's Secret War,* 1–3; Buchheit, *Der deutsche Geheimdienst,* 242–49; Brammer, *Spionageabwehr Hamburg,* 89–95.

34. Brammer, *Spionageabwehr Hamburg,* 95–97.

35. Leverkuehn, *German Military Intelligence,* 27–37, and *Der geheime Nachrichtendienst,* 9–17; Leopold Bürkner, [Abwehr organization description], n.d., Bestand: Leopold Bürkner, N565/Nr. 2, and Leopold Bürkner, "Die Abwehr-Abteilung spätere Amtsgruppe Ausland," August 22, 1960, OKW/Amt Ausland/Abwehr, RW5/278, Bundesarchiv, Militärarchiv, Freiburg; Rout and Bratzel, *Shadow War,* 16; Kahn, *Hitler's Spies,* 57–63; Hilton, *Hitler's Secret War,* 15; Freud, "OKW/Amt für Auslandsnachrichten/Abwehr."

36. Messick, *John Edgar Hoover,* 252–55; Powers, *G-Men,* xi–xix; Potter, *War on Crime,* 196–202; Summers, *Official and Confidential,* 9–14, 432–38.

37. Powers, *Secrecy and Power,* 252; MacDonnell, *Insidious Foes,* 165–77.

38. Persico, *Roosevelt's Secret War,* 16–17; Friedman, *Nazis and Good Neighbors;* Jakub, *Spies and Saboteurs,* 30.

39. Braden, *Diplomats and Demagogues,* 280–86; [Spruille Braden], "Memorandum" Strictly Confidential, September 4, 1942, Cuba: Havana Embassy, Super Confidential (1940–44), entry 2359, box 2, RG 84, NARA.

40. Persico, *Roosevelt's Secret War,* 86–87.

41. Hitler, *Hitlers zweites Buch,* and *Hitler's Second Book;* Goda, *Tomorrow the World,* xiii–xxvi, 12, 16–17, 194–202.

42. Dorril, *MI6,* 4.

43. Telegram, February 25, 1942, HS 8/61, "Reorganization of S.O. in Latin America," November 20, 1942, Central and South America, December 1942–January 1945, HS 8/25, and C. G. des Graz to W. Preston Corderman, January 13, 1942, British and American Censorship Cooperation, November 1940–December 1942, DEFE 1/175, PRO.

44. West, *MI6,* 225–26; Dorril, *MI6,* 7.

45. West, *MI6,* 225, 382.

46. Hinsley et al., *British Intelligence,* 4:146, 159–60; West, *MI6,* 225.

47. Hyde, *Quiet Canadian,* 50–52, 56, 163–66, and *Room 3603,* 50–57, 134–35.

48. Gellman, *Good Neighbor Diplomacy,* 115; Persico, *Roosevelt's Secret War,* 126–28 (quote, 128).

49. F. C. Holloman to D. M. Ladd, December 13, 1941, and drafts of proposed intelligence exchange arrangements, box 16, sec. 2, RG 65, NARA; Hinsley et al., *British Intelligence,* 1:313–14, 4:143–44 (quote, 143); Jakub, *Spies and Saboteurs,* 31.

50. Hinsley et al., *British Intelligence,* 4:143–44; Jakub, *Spies and Saboteurs,* 13.

51. Hinsley et al., *British Intelligence,* 4:158–59; British Security Coordination, *Secret History of British Intelligence,* ix–x, xxxiv–xxxv; Andrew, *Her*

Majesty's Secret Service, 459–65; Penrose and Freeman, *Conspiracy of Silence,* 364–67.

52. Braden, *Diplomats and Demagogues,* 281–85; Larry Daley, e-mail to the author, September 30, 2005.

53. *New Orleans Times-Picayune,* September 6, 1942, 1; *Atlanta Constitution,* September 6, 1942, 1; *New York Times,* June 11, 1944, 46, June 14, 1944, 8, and November 23, 1944, 12; Leading Personalities, Cuba, 1943, p. 3, FO 371/33840, PRO.

54. Pérez, *On Becoming Cuban,* 413; Levine, "Cuba," 788–90; Newton, *"Nazi Menace,"* xiii–xix; Thomas, *Cuba,* 724–26; Benítez, "On Radio Berlin."

55. Friedman, *Nazis and Good Neighbors,* 1–73.

3. Back to School!

1. Hoover to Berle, November 24, 1942, MID 201 Lüning, file x8536413, box 131E, RG 319, NARA; memo on Lüning, October 26, 1942, file 65-44610-385, sec. 10, FBI summary report, November 9, 1942, p. 14, file 65-44610-[illegible], sec. 18, SIS 253, FBI memo, September 4, 1942, p. 1, file 65-44610-16, sec. 2, and memo, n.d. [1943?], file 65-44610-635, sec. 17, FBI HQ Archive.

2. SIS 253, FBI memo, September 4, 1942, p. 1, file 65-44610-16, sec. 2, FBI summary report, November 9, 1942, pp. 7–8, file 65-44610-[illegible], sec. 18, SIS 253, FBI summary report, October 6, 1942 [censored], pp. 6–14, file 65-44610-164, sec. 5, and unsigned memo, September 26, 1942, pp. 1–3, file 65-44610-126, sec. 4, FBI HQ Archive.

3. FBI summary report, November 9, 1942, pp. 7–8, file 65-44610-[illegible], sec. 18, [censored name] to [censored name], September 30, 1942, SIS 253, FBI summary report, October 6, 1942 [censored], pp. 6–14, files 65-44610-148 and -164, sec. 5, and unsigned memo, September 26, 1942, pp. 1–3, file 65-44610-126, sec. 4, FBI HQ Archive; Brammer, *Spionageabwehr Hamburg,* 99.

4. SIS 253, FBI summary report, October 6, 1942 [censored], p. 7, file 65-44610-164, sec. 5, FBI HQ Archive; Brammer, *Spionageabwehr Hamburg,* 99.

5. Military Attaché Report, J. W. Pumpelly, February 16, 1943, enclosing a memo, September 11, 1942, 33 MID 201 Lüning, 16-Feb-43, file x8536413, box 131E, RG 319, NARA; memo, September 14,1942, pp. 2–3, file 65-44610-12, sec. 2, FBI HQ Archive.

6. SIS 253, FBI summary report, October 6, 1942 [censored], p. 7, file 65-44610-164, sec. 5, FBI HQ Archive.

7. Hoover to Berle, November 24, 1942 (quote), MID 201 Lüning, file x8536413, box 131E, RG 319, NARA; Hoover to Harry L. Hopkins, November 2, 1942, pp. 1–2, and Hoover to Berle, November 2, 1942, pp. 1–2, attached signed statement by Lüning, files 65-44610-258 and -270, sec. 7, FBI HQ Archive.

8. SIS 253, FBI summary report, October 6, 1942 [censored], p. 34, file 65-44610-164, sec. 5, memo on Lüning, November 10, 1942, file 65-44610-296, sec. 8, and FBI summary report, November 9, 1942, p. 13, file 65-44610-[illegible], sec. 18, FBI HQ Archive.

9. SIS 253, FBI summary report, October 6, 1942 [censored], p. 34, file 65-44610-164, sec. 5, FBI HQ Archive.

10. Hoover to Berle, September 11, 1942, MID 201 Lüning, file x8536413, box 131E, RG 319, NARA; Little to Ladd, November 18, 1942, file 65-44610-393, sec. 10, memo on Lüning, November 10, 1942, file 65-44610-296, sec. 8, FBI summary report, November 9, 1942, p. 13, file 65-44610-[illegible], sec. 18, and SIS 253 to FBI, memo, September 4, 1942, file 65-44610-16, sec. 2, FBI HQ Archive.

11. Memo on Lüning, with Hoover to Berle, November 13, 1942, file 65-44610-381, sec. 10, and copy of Lüning's Honduran passport in C. H. Carson, memo for Ladd, October 20, 1942, file 65-44610-235, sec. 6, FBI HQ Archive.

12. Hoover to Berle, September 11, 30, 1942, and "Who's Who Card Summary," November 24, 1942, MID 201 Lüning, file x8536413, box 131E, RG 319, NARA; Hoover to U.S. Attorney General, September 16, 1942, DOJ case file, 146-7-0, NARA; SIS 253, memo, September 4, 1942, p. 1, and La bohemia (Havana), September 13, 1942, files 65-44610-16 and -20, sec. 2, and FBI to SIS 253, September 28, 1942, file 65-44610-157, sec. 5, FBI HQ Archive; Diario de la marina (Havana), September 6, 1942, 1, 16, September 16, 1942, 3, and October 8, 1942, 2; copy of Lüning's Honduran passport in Carson, memo for Ladd, October 20, 1942, file 65-44610-235, sec. 6, FBI HQ Archive.

13. SIS 253, FBI summary report, October 6, 1942 [censored], p. 8, file 65-44610-164, sec. 5, Carson, memo for Ladd, October 20, 1942, file 65-44610-235, sec. 6, and T. J. Donegan to Hoover, January 26, 1943, and State Department official to Secretary of State, October 16, 1942, files 65-44610-459 and -470, sec. 12, FBI HQ Archive.

14. FBI summary report, November 9, 1942, p. 7, file 65-44610-[illegible], sec. 18, and SIS 253, FBI summary report, October 6, 1942 [censored], pp. 22–27, file 65-44610-164, sec. 5, FBI HQ Archive.

15. SIS 253, FBI summary report, October 6, 1942 [censored], pp. 14–15, file 65-44610-164, sec. 5, and Hoover to [?], December 4, 1942, enclosing a memo on Lüning, October 26, 1942, file 65-44610-386, sec. 10, FBI HQ Archive.

16. SIS 253, FBI summary report, October 6, 1942 [censored], pp. 14–15, file 65-44610-164, sec. 5, FBI HQ Archive.

17. Incoming reports from Abwehr agent A-3779, Havana, Cuba, Heeres-Fernschreibnetz, RW49/525, microfilm 561, Bundesarchiv, Freiburg.

18. Hoover to Berle, November 24, 1942, MID 201 Lüning, file x8536413, box 131E, RG 319, NARA; FBI summary report, November 9, 1942, p. 14, file

65-44610-[illegible], sec. 18, and SIS 253, FBI memo, September 4, 1942, p. 1, file 65-44610-16, sec. 2, FBI HQ Archive.

19. SIS 253, FBI memo, September 4, 1942, p. 1, file 65-44610-16, sec. 2, FBI HQ Archive.

20. Hoover to Berle, November 24, 1942, MID 201 Lüning, file x8536413, box 131E, RG 319, NARA; FBI summary report, November 9, 1942, p. 14, file 65-44610-[illegible], sec. 18, and Alfonso Hernández Cata and Juan Valdés Díaz, report, September 17, 1942 (quote, my translation), file 65-44610-220, sec. 6, FBI HQ Archive.

21. Signed statement of Heinz August Lüning, October 27, 1942, and Hoover to Berle, November 24, 1942, MID 201 Lüning, file x8536413, box 131E, RG 319, NARA.

4. Tested in Action

1. Military Attaché Report, Pumpelly to Kerr, February 16, 1943 (quote), MID 201 Lüning, file x8536413, box 131E, RG 319, NARA; SIS 491, report on Lüning, August 9, 1943, p. 2, file 65-44610-630x, sec. 17, FBI HQ Archive.

2. Military Attaché Report, Pumpelly to Kerr, February 16, 1943 (quote), MID 201 Lüning, file x8536413, box 131E, RG 319, NARA; SIS 491, report on Lüning, August 9, 1943, p. 2, file 65-44610-630x, sec. 17, FBI HQ Archive.

3. Benítez, "On Radio Berlin," 11–12.

4. Foxworth to Hoover, October 3, 1942, file 65-44610-124, sec. 4, and [censored] to Hoover, October 6, 1942, including report of October 3, 1942, file 65-44610-164, sec. 5, FBI HQ Archive; Enrique Rodríguez, e-mail to the author, October 17, 2005; Bochow, *FBI,* 255–62.

5. Report, November 9, 1942, file 65-44610-644, sec. 18, FBI Archive.

6. SIS 396 [Leddy?], report, September 7, 1942, SIS 396, report, September 11, 1942, and SIS 253, memo, September 4, 1942, files 65-44610-8, -9, and -16, sec. 2, and Hoover to Berle, September 30, 1942, file 65-44610-111, sec. 4, FBI HQ Archive; Hoover to Berle, November 24, 1942, 800.20237/222, box 3220, December File (1940–44), RG 59, NARA; *Diario de la marina,* September 6, 1942, 1, 16.

7. Hyde, *Quiet Canadian,* 79ff., and *Room 3603,* 55–57, 134–36; British Security Coordination, *Secret History of British Intelligence,* 330–32, 354–58, 462–63.

8. Koop, *Weapon of Silence,* 3–15; Kahn, *The Codebreakers,* 513–15.

9. C. H. Carson to D. M. Ladd, June 5, 1942, Hoover to Ladd, June 3, 1942 (quote), and memo for Stott, June 22, 1943, file 65-44610-x30, sec. 1, FBI HQ Archive.

10. Partial transcript of Faget and SIS 253 interrogation of Luni in Spanish, October 1942, file 65-44610-130, sec. 4, FBI HQ Archive.

11. SIS 253, FBI summary report, October 6, 1942 [censored], p. 17, file 65-44610-164, sec. 5, John B. Little to Ladd, October 9, 1942 (quote), file 65-44610-170, sec. 6, copies of secret ink messages, December 1941–August 1942, files 65-44610-x to -x46, sec. 1, and copies of secret ink messages, December 1941–August 1942, files 65-44610-x47 to -x66, sec. 2, FBI HQ Archive.

12. Hoover to Berle, September 11, November 24, 1942, MID 201 Lüning, file x8536413, box 131E, RG 319, NARA.

13. SIS 253, memo, September 4, 1942, file 65-44610-16, sec. 2, Hoover to SAC (New York), September 30, 1942, and 17 attachments, file 65-44610-128, sec. 4, and H. H. Clegg to Ladd, September 11, 1942, and SIS 396 to Hoover, October 6, 1942, files 65-44610-150 and -156, sec. 5, FBI HQ Archive; Hoover to Berle, September 11, 30, 1942, and "Who's Who Card Summary," November 24, 1942, MID 201 Lüning, file x8536413, box 131E, RG 319, NARA; Hoover to U.S. Attorney General, September 16, 1942, DOJ Case file, 146-7-0, RG 65, NARA; *Diario de la marina,* September 6, 1942, 1, 16, September 8, 1942, 3, September 16, 1942, 3, and October 8, 1942, 2; *New York Times,* October–December 1942.

14. S.O. Organization in Latin America, n.d. [September 1942], America: South American Reports, April–September 1942, p. 18, HS 8/39, cipher telegrams nos. 39–42, February 26, 1942, and "S.O.E. in Latin America," n.d. [March 1942?], p. 6, Latin America, January–March 1942 (quote), HS 8/61, "Memorandum by S.O.E. on Axis Penetration in South and Central America," April 1, 1942, America, South, December 1941–September 1942, HS 8/24, and G. Ogilvie-Forbes to Foreign Office, May 4, 1942, cipher, A4846, FO 371/30455, PRO.

15. British agents in Cuba, late 1941–mid-1942, March 3, 1942, cipher A2136, FO 371/30455, PRO.

16. SIS 491 to U.S. Embassy, August 9, 1943, file 65-44610-630x, FBI HQ Archive; Koop, *Weapon of Silence,* 3–15, 77, 90–91.

17. MID memo re: Lüning from September 16, 1942, and Hoover to Berle, September 16, 1942, enclosing a memo "from a reliable and confidential source," MID 201 Lüning, file x8536413, box 131E, RG 319, NARA; SIS 491 to U.S. Embassy, August 9, 1943 (quote), file 65-44610-630x, sec. 17, FBI HQ Archive; Koop, *Weapon of Silence,* 3–15, 77, 90–91.

18. Memo re: Lüning with Hoover to Berle, December 12, 1942, MID 201 Lüning, file x8536413, box 131E, RG 319, NARA; unsigned memo, n.d., file 65-44610-[160], sec. 5, and Hoover to ONI, January 29, 1943, and SIS to Hoover, February 15, 1943, files 65-44610-494 and -508, sec. 13, FBI HQ Archive; *Diario de la marina,* September 6, 1942, 1, 16.

19. SIS 253, memo, September 4, 1942, file 65-44610-16, sec. 2, and FBI summary report, November 9, 1942, p. 16, file 65-44610-[illegible], sec. 18, FBI HQ Archive; memo with Hoover to Berle, November 20, 1942, and Hoover to

Berle, December 11, 1942, 862.20210 Beilin, George/1, box 5525, and Hoover to Berle, March 3, 1943, 862.20210 Beilin, George/2, box 5525, December File (1940–44), RG 59, NARA; Rodríguez, e-mail to the author, October 17, 2005; *Diario de la marina,* September 6, 1942, 1, 16; Greene, *Our Man in Havana,* 1. The University of Louisiana at Lafayette English Professor John Greene reports from his visit to Havana in January 2003 that the Wonder Bar no longer exists.

20. Hoover to [censored], September 14, 1942, pp. 1–3, file 65-44610-[264], sec. 7, and Hoover to Berle, December 1942, and memo, file 65-44610-456, sec. 12, FBI HQ Archive. Bochow (*FBI,* 255–62) erroneously indicated a tie to the Gough brothers.

21. Memo re: Lüning, December 3, 1942, with Hoover to Berle, December 3, 1942, 800.20237/224, box 3320, and Hayne D. Boyden, Lieutenant Commander, to MID, October 5, 1942, 862.20237/388, box c356, December File (1940–44), RG 59, NARA. See also reports in files 65-44610-299, -324, and -336, FBI HQ Archive.

22. FBI summary report, November 9, 1942, p. 7, file 65-44610-[illegible], sec. 18, SIS 253, FBI summary report, October 6, 1942 [censored], pp. 22–27, file 65-44610-164, sec. 5, SIS 284, memo, July 13, 1942, p. 1, file 65-44610-620, sec. 17, and James P. McMahon to Hoover, March 14, 1947, file 65-44610-712, sec. 19, FBI HQ Archive; Benítez, "On Radio Berlin," 73; Farago, *Game of the Foxes,* 505.

23. *Diario de la marina,* November 1, 1942, 2, November 10, 1942, 1, and November 11, 1942, 2; *Washington Times Herald,* December 7, 1942, file 65-44610, sec. Sub A, and partial transcript of Faget and SIS 253 interrogation of Lüning in Spanish (quote), October 1942, file 65-44610-130, sec. 4, FBI HQ Archive; Benítez, "On Radio Berlin," 73; Singer, *Spies and Traitors,* 110, 113–14 (which is unreliable); Rodríguez, e-mails to the author, November 20, 24, 2003, August 15, September 15, 2005.

24. SIS 396, report, September 7, 1942, file 65-44610-8, sec. 2, and SIS 253, FBI summary report, October 6, 1942 [censored], pp. 7, 34, file 65-44610-164, sec. 5, and Alfredo Hernández Cata and Juan Valdes Díaz, report, September 17, 1942, file 65-44610-220, sec. 6, FBI HQ Archive.

25. Abstracts of agent A-3779 letters, Havana, A-3779, RW 49/561, microfilm FB2199P RW 49/532, 533, 534, and summaries of eight secret ink messages on reel 24, RW49/950, Cuba, Abwehr records, Bundesarchiv, Freiburg; Hoover to Berle, September 11, 1942, enclosing a memo, September 11, 1942, MID 201 Lüning, 9-11-42, file x8536413, box 131E, RG 319, NARA; Koop, *Weapon of Silence,* 3–15.

26. Hoover to ONI, January 29, 1943, files 65-44610-494 and -495, sec. 13, FBI HQ Archive.

27. Ladd to Hoover, memo, December 14, 1942, p. 2, file 65-44610-426, sec.

11, FBI HQ Archive; Benítez, "On Radio Berlin," 11–12. Benítez claimed that the headache powder was in the ink, but various FBI-SIS reports, including one from Hoover, suggest that the ink was weak because the powder was left out.

28. Hoover to Berle, November 24, 1942, MID 201 Lüning, file x8536413, box 131E, RG 319, NARA.

29. Isabel to Enrique Augusto Luni, March 26, 1942, secret ink intercepts, Name index, Heinz August Lüning file, RG 216.2, Justice Department, NARA.

30. Ibid.

31. Ibid.

32. Ladd to Hoover, memo, December 14, 1942, p. 2, file 65-44610-426, sec. 11, FBI HQ Archive.

33. Memo, September 17, 1943, 800.20225/222a, box 3211, December File (1940–44), RG 59, NARA; Hoover to Berle, September 11, 1942, November 24, 1942, MID 201 Lüning, file x8536413, box 131E, RG 319, NARA; FBI summary report, November 9, 1942, pp. 9–11, file 65-44610-[illegible], sec. 18, FBI report, Richard L. Johnson, October 30, 1942, pp. 1–3, file 65-44610-273, sec. 7, *La bohemia,* September 13, 1942, file 65-44610-20, sec. 2, and *Washington Times-Herald,* December 7, 1942, file 65-44610, sec. Sub A, FBI HQ Archive; *Chicago Tribune,* June 17, 1900, 39, and *Chicago Daily Tribune,* January 8, 1902, 4 (on Moritz Lassig, Helga's great-grandfather); numerous items in the Philip Bartholomae clipping folder, Theater Collection, New York Public Library, Performing Arts Branch, NY; Rogan, e-mail to the author, December 13, 2005; marriage licence for George Bartholomae and Emma Lassig, Chicago, September 12, 1878, Cook County Clerk of Court, Chicago.

34. Johnson, report, October 30, 1942, file 65-44610-273, sec. 7, and Benvenido Alegría (Hijo) to Luni, c/o Honduran Consul-General, Havana, Hoover to SAC (New York), January 8, 1943, and Hoover to U.S. Embassy (Santiago, Chile), March 4, 1943, files 65-44610-446, -457, and -462, sec. 12, FBI HQ Archive.

35. SIS 396 to Hoover, November 20, 1942, file 65-44610-446, sec. 11, FBI HQ Archive.

36. Memo re: Lüning with Hoover to Berle, December 12, 1942, MID 201 Lüning, file x8536413, box 131E, RG 319, NARA; Bienvenido Alegría (Hijo) to Luni, n.d. (quote), with unsigned memo, n.d., file 65-44610-[160], sec. 5, and Hoover to ONI, January 29, 1943, Hoover to SIS 396, February 6, 1943, file 65-44610-446, sec. 11, and SIS to Hoover, February 15, 1943, files 65-44610-494 and -508, sec. 13, FBI HQ Archive; *Diario de la marina,* September 6, 1942, 1, 16.

37. SIS 253 to FBI, memo, September 4, 1942, file 65-44610-16, sec. 2, and X-code cable, September 25, 1942, file 65-44610-218, sec. 6, FBI HQ Archive; Hoover to Berle, November 24, 1942, MID 201 Lüning, file x8536413, box 131E, RG 319, NARA.

38. SIS 253, FBI summary report, October 6, 1942 [censored], p. 31, file 65-44610-164, sec. 5, FBI HQ Archive.

39. SIS 253, FBI summary report, October 6, 1942 [censored], p. 18, file 65-44610-164, sec. 5, FBI HQ Archive; Hoover to Berle, November 24, 1942, MID 201 Lüning, file x8536413, box 131E, RG 319, NARA; *New York Times,* September 6, 1942, 19.

40. Foxworth to Carson, September 14, 1942, file 65-44610-91, sec. 4, FBI report by Johnson, October 31, 1942, file 65-44610-299, sec. 8, SIS 253, FBI summary report, October 6, 1942 [censored], p. 18, file 65-44610-164, sec. 5, secret ink messages, December 1941–August 1942, files 65-44610-x to -x46, sec. 1, secret ink messages, December 1941–August 1942, files 65-44610-x47 to -x66, sec. 2, and *Kansas City Star,* September 6, 1942, file 65-44610, sec. Sub A, FBI HQ Archive.

41. SIS 253, FBI memo, September 4, 1942, p. 1, secret ink messages, December 1941–August 1942, files 65-44610-16 and -x47 to -x66, sec. 2, and secret ink messages, December 1941–August 1942, files 65-44610-x to -x46, sec. 1, FBI HQ Archive.

42. Hernández Cata and Valdes Díaz, report, September 17, 1942, file 65-44610-220, sec. 6, FBI HQ Archive.

43. SIS 253, FBI summary report, October 6, 1942 [censored], p. 18, file 65-44610-164, sec. 5, secret ink messages, December 1941–August 1942, files 65-44610-x to -x46, sec. 1, and secret ink messages, December 1941–August 1942, files 65-44610-x47 to -x66, sec. 2, FBI HQ Archive.

44. SIS 253, FBI memo, September 4, 1942, p. 1, FBI reports re: Carlos Robinson, September 7, 11, 1941, U.S. Office of Censorship intercept, [February 6, 1942, p. 1], and BIC to Office of Censorship, February 6, August 12, 1942, files 65-44610-3, -8, -16, -x59, and -x66, sec. 2, FBI HQ Archive.

45. Secret ink messages, December 1941–August 1942, files 65-44610-x to -x46, sec. 1, and SIS 253, FBI memo, September 4, 1942, p. 1, and secret ink messages, December 1941–August 1942, files 65-44610-16 and -x47 to -x66, sec. 2, FBI HQ Archive.

46. SIS 253, FBI summary report, October 6, 1942 [censored], p. 17, file 65-44610-164, sec. 5, secret ink messages, December 1941–August 1942, files 65-44610-x to -x46, sec. 1, and secret ink messages, December 1941–August 1942, files 65-44610-x47 to -x66, sec. 2, FBI HQ Archive.

47. SIS 253, FBI summary report, October 6, 1942 [censored], p. 18, file 65-44610-164, sec. 5, secret ink messages, December 1941–August 1942, files 65-44610-x to -x46, sec. 1, and secret ink messages, December 1941–August 1942, files 65-44610-x47 to -x66, sec. 2, FBI HQ Archive; Hoover to Berle, November 24, 1942, MID 201 Lüning, file x8536413, box 131E, RG 319, NARA.

48. Hoover to Berle, November 24, 1942, MID 201 Lüning, file x8536413,

box 131E, RG 319, NARA; SIS 253, FBI summary report, October 6, 1942 [censored], p. 18, file 65-44610-164, sec. 5, secret ink messages, December 1941–August 1942, files 65-44610-x to -x46, sec. 1, and secret ink messages, December 1941–August 1942, files 65-44610-x47 to -x66, sec. 2, FBI HQ Archive.

49. BIC to U.S. government, Bermuda intercept, August 12, 1942, file 65-44610-x66, and other intercepts, files 65-44610-x47 to -x65, sec. 2, FBI HQ Archive.

50. SIS 396 to Hoover, October 6, 1942, file 65-44610-156, sec. 5, FBI HQ Archive.

51. H. Hobson to Foreign Office, June 19, 1942, A5820, and Hobson to Foreign Office, July 30, 1942, A7617, FO 371/30455, PRO.

52. Report of British naval attaché in Washington on visit to Havana, May 25, 1942, A6016/G, FO 371/30455, PRO.

53. Morison, *Two-Ocean War,* 109–10; Kelshall, *U-Boat War,* 13–15; Weinberg, *World at Arms,* 377–78.

54. Friedman, *Nazis and Good Neighbors,* 34–35.

55. Padfield, *Dönitz et la guerre des U-Boote,* 222–29; Frank, *Sea Wolves,* 149.

56. Frank, *Sea Wolves,* 149; Dönitz, *Zehn Jahre und zwanzig Tage,* 196–97, 215, 217.

57. Keegan, *Intelligence in War,* 234; Baptiste, *War, Cooperation and Conflict;* 144; Hinsley et al., *British Intelligence,* 2:228–29, 233; Syrett, ed., *Battle of the Atlantic,* 1–187.

58. Maingot, *The United States and the Caribbean,* 56–57; Mollman-Showell, *Kriegsmarine,* 33.

59. Kurowski, *An alle Wölfe,* 14–15, and *Krieg unter Wasser,* 154; Blair, *Hitler's U-Boat War: The Hunted,* 51–54; Hoover to Berle, December 3, 1942, and attachments, 800.20237/224, box 3220, December File (1940–44), RG 59, NARA.

60. *Time* 40, no. 2 (July 13, 1942): 34; *New York Times,* July 3, 1942, 1–2, July 4, 1942, 7, and February 27, 1943, 4; *Washington Post,* July 3, 1942, 1, 4, and July 4, 1942, 2; Hoover to Berle, December 3, 1942, file 65-44610-456, sec. 12, FBI HQ Archive; Dönitz, *Zehn Jahre und zwanzig Tage,* 213; Frank, *Sea Wolves,* 169; Latin America, Memorandum on S.O.E., June 1942, HS 8/62, PRO.

61. Bishop, *Prints in the Sand,* 1–22, 73–75; Wiggins, *Torpedoes in the Gulf,* 124–29; Willoughby, *U.S. Coast Guard,* 47–48.

62. Dönitz, *Zehn Jahre und zwanzig Tage,* 192; Padfield, *Dönitz et la guerre des U-Boote,* 216–17, 224.

63. Baptiste, *War, Cooperation and Conflict,* 144; Dönitz, *Zehn Jahre und zwanzig Tage,* 196–97, 210; Maingot, *The United States and the Caribbean,* 58–61 (all three quotes); Rohwer, *Axis Submarine Successes,* and *Die U-Boot-*

Erfolge der Achsenmächte, 84–85, 97, 107, 110, 112–13; Benítez, "On Radio Berlin," 10.

64. ONI Intelligence Report, December 26, 1942, file 65-44610-487, sec. 12, FBI HQ Archive.

65. Baptiste, *War, Cooperation and Conflict,* 144; Dönitz, *Zehn Jahre und zwanzig Tage,* 196–97, 210.

66. Hinsley et al., *British Intelligence,* 2:228–30.

67. Blair, *Hitler's U-Boat War: The Hunter,* 771, and *Hitler's U-Boat War: The Hunted,* ix–xii, 820; Hashimoto, *Sunk,* 193–98; Rohwer, *Axis Submarine Successes.*

68. Maingot, *The United States and the Caribbean,* 58–61.

5. Failure and Fatality

1. Koop, *Weapon of Silence,* 3–15; Kahn, *The Codebreakers,* 513–15; "Who's Who Card Summary," 33 MID 201 Lüning, Heinz August, file x8536413, box 131E, RG 319, NARA.

2. C. A. Carson, memo for D. M. Ladd, June 21, 1943, Ernest Hemingway file, file 64-23312-6x, FBI HQ Archive.

3. Ibid.

4. Ibid.

5. Ibid.

6. R. G. Leddy to Hoover, October 8, 1942, Ladd, memo for Hoover, December 17, 1942, Hoover memo, December 19, 1942, Hoover to SIS 396, December 17, 1942, Ladd, memo for Hoover, April 27, 1943, and Carson, memo for Ladd, June 13, 21, 1943, files 64-23312-x1, -x2, -1, -3, -6x, and -6x1, FBI HQ Archive.

7. Boyden ONI Intelligence Report, September 9, 1942, file 65-44610-103, sec. 4, and John B. Little to Ladd, September 23, 1942, file 65-44610-149, sec. 5, FBI HQ Archive; Hoover to Braden, September 17, 1942, MID 201 Lüning, file x8536413, box 131E, RG 319, NARA; Braden to Secretary of State, September 18, 1942, 103.02, box 1, entry 2359, Cuba: Havana Embassy, Super Confidential, December File (1940–44), RG 59, NARA.

8. C. R. Watkins-Mence, "Censorship History of Bermuda," March 1944, pp. 2–52, DEFE 1/323, "History of Caribbean Imperial Censorship," [1944–1945], DEFE 1/329, and Charles des Graz, "Report on Operations in the Western Hemisphere, 1941–42," March 1943, DEFE 1/156, PRO; "Who's Who Card Summary," November 24, 1942, MID 201 Lüning, file x8536413, box 131E, RG 319, NARA; FBI summary report, November 9, 1942, p. 17, file 65-44610-[illegible], sec. 18, FBI HQ Archive.

9. Watkins-Mence, "Censorship History of Bermuda," March 1944, pp.

2–52, DEFE 1/323, "History of Caribbean Imperial Censorship," [1944–1945], DEFE 1/329, and des Graz, "Report on Operations in the Western Hemisphere, 1941–42," March 1943, DEFE 1/156, PRO; Ladd to Hoover, memo, December 14, 1942, pp. 3–4, file 65-44610-426, sec. 11, FBI HQ Archive.

10. Koop, *Weapon of Silence*, 3–15; Kahn, *The Codebreakers*, 513–15; "Who's Who Card Summary," 33 MID 201 Lüning, file x8536413, box 131E, RG 319, NARA.

11. Koop, *Weapon of Silence*, 3–15; *Diario de la marina* and *New York Times* for September, October, and November 1942; Gellman, *Roosevelt and Batista*, 148–49.

12. MID memo re: Lüning, September 16, 1942, and Hoover to Berle, September 11, 1942, enclosing a memo, September 11, 1942, MID 201 Lüning, 9-11-42, file x8536413, box 131E, RG 319, NARA.

13. SIS 253 to FBI, memo, September 4, 1942, pp. 1–2, decode of cable from SIS 396, August 31, 1942, FBI to SIS 396, September 1, 1942, and Carson memo to Ladd, September 2, 1942, files 65-44610-250X1, -x56, -x57, and -6, sec. 2, FBI HQ Archive; *Christian Science Monitor,* September 8, 1942, 3.

14. Ellis O. Briggs to Secretary of State, April 27, 1942, Cuba: Havana Embassy, General Records, Confidential files, box 4, December Files (1940–44), RG 84, NARA; Hoover to Berle, September 11, 1942, MID 201 Lüning, file x8536413, box 131E, RG 319, NARA; Singer, *Spies and Traitors,* 110; *New York Times,* December 10, 1942, 14; *Christian Science Monitor,* December 10, 1942, 8; *Diario de la marina,* September 6, 1942, 16; Louis Pérez (University of North Carolina, Chapel Hill), e-mail to the author, November 3, 2003.

15. Memo re: Lüning, n.d., file 65-44610-160, sec. 5, FBI HQ Archive; *Diario de la marina,* September 1, 1942, 1, and September 3, 1942, 2; *New York Times,* September 2, 1942, 29, September 5, 1942, 5, and September 6, 1942, 19.

16. SIS 253 to FBI, memo, September 4, 1942, p. 3, file 65-44610-16, sec. 2, Hayne D. Boyden, ONI Report, September 9, 1942, file 65-44610-103, sec. 4, and memo: re: Lüning, n.d., file 65-44610-160, sec. 5, FBI HQ Archive; *New York Times,* September 6, 1942, 19; *Washington Post,* September 6, 1942, 3; *New Orleans Times-Picayune,* September 6, 1942, 1; *Atlanta Constitution,* September 6, 1942, 1.

17. Benítez, "On Radio Berlin," 73.

18. [Censored] to Hoover, September 8, 1942, and SIS 396 to Hoover, September 7, 11, 1942, p. 1, files 65-44610-8 and -9, Carson memo for Ladd, September 5, 1942, p. 3, file 65-44610-11, sec. 2, and Benítez telegram to Santiago, Chile, Chief of Police, September 29, 1942, and translation, file 65-44610-366, sec. 10, FBI HQ Archive.

19. [Censored] to Hoover, September 8, 1942, and SIS 396 to Hoover, September 7, 11, 1942, p. 1 (quote, September 11), files 65-44610-8 and -9, sec. 2,

Havana Post, October 8, 1942, *La nación* (Santiago de Chile), October 8, 1942, *La hora* (Santiago de Chile) in *Noticiero Mercantil* (Havana), October 9, 1942, and William Philips Simms, "Welles' Charges," *Washington News,* October 13, 1942, 15, file 65-44610, sec. Sub A, FBI HQ Archive.

20. Boyden, ONI Report, September 9, 1942, file 65-44610-103, sec. 4, FBI HQ Archive; "Who's Who Card Summary," November 24, 1942 (quote), MID 201 Lüning, file x8536413, box 131E, RG 319, NARA.

21. "Benítez, Manuel, Police chief of Cuba," Kartei über Cuba/Personen, fiches 1–3, RH2/1863, Bundesarchiv, Freiburg; "Leading Personalities, Cuba, 1941," FO 371/25935, and "Leading Personalities, Cuba, 1943," FO 371/33840, PRO.

22. [Censored] to Hoover, September 8, 1942, and SIS 396 to Hoover, September 7, 11, 1942 (quote, September 11), files 65-44610-8 and -9, sec. 2, FBI HQ Archive.

23. Boyden, ONI Report, September 19, 1942, file 65-44610-269, sec. 7, FBI HQ Archive; Carson, memo for Ladd, June 21, 1943, file 64-23312-6x, FBI HQ Archive; Lynn, *Hemingway,* 502–3; Mellow, *A Life without Consequences,* 526; Cirules, *Hemingway in Cuba,* 73–74.

24. Boyden, ONI Report, September 19, 1942, file 65-44610-269, sec. 7, FBI HQ Archive.

25. Hoover to Berle, September 11, 1942, enclosing a memo, September 11, 1942, MID 201 Lüning, file x8536413, box 131E, RG 319, NARA; Koop, *Weapon of Silence,* 3–15.

26. MID memo re: Lüning, September 16, 1942, and Hoover to Berle, September 11, 1942, enclosing a memo, September 11, 1942, MID 201 Lüning, file x8536413, box 131E, RG 319, NARA; *New York Times,* September 6, 1942, and *New York Journal American,* September 6, 1942, file 65-44610, sec. Sub A, FBI HQ Archive; boxes 4 and 5, SIS records (1942–1945), RG 38, NARA.

27. *New Orleans Times-Picayune,* September 6, 1942, 1; *Atlanta Constitution,* September 6, 1942, 1; *New York Times,* September 6, 1942, 19, September 18, 1942, 7, September 19, 1942, 2, October 13, 1942, 1, 10, and November 1, 1942, 20; *Washington Post,* September 6, 1942, 3 (quotes, "most important spies," "escape the firing squad"), September 20, 1942, 5, October 13, 1942, 1–2, and November 11, 1942, 4; Rockefeller, "Fighting the Traitors Within."

28. *New York Times,* September 6, 1942, 19 (quote); Memo on Lüning, October 26, 1942, file 65-44610-385, sec. 10, and *Chicago Daily Tribune,* September 6, 1942, 2, "Cubans Grab Spy Sending Out Data on Ship Sailings," *New Orleans Times-Picayune,* September 6, 1942, p. 1 (from AP), *Washington Daily News,* September 11, 1942, 11, and *Kansas City Star,* September 6, 1942, file 65-44610, sec. Sub A, FBI HQ Archive; Benítez, "On Radio Berlin."

29. Memo on Lüning, October 26, 1942, file 65-44610-385, sec. 10, and *Chicago Daily Tribune,* September 6, 1942, 2, "Cubans Grab Spy Sending Out Data

on Ship Sailings," *New Orleans Times-Picayune,* September 6, 1942, 1 (from AP), *Washington Daily News,* September 11, 1942, 11, and *Kansas City Star,* September 6, 1942, file 65-44610, sec. Sub A, FBI HQ Archive.

30. Hoover to Chief, Radio Intelligence Division, FCC, September 23, 1942, file 65-44610-93, sec. 4, SIS 253, FBI summary report, October 6, 1942 [censored], pp. 2, 20, 33, file 65-44610-164, sec. 5, and SIS 253, "Partial transcript of questions and answers in Spanish of subject, Heinz August Lüning, questioned by Captain [Mariano Faget] and [SIS 253]," n.d., file 65-44610-16, sec. 2, FBI HQ Archive.

31. Hoover to Berle, November 24, 1942, 800.20237/222, box 3220, December File (1940–44), RG 59, NARA; SIS 253 to Hoover, October 6, 1942, pp. 7, 20, file 65-44610-164, sec. 5, FBI HQ Archive; *Diario de la marina,* September 6, 1942, 1, 16.

32. Hoover to [?], November 16, 1942, file 65-44610-392, sec. 10, FBI HQ Archive.

33. Briggs to Secretary of State, April 27, 1942, Cuba: Havana Embassy, General Records, Confidential files, box 4, December Files (1940–44), RG 84, NARA; Hoover to Berle, September 11, 1942, MID 201 Lüning, file x8536413, box 131E, RG 319, NARA; Singer, *Spies and Traitors,* 110; *Diario de la marina,* September 6, 1942, 16.

34. *Diario de la marina,* September 6, 1942, 16; Boyden, ONI Report, September 9, 1942, file 65-44610-103, sec. 4, FBI HQ Archive.

35. Hoover to U.S. Attorney General, September 16, 1942, DOJ Case file, 146-7-0, RG 65, NARA; Hoover to Chief, Radio Intelligence Division, FCC, September 23, 1942, file 65-44610-93, sec. 4, FBI HQ Archive; Hoover to Berle, September 11, 1942, MID 201 Lüning, file x8536413, box 131E, RG 319, NARA.

36. SIS 396 report, September 7, 1942, and X-code cable, September 11, 1942, files 65-44610-8 and -3, sec. 2, SIS 253 to Hoover, October 6, 1942, pp. 7, 20, file 65-44610-164, sec. 5, and Ladd, memo, December 14, 1942, file 65-44610-424, sec. 11, FBI HQ Archive.

37. Alfonso Hernández Cata and Juan Valdes Díaz, report, September 17, 1942, file 65-44610-220, sec. 6 (quotes), and Hoover to W. C. Spears, September 12, 1944, file 65-44610-681, sec. 19, FBI HQ Archive.

38. SIS 396 report, September 7, 1942, and X-code cable, September 11, 1942, files 65-44610-3 and -8, sec. 2, FBI HQ Archive.

39. FBI summary report, November 9, 1942, p. 1, file 65-44610-[illegible], sec. 18, and FBI reports, September 7, 11, 1942, re: Carlos Robinson cables from Chile, files 65-44610-3 and -8, sec. 2, FBI HQ Archive.

40. Hoover to Berle, September 11, 30, 1942, and "Who's Who Card Summary," November 24, 1942, MID 201 Lüning, file x8536413, box 131E, RG 319, NARA; Hoover to U.S. Attorney General, September 16, 1942, DOJ Case file,

146-7-0, RG 65, NARA; *Diario de la marina,* September 6, 1942, 1, 16, September 16, 1942, 3, and October 8, 1942, 2, and Carson memo for Ladd, September 5, 1942, p. 3, file 65-44610-11, sec. 2, and G. E. Sterling (Chief FCC) to E. P. Coffey, September 21, 1942 (quote), file 65-44610-93, sec. 4, FBI HQ Archive.

41. Koop, *Weapon of Silence,* 3–15; Kahn, *The Codebreakers,* 513–15; Braden, *Diplomats and Demagogues,* 287 (his discredited allegation of Lüning's radio work); Isabel to Luni, March 26, 1942, RG 216, NARA; FBI reports, September 7, 11, 1942, re: Robinson cables from Chile, files 65-44610-3 and -8, sec. 2, and SIS 253 to Hoover, October 6, 1942, pp. 7, 20, file 65-44610-164, sec. 5, FBI HQ Archive. A dramatic, part-fictionalized version of Lüning's story is found in Singer, *Spies and Traitors,* 108–14.

42. Memo, September 4, 1942, file 65-44610-16, sec. 2, and Hernández Cata and Valdes Díaz, report, September 17, 1942, file 65-44610-220, sec. 6, FBI HQ Archive; *Noticias de hoy* (Havana), November 6, 1942, 8, November 10, 1942, 8, and November 11, 1942, 1, 8; *New York Times,* September 18, 1942, 7, September 19, 1942, 2, and October 13, 1942, 1, 10; *Washington Post,* September 20, 1942, 5, and October 13, 1942, 1–2; *Boston Daily Globe,* November 10, 1942, 39; *Los Angeles Herald Express,* November 10, 1942, 2.

43. SIS 396 report, September 7, 1942, and X-code cable, September 11, 1942, files 65-44610-3 and -8, sec. 2, and Ladd, memo, December 14, 1942, file 65-44610-426, sec. 11, FBI HQ Archive.

44. Singer, *Spies and Traitors,* 109; Braden, *Diplomats and Demagogues,* 287–88; Farago, *Game of the Foxes,* 505; Koop, *Weapon of Silence,* 3–15; Hoover to Berle, November 24, 1942, 800.20237/223, box 3220, December File (1940–44), RG 59, NARA; Hoover to Berle, November 24, 1942, MID 201 Lüning, file X8536413, box 131E, RG 319, NARA.

45. Boyden, ONI Report, September 5, 1942, file 65-44610-104, sec. 4, and SIS 253 to FBI, memo, September 4, 1942, p. 3, file 65-44610-16, sec. 2, FBI HQ Archive; Hoover to Berle, November 24, 1942, 800.20237/222, box 3220, December File (1940–44), RG 59, NARA.

46. Hoover to Berle, November 13, 1942, enclosing memo, n.d., pp. 1–2, file 65-44610-381, sec. 10, and SIS 138, memo, October 27, 1942, pp. 1–2, file 65-44610-266, sec. 7, FBI HQ Archive.

47. SIS 253, FBI summary report, October 6, 1942 [censored], p. 20, file 65-44610-164, sec. 5, FBI HQ Archive.

48. FBI report file 65-248, April 24, 1944, 702.3711c/33, box 1914, December File (1940–44), RG 59, NARA; *New York Times,* September 15, 1942, 16.

49. Rohwer, *Axis Submarine Successes; Diario de la marina,* September 19, 1942, 3; FBI report file 65-248, April 24, 1944, 702.3711c/33, box 1914, December File (1940–44), RG 59, NARA.

50. *Diario de la marina,* September 16, 1942, 3, September 17, 1942, 2, Sep-

tember 19, 1942, 3, and October 3, 1942, 2; German Ambassador in Madrid, for-warding message from Buenos Aires, November 12, 1942, Inland Iig, 74, Nr. 1922, and von Grote to OKW Amt Ausland/Abwehr, February 5, 1943, Agenten und Spionagewesen, R102073, PAAA; *Noticias de hoy,* September 29, 1942, 4, October 1, 1942, 3, and October 30, 1942, 3; *La correspondencia* (Cienfuegos), September 22, 1942, 1. See also the editorial, *Noticias de hoy,* November 3, 1942, 2.

51. *Chicago Daily Tribune,* September 20, 1942, 2; Hoover to Berle, September 30, 1942, MID 201 Lüning, file x8536413, box 131E, RG 319, NARA; FBI summary report, November 9, 1942, p. 21, file 65-44610-[illegible], sec. 18, FBI HQ Archive; *Noticias de hoy,* November 6, 1942, 1, 8; *Carteles* (Havana), no. 39 (September 27, 1942): 28–29 (seven photographs of Lüning and his trial).

52. SIS [censored] to Hoover, September 19, 1942 (quote), and Hoover to Berle, September 26, 1942, file 65-44610-155, sec. 5, and SIS 396, FBI, communications section, p. 1, file 65-44610-21, sec. 2, FBI HQ Archive.

53. Braden, *Diplomats and Demagogues,* 287–88; *New York Times,* October 18, 1942, 26, and November 11, 1942, 2; *Diario de la marina,* October 31, 1942, 2; *La correspondencia,* November 6, 1942, 1–2; *Chicago Daily Tribune,* November 8, 1942, 21, and November 10, 1942, 1; *Havana Post,* October 31, 1942, 1.

54. *Diario de la marina,* September 19, 1942, 3, and October 3, 1942, 2, *Noticias de hoy,* September 29, 1942, 4, October 1, 1942, 3, October 30, 1942, 3, and November 3, 1942, 2, *La correspondencia,* September 22, 1942, 1, *Havana Post,* November 5, 1942, and *Avance* (Havana), September 18, 1942, 1, 9, file 65-44610, sec. Sub A, FBI HQ Archive.

55. Braden, *Diplomats and Demagogues,* 287–88 (quote); file 65-44610-677, sec. 18, FBI HQ Archive.

56. A. George Hauer, report, August 4, 1944, file 65-44610-677, sec. 18, FBI HQ Archive.

57. Hauer, report, August 4, 1944, file 65-44610-677, sec. 18, FBI HQ Archive; *Wall Street Journal,* October 29, 1942, 10; *Chicago Daily Tribune,* November 8, 1942, 26; *New York Times,* December 15, 1942, 48, December 16, 1942, 11, and December 19, 1942, 3; *Washington Post,* December 10, 1942, 9.

58. Boyden, ONI Report, September 9, 1942, file 65-44610-103, sec. 4, FBI HQ Archive.

59. *El mundo* (Havana), November 11, 1942, file 65-44610, sec. Sub A, FBI HQ Archive.

60. Benítez, "On Radio Berlin," 73; Singer, *Spies and Traitors,* 113–14; Phillips, *Cuba,* 216–17; [Benítez], "On Radio Berlín"; Rodríguez, e-mails to the author, November 24, December 17, 2003, and August 24, 2005; SIS 253, FBI summary report, October 6, 1942 [censored], pp. 22–27, file 65-44610-164, sec. 5, and *Washington Times-Herald,* December 7, 1942, file 65-44610, sec. Sub A, FBI HQ Archive.

61. G-2 Report, Roberts to MID, November 28, 1942, War Department, General Staff, MID 201 Lüning, file x8536413, box 131E, RG 319, NARA; report, February 2, 1943, 800.20210/1477, box 3136, December File (1940–44), RG 59, NARA; *Diario de la marina,* November 11, 1942, 2; *Carteles,* 47 (November 22, 1942): 25 (photographs of Rey and Romero).

62. *Los Angeles Times,* November 9, 1942, 9, *Washington Times-Herald,* November 11, 1942, 1, and *El mundo,* November 11, 1942, file 65-44610, sec. Sub A, FBI HQ Archive; Singer, *Spies and Traitors,* 113–14; *Diario de la marina,* November 1, 1942, 2; *Noticias de hoy,* November 10, 1942, 1, 8, and November 11, 1942, 1, 8. After Lüning's death, a U.S. official listed six photographs in the weekly *La bohemia* (for mid-November) that documented his death as "(*a*) Lüning being interviewed by Cuban reporter; (*b*) Lüning just before execution; (*c*) Fathers Angel Rey and José Romero; (*d*) Lüning being led to face firing squad; (*e*) Lüning being led to face firing squad; and (*f*) coffin containing remains of Lüning" (G-2 Report, Roberts to MID, November 28, 1942, War Department, General Staff, MID 201 Lüning, file x8536413, box 131E, RG 319, NARA).

63. *New York Times,* October 18, 1942, 26, and November 11, 1942, 2; *Diario de la marina,* October 31, 1942, 2; *La correspondencia,* November 6, 1942, 1–2; *Noticias de hoy,* November 10, 1942, 1, 8.

64. Acta de Identificación (death certificate), November 10, 1942, Director Jefe del Servicio Médico Forense de la Habana [director of forensic medicine in Havana] to Hoover, November 13, 1942, file 65-44610-379, sec. 10, SIS 348 to FBI, November 16, 1942, and SIS 396 to Nelson Rockefeller, November 23, 1942, file 65-44610-416, sec. 11, and *El mundo,* November 11, 1942, file 65-44610, sec. Sub A, FBI HQ Archive.

65. Von Grote to OKW Amt Ausland/Abwehr, February 5, 1943, and Klemse to AA, February 24, 1943, R102073 "Agenten und Spionagewesen, Einzelfälle," and German Ambassador in Madrid to AA, enclosing telegram from the Spanish chargé, Havana, Akten Lüning, Inland IIg, 74, microfiche no. 1922, PAAA; Joyce to Secretary of State, January 19, 1943, 800.20237/241, box 3220, December File (1940–44), RG 59, NARA; Brammer, *Spionageabwehr Hamburg,* 31; *Diario de la marina,* November 10, 1942, 1, and November 11, 1942, 2 (mistakenly identifying Lüning's wife with the names Lyli and Edna Barbara and his six-year-old son as Bartolomé).

66. Original Lüning letter to his family with James P. McMahon, legal attaché in Havana, to Hoover, March 14, 1947, file 65-44610-712, sec. 19, FBI HQ Archive; Joyce to Secretary of State, January 19, 1943, 800.20237/241, box 3220, December File (1940–44), RG 59, NARA.

67. Lethe (?), I-Dienst, November 10, 1942, "Heinz August Lüning in Havana hingerichtet," R 41789, Deutsche Zivilgefangenen Cuba, PAAA; Memo: "Meth-

ods used by German Spy apprehended in Cuba," MID 201 Lüning, file x8536413, box 131E, RG 319, NARA; Benítez, "On Radio Berlin," 73.

68. *Diario de la marina,* October 27, 1942, 1; *New York Times,* December 10, 1942, 14; *Christian Science Monitor,* December 10, 1942, 8.

69. SIS 491, report on Lüning, August 9, 1943, 1, 3, file 65-44610-630x, sec. 17, and *Washington Post,* September 6, 1942, *San Francisco Examiner,* September 6, 1942, and *New York Times,* September 6, 1942, file 65-44610, sec. Sub A, FBI HQ Archive.

70. FBI summary report, November 9, 1942, p. 17, Hoover to John W. Speakes, May 14, 1945, and R. F. Cartwright to Nichols, February 5, 1946, files 65-44610-[illegible] and -663, sec. 18, and -704, sec. 19, FBI HQ Archive.

6. Their Man in Havana

1. Rohwer, *Die U-Boot-Erfolge der Achsenmächte,* 72–185; Koop, *Weapon of Silence,* 3–15, 77, 90–91; Morison, *Two-Ocean War,* 108–18; Weinberg, *World at Arms,* 377–79; Boog, *Der globale Krieg,* 319; *Christian Science Monitor,* December 10, 1942, 8.

2. *Diario de la marina,* September 6, 1942, 16, and September 8, 1942, 3; *New York Times,* October–December 1942; "Who's Who Card Summary," November 24, 1942, MID 201 Lüning, file x8536413, box 131E, RG 319, NARA; SIS 396 to FBI, report, September 2, 1942, and clipping from *El mundo,* file 65-44610-22, sec. 2, and Bureau radio, October 10, 1942, file 65-44610-434, sec. 11, FBI HQ Archive.

3. C. H. Carson to Ladd, November 13, 1942, and Ladd to Hoover, November 13, 1942, Records of the FBI, box 16, sec. 5, RG 65, NARA; *Chicago Daily Tribune,* August 23, 1942, 4; Briggs to W. N. Walmsley, October 23, 1942 (2nd, 3rd quotes), Cuba: Havana Embassy: General Records, Confidential, box 3, December Files (1940–44), RG 84, NARA; *New York Times,* October 8, 1942, 7, October 24, 1942, 4, November 1, 1942, 20 (1st quote), and November 5, 1942, 15; *Diario de la marina,* October 27, 1942, 1.

4. *Chicago Daily Tribune,* August 17, 1942, 5; *Diario de la marina,* September 6, 1942, 16, and September 8, 1942, 3; *New York Times,* October and December 1942; SIS 396 to FBI, report, September 2, 1942, file 65-44610-22, sec. 2, and Bureau radio, October 10, 1942, file 65-44610-434, sec. 11, FBI HQ Archive; *Christian Science Monitor,* December 10, 1942, 8.

5. *New York Times,* December 7, 1942, 42; Alfonso Hernández Cata and Juan Valdes Díaz, report, September 17, 1942, file 65-44610-220, sec. 6, FBI HQ Archive.

6. *Washington Post,* December 10, 1942, 9; *New York Times,* December 10, 1942, 14, and December 15, 1942, 48.

7. MID report, November 19, 1942, file 65-44610-354, sec. 9, and Carson to

Ladd, January 29, 1943, and memo re: Heinz August Lüning, January 29, 1943, file 65-44610-505, sec. 13, FBI HQ Archive.

8. Cordell Hull to U.S. Minister in Honduras, September 12, 1942, 862.20215/190, John D. Erwin to Secretary of State, September 23, 1942, 862.20215/195, State Department to U.S. Consul, Barcelona, September 25, 1942, 862.20215/195A, Hoover to Berle and memo, December 12, 1942, 862.20215/206, and Hoover to Berle, January 29, 1943, 862.20215/209, box c322, December File (1940–44), RG 59, NARA; Hoover to Berle, September 11, 1942, MID 201 Lüning, file x8536413, box 131E, RG 319, NARA; *La bohemia,* September 13, 1942, file 65-44610-20, sec. 2, and Hoover memo, December 19, 1942, and Hoover to Berle, January 25, 1943, 4, files 65-44610-437 and -439, sec. 11, FBI HQ Archive.

9. [Unnamed in Barcelona] to Secretary of State, October 16, 1942, and T. J. Donegan to Hoover, January 26, 1943, files 65-44610-459 and -470, sec. 12, FBI HQ Archive.

10. Hoover to Berle, September 11, 1942, MID 201 Lüning, file x8536413, box 131E, RG 319, NARA; Hoover to SAC (NY), December 9, 1942, Hoover memo, December 19, 1942, and Hoover to Berle, January 25, 1943, p. 4, files 65-44610-417, -435, -437, and -439, sec. 11, and Erwin to Secretary of State, January 7, 1943, file 65-44610-498, sec. 12, FBI HQ Archive.

11. SIS 253, memo, September 17, 1942, pp. 1–5, file 65-44610-15, sec. 2, and Hoover to SIS 187, SIS 206, and SIS 250, September 24, 1942, files 65-44610-106, -107, -108, sec. 4, FBI HQ Archive.

12. [Censored] to [censored], October 7, 1942, file 65-44610-159, sec. 5, SIS 138, memo, October 27, 1942, SIS 129 to Hoover, October 23, 1942, SIS 72 to State Department, October 28, 1942, and SIS 9, memo, October 27, 1942, files 65-44610-266, -268, -280, and -284, sec. 7, and memo to [censored], January 25, 1943 (quote), file 65-44610-476, sec. 12, FBI HQ Archive.

13. SIS 180 to Hoover, September 30, 1942, [agent in Asunción] report, October 2, 1942, and [agent in Rio de Janeiro] to Hoover, September 25, 1942, files 65-44610-169, -176x, and -197, sec. 6, [agent in Bogotá] to Hoover, November 28, 1942, file 65-44610-390, sec. 10, and Carson to Ladd, January 29, 1943, and memo, January 29, 1943, file 65-44610-505, sec. 13, FBI HQ Archive.

14. Carson to Ladd, January 29, 1943, and memo, January 29, 1943, file 65-44610-505, sec. 13, FBI HQ Archive.

15. Memo, SIS 9 to FBI, October 27, 1942, file 65-44610-284, sec. 7, decrees of President Elie Lescot, Nos. 108, 178, February 5, 1942, August 6, 1942, from *Le moniteur,* files 65-44610-291 and -292, sec. 8, [Port au Prince agent] to Hoover, October 9, 1942, file 65-44610-327, sec. 9, [Port au Prince agent] to Hoover, November 21, 1942, file 65-44610-373, sec. 10, Carson to Ladd, January 29, 1943, and memo, January 29, 1943, file 65-44610-505, sec. 13, and SIS summary report, August 1, 1945, file 65-44610-699, sec. 19, FBI HQ Archive.

16. Boyden, ONI Report, September 5, 1942, file 65-44610-104, sec. 4, and SIS 253 to FBI, memo, September 4, 1942, p. 3, file 65-44610-16, sec. 2, FBI HQ Archive; Hoover to Berle, November 24, 1942 (quote), 800.20237/222, box 3220, December File (1940–44), RG 59, NARA.

17. [Censored] to [censored], October 7, 1942, file 65-44610-159, sec. 5, and SIS 138, memo, October 27, 1942, SIS 129 to Hoover, October 23, 1942, SIS 72 to State Department, October 28, 1942, and SIS 9, memo, October 27, 1942, files 65-44610-266, -268, -280, and -284, sec. 7, FBI HQ Archive; Hoover to Berle, November 6, 1942, 862.20210 Annie Lehmann, box 5568, December File (1940–44), RG 59, NARA.

18. Rubinstein, *Myth of Rescue,* 206–16; Eck, "Rescue of Jews," 151; Friedman, "Failure to Rescue," 40–42.

19. Hoover to Berle, November 24, 1942, MID 201 Lüning, file x8536413, box 131E, RG 319, NARA; SIS 396, report, September 7, 1942, file 65-44610-8, sec. 2, and John N. Speakes to Hoover, May 7, 1945, and Hoover to Speakes, May 14, 1945, file 65-44610-704, sec. 19, FBI HQ Archive; *Christian Science Monitor,* October 8, 1942, 13, October 12, 1942, 3, and November 4, 1942, 10; *New York Times,* October 8, 1942, 5, and October 13, 1942, 1; *Chicago Daily Tribune,* October 8, 1942, 4, and October 13, 1942, 5.

20. Braden to Secretary of State, October 11, 1942 (quote), 862.20225/721, box c333, Hoover to Berle, August 30, 1943, memo, September 17, 1943, 800.20225/222a, box 3211, and Hoover to Berle, October 29, 1942, 862.20210 Alfred Klaiber, box 5572, December File (1940–44), RG 59, NARA; memo re: Lüning, October 20, 1942, and memo re: Lüning with Hoover to Berle, December 12, 1942, MID 201 Lüning, file x8536413, box 131E, RG 319, NARA; [censored] to Hoover, October 6, 1942, file 65-44610-163, sec. 5, report on Chilean aspect of Lüning case, March 4, 1944, file 65-44610-663, sec. 18, and *Havana Post,* October 8, 1942, *La nación,* October 8, 1942, *La hora* in *Noticiero mercantil,* October 9, 1942, 1, and William Philips Simms, "Welles' Charges," *Washington News,* October 13, 1942, 15, file 65-44610, sec. Sub A, FBI HQ Archive; *Christian Science Monitor,* October 8, 1942, 15, October 13, 1942, 3, and November 4, 1942, 10; *New York Times,* October 8, 1942, 5, October 9, 1942, 7, and October 13, 1942, 1.

21. Memo re: Lüning, October 20, 1942, MID 201 Lüning, file x8536413, box 131E, RG 319, NARA; *Diario de la marina,* October 8, 1942, 2.

22. Hoover to Berle, October 29, 1942, 862.20210 Maier, Alfredo Klaiber/2, box 5572, December File (1940–44), RG 59, NARA.

23. Hoover to Berle, November 20, 1942, 862.20210 Beilin, Georges/1, and Hoover to Berle, March 3, 1943, Beilin, Georges/2, box 5525, December File (1940–44), RG 59, NARA.

24. Hoover to Berle, November 24, 1942, MID 201 Lüning, file x8536413,

box 131E, RG 319, NARA; Hoover to SAC, January 25, 1943, and memo, file 65-44610-476, sec. 12, FBI HQ Archive.

25. Memo: "Mrs. Henri Philippe Lehmann" with Hoover to Berle, November 6, 1942, 862.20210 Lehmann, Annie /1, box 5568, December File (1940–44), RG 59, NARA.

26. U.S. Chargé to Secretary of State, August 14, 1943, 862.20210/2509, box 5515, December File (1940–44), RG 59, NARA; SIS agent report, February 2, 1943, file 65-44610-502, sec. 13, FBI HQ Archive.

27. Memo, Hoover to Assistant Attorney General Wendell Berge, November 13, 1942, file 65-44610-257, sec. 7, FBI HQ Archive.

28. *Christian Science Monitor,* December 10, 1942, 8, December 15, 1942, 3, and December 18, 1942, 18; *Los Angeles Times,* December 15, 1942, 2; Dr. Priese to Reichsführer SS and AA Luther, December 29, 1942, Inland IIg, 454, microfiche Nr. 2970, PAAA.

29. German Ambassador to Madrid to AA, enclosing telegram from the Spanish chargé, Havana, November 12, 1942, Akten Lüning, Inland IIg, 74, microfiche Nr. 1922, PAAA.

30. Von Grote to OKW Amt Ausland/Abwehr, February 5, 1943, and Klemse to AA, February 24, 1943, R102073 "Agenten und Spionagewesen, Einzelfälle," PAAA; Joyce to Secretary of State, January 19, 1943, 800.20237/241, box 3220, December File (1940–44), RG 59, NARA; *Diario de la marina,* November 10, 1942, 1, and November 11, 1942, 2.

31. Koop, *Weapon of Silence,* 3–15, 77, 90–91; Singer, *Spies and Traitors,* 108–15; Knight, "Secret War"; Hoover to Berle, September 11, 1942, MID 201 Lüning, file x8536413, box 131E, RG 319, NARA; *New York Times,* September 6, 1942, 19; Greene, *Our Man in Havana.*

32. Bochow, *FBI,* 255–63; Paredes, *Mis 300 Pasaportes,* 5–7, 12–15; José R. Castro, "[Heinz] August Lunning [Lüning], El tenebroso espía Nazi, fusilado en Cuba," *Diario latino* (San Salvador), September 27, 1944, file 65-44610-683, sec. 19, FBI HQ Archive.

33. Benítez, "On Radio Berlin"; W. C. Spears to Hoover, June 23, 1947, enclosing clippings from *Mañana* (Havana), June 12–21, 1947, file 65-44610-713, sec. 19, FBI HQ Archive; Bochow, *FBI,* 255–63.

34. Speakes to Hoover, May 7, 31, 1945, files 65-44610-x704 and -x708, sec. 19, FBI HQ Archive.

35. *New York Times,* September 6, 1942, 19.

7. Graham Greene's Man in Havana

1. Greene, *Ways of Escape,* 239 (quote), 297; Sheldon, *Graham Greene,* 299–301.

2. Benítez, "On Radio Berlin"; Koop, *Weapon of Silence,* 3–15, 77, 90–91;

Hoover to Berle, September 11, 1942, MID 201 Lüning, file x8536413, box 131E, RG 319, NARA; *New York Times,* September 6, 1942, 19.

3. Ladd to Hoover, memo, December 14, 1942, p. 2, file 65-44610-426, sec. 11, FBI HQ Archive; Benítez, "On Radio Berlin," 11–12.

4. Falk, *Travels in Greeneland,* 147.

5. Van der Linde, telephone conversation with the author, July 29, 2004.

6. Fermoselle, *Evolution of the Cuban Military,* 226–27, 243, 258. Rodríguez, e-mail to the author, November 20, 2003.

7. Greene, *Our Man in Havana,* 177, 186, 188–89, 217; SIS 253 to Hoover, October 6, 1942, enclosing 34-page report, pp. 4–5, file 65-44610-164, sec. 5, FBI HQ Archive.

8. Sheldon, *Graham Greene,* 299–301.

9. Greene, *Ways of Escape,* 250.

10. Sherry, *Life of Graham Greene,* 2:109, 116; West, *Quest for Graham Greene,* 169; Graham Greene to James Michie, June 5, 1958, box 45, folder 1, correspondence, Graham Greene Papers, Boston College, Boston.

11. Benítez, "On Radio Berlin"; map of Havana and surrounding area (American Geographical Society of New York, 1942), box 80, folder 12, Graham Greene Papers, Boston College.

12. Falk, *Travels in Greeneland,* 146–48 (quote, 146); Allain, *The Other Man,* 59; Adamson, *Graham Greene: The Dangerous Edge,* 144–46, and *Graham Greene and Cinema,* 92–94.

13. Greene, *End of the Affair,* 34.

14. Cloetta, foreword, ix, 1.

15. Allain, *The Other Man,* 139.

16. Ibid., 126, 150.

17. Greene, *Ways of Escape,* 221.

18. Interview with Gloria Emerson in 1978, in Donaghy, ed., *Conversations with Graham Greene,* 125.

19. Greene, *World of My Own,* 15.

20. Greene, *Tenth Man,* 13 (introduction).

21. Ibid., 19.

22. Ibid., 20–33.

23. Greene, *Ways of Escape,* 257.

24. Sherry, *Life of Graham Greene,* 2:128–29; Rodríguez, e-mail to the author, August 24, 2005.

25. Sherry, *Life of Graham Greene,* 2:172–73, 176n; Greene, *Tenth Man,* 20–33.

26. Greene, *Ways of Escape,* 238–39 (quote, 239).

27. Sherry, *Life of Graham Greene,* 2:169.

28. Adamson, *Graham Greene: The Dangerous Edge,* 139–47; Greene, *Ways of Escape,* 238–44.

29. Falk, *Travels in Greeneland,* 146–48; Allain, *The Other Man,* 59 (quote); Adamson, *Graham Greene: The Dangerous Edge,* 144–46, and *Graham Greene and Cinema,* 92–94.

30. Fermoselle, *Evolution of the Cuban Military,* 226–27, 243, 258. Faget fled to Florida when Batista's government fell.

Conclusion

1. A. E. Leonard to Nichols, "SIS Statistical Accomplishments," January 17, 1946, Table 1, box 16, sec. 10, Records of the FBI, RG 65, NARA.

2. FBI summary report, November 9, 1942, p. 1, file 65–44610-[illegible], sec. 18, FBI HQ Archive.

Bibliography

Although German records were seized and microfilmed at the end of World War II, this apparent good fortune is less fruitful for the study of Heinz Lüning's espionage in Havana than it might appear. Before the war's end, some records were destroyed by Allied attacks or German acts of political self-defense. In fact, a general order for the destruction of records, issued on April 10, 1945, was poorly distributed and often ignored. Nevertheless, regretfully, the records of the staff of the Oberkommando der Wehrmacht [OKW, Supreme Command of the Armed Forces], the materials of General Alfred Jodl (chief of staff of the OKW), the Gestapo archives, and the Abwehr files for the Hamburg AST stored at Flensburg and Zossen succumbed to acts of war or to willful destruction. The records of the Hamburg AST (Wehrkreis X, Military District 10)—which trained and employed Lüning—were near totally destroyed. The loss of Hamburg AST records meant that most Abwehr records related to the Caribbean are missing. This loss is lamentable but of modest consequence because few of Lüning's secret ink messages made it to Germany in legible form.

In 1986, the historian Uwe Brammer found fewer than two hundred pages of original Abwehr documents for the Hamburg AST. The surviving records do not mention Lüning by name. Allied sources supply most of our information about him. The Allied intelligence agencies had copies of perhaps seventy pieces of correspondence between Lüning, the Abwehr, and Abwehr agents. The SIS interviewed him scores of times about his Abwehr training, his activities, his contacts, and his espionage work. In addition, Brammer interviewed numerous former Hamburg AST employees to supplement the sparse paper record (Brammer, *Spionageabwehr Hamburg*, 11–21). The loss of German government records does make it difficult to assess the relationship between Lüning and his Abwehr handlers.

The German Foreign Ministry files for 1942–1945 suffered extensive damage when an Allied air attack destroyed Foreign Minister Joachim von Ribbentrop's train, which held the originals of recent and pending Foreign Ministry records. Late in the war, Ribbentrop's special train followed Hitler's special train through Germany. (See various items in the Politisches Archiv des Aus-

187

wärtigen Amts [PAAA] and record groups RH2 [Reichsheer], RW5 [Oberkom-
mando Wehrmacht, Auslandsamt/Abwehr], and RW49, microfilm M-3811, and
Bestand: Leopold Bürkner in the Militärarchiv, Bundesarchiv, Freiburg; and
Kahn, "Secrets of the Nazi Archives.") Despite these misfortunes, some materials about Lüning and his mission remain in the Foreign Ministry archives
in Berlin and in the Military Archives in Freiburg. These documents must be
supplemented from Allied sources. Thus, reconstructing Lüning's relationship
with Abwehr officials required foreign materials to a large extent.

Public sources in the United States, Cuba, and Britain hold abundant docu-
mentation on Lüning and his activity in 1941 and 1942. The most extensive
records related to Lüning are those of the FBI-SIS. The FBI-SIS and other
U.S. intelligence agencies received copies of Lüning's secret ink messages to the
Hamburg AST that the British Bermuda station intercepted. After Lüning's arrest, FBI-SIS agents interviewed scores of people in Cuba and Santo Domingo,
throughout Latin America, and in the United States who knew or had contact with Lüning. This investigation produced a four-thousand-page file about
Lüning and his Abwehr activity in the Americas.

Despite the lapse of sixty-five years, this large FBI headquarters file is,
however, available only in censored form. The highly secret Office of Censorship records (RG 216, National Archives) contain hundreds of thousands of
intercepted secret ink and radio messages from World War II (an archival description of RG 216 is available). Since U.S. censors intercepted only a couple
of Lüning's messages, RG 216 may hold little of use. However, these materials
are closed even to Freedom of Information/Privacy Act (FOIA) requests; only
the U.S. president can approve the use of RG 216 intercepts (J. Edgar Hoover
to Adolf Berle Jr., September 11, 1942, enclosing a memorandum, September
11, 1942, MID 201, Lüning, Heinz August 9-11-42, file x8536413, box 131E,
RG 319, NARA; Kahn, "Secrets of the Nazi Archives"; Farago, *Game of the
Foxes*, xi–xv).

The nearly inaccessible British Imperial Censorship records at the Public
Records Office likewise do not show the intercepts of 1941–1942. But many
British records are closed for seventy-five years. The British Foreign Office
holdings at the Public Records Office had at least five files about Lüning's case,
but these files were removed from use until 2017.

Finding copies of Lüning's forty-nine secret ink messages (the actual number of secret ink reports is uncertain because Lüning frequently misnumbered
his messages and repeated numbers on occasion) has proved difficult. The British Imperial Censorship station in Bermuda, called the *Bermuda station,* first
uncovered the secret ink messages and continued to track Lüning's writing until
he was captured. The censors intercepted, photographed, and copied forty-four
of what they consider the forty-nine messages sent by Lüning. There are cop-

ies of the British intercepts in the FBI headquarters file on Lüning. Volume 1 of that file, released under my first FOIA request, had about a hundred pages of text entirely blackened out (only the sender, the recipient, the date, and the letterhead were not darkened) and seventy-five pages withheld. On appeal, I received a copy with all pages included and only a few names blackened out. This volume contained copies or photostats of about half of Lüning's secret messages. I assume the second half of his secret ink messages are in the heavily censored volume 2. My appeal to see the censored and excluded materials in volume 2 was turned down. Even when other material is released, censored text will reduce its value. Still, a general idea of these secret messages is available because Koop's *Weapon of Silence* and other FBI documents contain abstracts of most of the secret ink messages.

Another great loss for the reconstruction of Lüning's activity in Havana occurred in Cuba. The Cuban records of the arrest, the investigation, and the trials of Lüning seem to have been discarded, misplaced, destroyed, or held without access. (Enrique Rodríguez, a Cuban historian of Lüning's time in Havana, claims that the trial record of the German agent, case no. 1366, has disappeared from the Cuban Judicial Archives.) Since the Cubans had severed relations with Nazi Germany in December 1941, the Spanish government represented German interests during World War II. In late 1942, the Spanish chargé in Havana sent several reports on Lüning's capture and execution to Madrid for forwarding to Berlin. Unfortunately, the German Foreign Ministry archives retained only brief memos. The originals were apparently destroyed on Ribbentrop's train. The Spanish Foreign Ministry apparently did not retain copies of the correspondence about Lüning (González, email, November 22, 2001; www.mae.es [Spanish Foreign Ministry archives Web site]; von Grote to OKW Amt Ausland/Abwehr, February 5, 1943, and Klemse to AA, February 24, 1943, R102073 "Agenten und Spionagewesen, Einzelfälle," and German Ambassador to Madrid to AA, enclosing telegram from the Spanish chargé, Havana, November 12, 1942, Akten Lüning, Inland IIg, 74, microfiche Nr. 1922, PAAA.)

In summary, while the Abwehr records with regard to German espionage in Latin America were decimated during World War II, some of the story can be reconstructed from U.S., British, Cuban, and Spanish sources.

Manuscript Materials

Germany

Archiv des Auswärtigen Amts, Berlin:
    Politisches Archiv:

Inland IIg;
R102027, 102073, 417789.
Bezirksamt Hamburg, Hamburg:
Melderegister, Eimsbüttel 540/61;
Wellingsbüttel (now Hamburg-Wandsbek), 171/45.
Bundesarchiv, Militärarchiv, Freiburg im Breisgau:
Bestand: Leopold Bürkner;
RH2 (Reichsheer);
RW5 (OKW/Amt Ausland/Abwehr);
RW49 (OKW/Amt Ausland/Abwehr);
Microfilm: M-3811.
Commerzbibliothek, Handelskammer, Hamburg:
Hamburger Adressbücher;
Handelsregister Bekanntmachungen—Auszüge;
H R Nr. A-32325, "Gustav Adolf Lüning."
Staatsarchiv Bremen:
Adressbücher;
Anmeldekarten: 4,8211-3/205; 4,8211-1/945.
Staatsarchiv Hamburg:
Adressbücher;
Anmeldekarten;
Plankammer-Archivalien, 131-4GRO411.
Standesamt Bremen-Mitte:
Heiratsregister, 1906.
Standesamt Hamburg (Barmek/Uhlenhort):
Sterbefälle, 2722/1997.
Standesamt Hamburg (Eimsbüttel):
Geburtseintrag, 748/1936.

Great Britain

British Library, London.
Public Record Office (PRO)/National Archives, Kew Gardens, London:
Records of the Minister of Defence:
DEFE 1: Postal and Telegraph Censorship Department.
Records of the Foreign Office:
FO 371: Political Department, General Correspondence from 1906.
Records of Special Operations Executive:
HS 8: Ministry of Economic Warfare, Special Operations Executive.
Records of the Security Service:
KV 2: The Security Service: Personal Files (PF).

Records of the War Office:
   WO 208: Directorate of Military Operations and Intelligence and
   Directorate of Military Intelligence;
   WO 216: Office of the Chief of the Imperial General Staff.

United States

Boston College, John J. Burns Library, Boston:
   Graham Greene Papers.
City of New York, Department of Records and Information Service:
   Marriage Records, H. A. Lüning and Helga Barbara Lüning, May 8, 1936.
Columbia University, Rare Book and Manuscript Library, New York:
   Spruille Braden Papers.
Cook County Clerk of Court, Division of Vital Statistics, Cook County, IL:
   Birth, Marriage, and Death Records.
Defense Intelligence Agency:
   Documents from the FBI Headquarters File 65-44610.
Department of Justice, Federal Bureau of Investigation:
   Headquarters File 64-23312, Ernest Hemingway;
   Headquarters File 65-44610, Heinz August Lüning.
Department of the Army:
   Documents from the FBI Headquarters File 65-44610.
Department of the Navy:
   Documents from the FBI Headquarters File 65-44610.
Federal Communications Commission:
   Documents from the FBI Headquarters File 65-44610.
Georgetown University, Special Collections, Washington, DC:
   Catherine Walston/Graham Greene Papers;
   Graham Greene Papers.
National Archives Records Administration (NARA):
   RG (Record Group) 38 (Office of Naval Intelligence);
   RG 59 (State Department);
   RG 65 (Federal Bureau of Investigation):
   Headquarters File from World War II;
   Case file 146-7-0, "Lüning."
   RG 84 (State Department, Post Records):
   Cuba: Havana Embassy, Super Confidential (1940–44), Entry 2359.
   RG 165 (War Department General and Special Staffs—includes
   Military Intelligence Division [MID]).
   RG 216 (Office of Censorship):
   216.2, Intercepts: Record NY-X-8.

RG 319 (Military Intelligence Department):
    Box 131E, file x8536413, Lüning, H. A.
New York Public Library, Performing Arts Branch, New York.
University of Texas Henry Ransom Humanities Resource Center, Austin:
    Graham Greene archives.

Printed Sources

Abhagen, Karl Heinz. *Canaris.* London: Hutchinson, 1956.
Acosta Rubio, Raul. *Cuba, Todos Culpables.* Miami: Ediciones Universal, 1977.
Adamson, Judith. *Graham Greene: The Dangerous Edge: Where Art and Politics Meet.* London: Macmillan, 1990.
————. *Graham Greene and Cinema.* Norman, OK: Pilgrim, 1984.
Aguilar, Luis E. *Cuba 1933: Prologue to Revolution.* Ithaca, NY: Cornell University Press, 1972.
Allain, Marie-Françoise. *The Other Man: Conversations with Graham Greene.* London: Bodley Head, 1983.
Andrew, Christopher. *Her Majesty's Secret Service: The Making of the British Intelligence Community.* New York: Viking Penguin, 1986.
————. "Introduction: Intelligence and International Relations, 1900–1945." In *Intelligence and International Relations, 1900–1945* (Exeter Studies in History, no. 15), ed. Christopher Andrew and Jeremy Noakes, 1–7. Exeter: University of Exeter, 1987.
————. "Introduction to 'The ISOS Years: Madrid, 1941–3.'" *Journal of Contemporary History* 30, no. 3 (July 1995): 355–58.
Astaire, Fred. *Steps in Time: An Autobiography.* New York: Cooper Square, 2000.
Avni, Haim. *Argentina and the Jews: A History of Jewish Immigration.* Tuscaloosa: University of Alabama Press, 1991.
————. *Argentina y la historia de la inmigración judía (1810–1950).* Jerusalem: Editorial universitaria magnes, 1983.
Axton, Charles B., and Otto Zehnder. *Reclams großes Musical-Buch.* Stuttgart: Philipp Reclam, 1997.
Baldridge, Cates. *Graham Greene's Fictions: The Virtues of Extremity.* Columbia: University of Missouri Press, 2000.
Baptiste, Fitzroy André. *War, Cooperation and Conflict: The European Possessions in the Caribbean, 1939–1945.* Westport, CT: Greenwood, 1988.
Bassett, Richard. *Hitler's Spy Chief: The Wilhelm Canaris Mystery.* London: Cassell Military, 2005.
Benítez, Manuel. "On Radio Berlin." *True Detective* 42, no. 2 (May 1944): 10–13, 70–73.

[Benítez, Manuel]. "On Radio Berlín: El caso Luning." *Mañana* (Havana), June 12–21, 1947. FBI HQ Archive.

Benton, Kenneth. "The ISOS Years: Madrid 1941–3." *Journal of Contemporary History* 30, no. 3 (July 1995): 359–410.

Berger, Henry W. "Crisis Diplomacy, 1930–1939." In *From Colony to Empire: Essays in the History of American Foreign Relations*, ed. William A. Williams, 293–336. New York: John Wiley, 1972.

Billman, Larry. *Fred Astaire: A Bio-Bibliography*. Westport, CT: Greenwood, 1997.

Bishop, Eleanor C. *Prints in the Sand: The U.S. Coast Guard Beach Patrol during World War II*. Missoula, Mont.: Pictorial Histories, 1989.

Blair, Clay. *Hitler's U-Boat War: The Hunted, 1942–1945*. New York: Random House, 1998.

———. *Hitler's U-Boat War: The Hunter, 1939–1942*. New York: Random House, 1996.

Bloom, Ken. *American Song: The Complete Musical Theatre Companion*. 2 vols. New York: Facts on File, 1985.

———. *Broadway: Its History, People, and Places, an Encyclopedia*. New York: Routledge, 2004.

Boardman, Gerald. *American Musical Theatre: A Chronicle*. New York: Oxford University Press, 2001.

———. *The Oxford Companion to American Theatre*. 2nd ed. New York: Oxford University Press, 1992.

Boardman, Gwenn R. *Graham Greene: The Aesthetics of Explanation*. Gainesville: University of Florida Press, 1971.

Bochow, Klaus-Peter. *FBI*. Berlin: C. A. Koch, 1968.

Böker, Uwe. *Loyale Illoyalität: Politische Elemente im Werk Graham Greenes*. Munich: Wilhelm Fink, 1982.

Boog, Horst. *Der globale Krieg: Die Ausweitung zum Weltkrieg und der Wechsel der Initiative*. Stuttgart: Deutsche Verlags–Anstalt, 1990.

Braden, Spruille. *Diplomats and Demagogues: The Memoirs of Spruille Braden*. New Rochelle, NY: Arlington House, 1971.

Bragadin, Marc'Antonio. *The Italian Navy in World War II*. Annapolis, MD: U.S. Naval Institute, 1957.

Brammer, Uwe. *Spionageabwehr und "Geheimer Meldedienst": Die Abwehrstelle im Wehrkreis X Hamburg, 1935–1945*. Freiburg: Rombach, 1989.

Breitman, Richard. *Official Secrets: What the Nazis Planned, What the British and Americans Knew*. New York: Hill & Wang, 1998.

Brennecke, Jochen. *Jäger—Gejagte: Deutsche U-Boote, 1939–1945: Die längste Schlacht im Zweiten Weltkrieg*. 7th ed. Herford: Koehlers, 1989.

Breuer, William B. *Undercover Tales of World War II*. New York: John Wiley, 1999.

Brissard, André. *Canaris: The Biography of Admiral Canaris, Chief of German Military Intelligence in the Second World War.* New York: Grosset & Dunlap, 1973.

British Security Coordination. *The Secret History of British Intelligence in the Americas, 1940–1945.* New York: Fromm International, 1999.

Buchheit, Gert. *Der deutsche Geheimdienst: Geschichte der militärischen Abwehr.* Munich: List, 1966.

Cadogan, Alexander. *The Diaries of Sir Alexander Cadogan.* Edited by David Dilks. London: Cassell, 1971.

Calic, Edouard. *Reinhard Heydrich: The Chilling Story of the Man Who Masterminded the Nazi Death Camps.* New York: Military Heritage, 1982.

Carter, Miranda. *Anthony Blunt: His Lives.* London: Macmillan, 2001.

Cassis, Awny F. *Graham Greene: Life, Work, and Criticism.* Fredericton, NB: York, 1994.

———, ed. *Graham Greene: Man of Paradox.* Chicago: Loyola University Press, 1994.

Chalou, George C., ed. *The Secrets War: The Office of Strategic Services in World War II.* Washington, DC: National Archives Records Administration, 1992.

Chester, Edmund A. *A Sergeant Named Batista.* New York: Henry Holt, 1954.

Cirules, Enrique. *Hemingway in Cuba.* Madrid: Libertarias-Prodhufi, 1999.

Clayton, Lawrence A., and Michael Conniff. *A History of Modern Latin America.* Fort Worth, TX: Harcourt Brace, 1999.

Cloetta, Yvonne. Foreword to *A World of My Own: A Dream Diary,* by Graham Greene, vii–xii. New York: Viking, 1992.

Collins, Frederick L. *The FBI in Peace and War.* New York: Putnam's, 1943.

Compton, James V. *The Swastika and the Eagle: Hitler, the United States, and the Origins of World War II.* Boston: Houghton Mifflin, 1967.

Couto, Maria. *Graham Greene on the Frontier: Politics and Religion in the Novels.* London: Macmillan, 1988.

Dallek, Robert. *Franklin D. Roosevelt and American Foreign Policy, 1932–1945.* New York: Oxford University Press, 1979.

D'Aumale, Geoffroy, and Jean-Pierre Taure. *Guide de l'espionage et du contre-espionage.* Paris: Le cherche midi, 1998.

Davis, Harold Eugene, and Larman C. Wilson, eds. *Latin American Foreign Policies: An Analysis.* Baltimore: Johns Hopkins University Press, 1975.

Devitis, A. A. *Graham Greene.* Rev. ed. Boston: Twayne, 1986.

Diemert, Brian. *Graham Greene's Thrillers and the 1930s.* Montreal: McGill-Queen's University Press, 1996.

Doerries, Reinhard. "Geheimdienste im 20. Jahrhundert." *Neue politische Literatur* 19, no. 3 (1974): 353–64.

Donaghy, Henry J., ed. *Conversations with Graham Greene*. Jackson: University Press of Mississippi, 1992.

Dönitz, Karl. *Mein wechselvolles Leben*. Göttingen: Musterschmidt, 1968.

———. *Zehn Jahre und zwanzig Tage*. Munich: Bernard & Graefe, 1975.

Dorril, Stephen. *MI6: Fifty Years of Special Operations*. London: Fourth Estate, 2001.

Dorwart, Jeffery M. *Conflict of Duty: The U.S. Navy's Intelligence Dilemma, 1919–1945*. Annapolis, MD: U.S. Navy Institute, 1983.

Dosal, Paul J. *Cuba Libre: A Brief History of Cuba*. Wheeling, IL: Harlan Davidson, 2006.

Dozer, Donald Marquand. *Are We Good Neighbors? Three Decades of Inter-American Relations, 1930–1960*. Gainesville: University of Florida Press, 1961.

Dülffer, Jost. *Weimar, Hitler und die Marine: Reichspolitik und Flottenbau, 1920–1939*. Düsseldorf: Droste, 1973.

Dur, Philip, and Christopher Gilcrease. "U.S. Diplomacy and the Downfall of a Cuban Dictator: Machado in 1933." *Journal of Latin American Studies* 34 (2002): 255–82.

Eck, Nathan. "The Rescue of Jews with the Aid of Passports and Citizenship Papers of Latin American States." *Yad Vashem Studies* 1 (1957): 125–52.

Elliff, John T. *The Reform of FBI Intelligence Operations*. Princeton, NJ: Princeton University Press, 1979.

Erasmus, Johannes. *Der geheime Nachrichtendienst*. Göttingen: Musterschmidt, 1952.

Ewen, David. *Richard Rodgers*. New York: Henry Holt, 1957.

Fagg, John Edwin. *Cuba, Haiti, and the Dominican Republic*. Englewood Cliffs, NJ: Prentice-Hall, 1965.

Falk, Quentin. *Travels in Greeneland: The Cinema of Graham Greene*. London: Quartet, 1984.

Farago, Ladislas. *The Game of the Foxes: The Untold Story of German Espionage in the United States and Great Britain during World War II*. New York: David McKay, 1971.

Farber, Samuel. *Revolution and Reaction in Cuba, 1933–1960*. Middletown, CT: Wesleyan University Press, 1976.

Fermoselle, Rafael. *The Evolution of the Cuban Military, 1492–1986*. Miami: Universal, 1987.

Fernández Artucio, Hugo. *La organización secreta Nazi en sudamérica*. Mexico, D.F.: Minerva, [1943?].

Floherty, John J. *Our FBI*. Philadelphia: J. B. Lippincott, 1951.

Foot, Michael R. D. *SOE: An Outline History of the Special Operations Executive, 1940–1946*. Rev. ed. Washington, DC: University Publishers of America, 1986.

———. "Was SOE Any Good?" *Journal of Contemporary History* 16, no. 1 (January 1981): 167–81.

Frank, Wolfgang. *The Sea Wolves: The Story of German U-Boats at War.* New York: Rinehart, 1955.

Freedland, Michael. *Fred Astaire.* London: W. H. Allen, 1976.

Freud, Hans. "OKW/Amt für Auslandsnachrichten/Abwehr." *Feldgrau* 11 (1963): 185–87.

Friedman, Max Paul. *Nazis and Good Neighbors: The United States Campaign against the Germans of Latin America in World War II.* New York: Cambridge University Press, 2003.

———. "There Goes the Neighborhood: Blacklisting Germans in Latin America and the Evanescence of the Good Neighbor Policy." *Diplomatic History* 27, no. 4 (September 2003): 569–97.

———. "The U.S. State Department and the Failure to Rescue: New Evidence on the Missed Opportunity at Bergen-Belsen." *Holocaust and Genocide Studies* 19 (Spring 2005): 26–50.

Frye, Alton. *Nazi Germany and the American Hemisphere, 1933–1941.* New Haven, CT: Yale University Press, 1967.

Fuentes, Norberto. *Ernest Hemingway: Jahre in Kuba.* Hamburg: Galgenberg, 1987.

Gänzl, Kurt. *The British Musical Theatre.* Vol. 2. London: Macmillan, 1986.

———. *The Encyclopedia of the Musical Theatre.* 3 vols. 2d ed. New York: Schirmer, 2001.

Gannon, Michael. *Operation Drumbeat: The Dramatic True Story of Germany's First U-Boat Attacks along the American Coast in World War II.* New York: Harper & Row, 1990.

Gardner, Lloyd C. *Economic Aspects of New Deal Diplomacy.* Boston: Beacon, 1964.

Gaston, Georg M. A. *The Pursuit of Salvation: A Critical Guide to the Novels of Graham Greene.* Troy, NY: Whitson, 1984.

Gellermann, Günther W. *Tief im Hinterland des Gegners: Ausgewählte Unternehmen deutscher Geheimdienste im Zweiten Weltkrieg.* Bonn: Bernard & Graefe, 1999.

Gellman, Irwin F. *Good Neighbor Diplomacy: United States Policies in Latin America, 1933–1945.* Baltimore: Johns Hopkins University Press, 1979.

———. *Roosevelt and Batista: Good Neighbor Diplomacy in Cuba, 1933–1945.* Albuquerque: University of New Mexico Press, 1973.

Gentry, Curt. *J. Edgar Hoover: The Man and the Secrets.* New York: Norton, 1991.

Germany. Auswärtiges Amt. *Akten zur Deutschen Auswärtigen Politik.* Ser. E, *1941–1945.* Vol. 4, pt. 1. Göttingen: Vandenhoeck & Ruprecht, 1975.

Goda, Norman J. W. *Tomorrow the World: Hitler, Northwest Africa, and the Path toward America.* College Station: Texas A&M University Press, 1998.

González del Valle, Antolín. *Fulgencio Batista: Trayectoria nacionalista.* Wilmington, NC: Patria, 1980.

Görlitz, Walter. *Karl Dönitz: Der Großadmiral.* Göttingen: Musterschmidt, 1972.

Graff, Frank Warren. *Strategy of Involvement: A Diplomatic Biography of Sumner Welles.* New York: Garland, 1988.

Grant, Mark N. *The Rise and Fall of the Broadway Musical.* Boston: Northeastern University Press, 2004.

Greene, Graham. *Collected Essays.* London: Bodley Head, 1969.

———. *The Comedians.* London: Vintage, 1999.

———. *The End of the Affair.* New York: Penguin, 1968.

———. *The Heart of the Matter.* Harmondsworth: Penguin, 1986.

———. *The Honorary Consul.* New York: Simon & Schuster, 1973.

———. *The Human Factor.* New York: Simon & Schuster, 1978.

———. *In Search of a Character.* New York: Penguin, 1975.

———. *Our Man in Havana.* New York: Viking, 1958.

———. *Reflections.* Edited by Judith Adamson. London: Reinhardt, 1990.

———. *A Sort of Life.* London: Vintage, 1999.

———. *The Tenth Man.* New York: Simon & Schuster, 1985.

———. *The Third Man; Loser Takes All.* New York: Viking, 1983.

———. *Ways of Escape.* New York: Simon & Schuster, 1980.

———. *A World of My Own: A Dream Diary.* New York: Viking, 1992.

———. *Yours, Etc.: Letters to the Press.* London: Reinhardt (Penguin), 1989.

Gruchmann, Lothar. *Totaler Krieg: Vom Blitzkrieg zur bedingungslosen Kapitulation.* Munich: dtv, 1991.

Gurevich, Beatriz, and Carlos Escudé, eds. *El genocidio ante la historia y la naturaleza humana.* Buenos Aires: Universidad Torcuarto de Tella, 1994.

Hashimoto, Mochitsura. *Sunk: The Story of the Japanese Submarine Fleet, 1941–1945.* London: Cassell, 1954.

Havemann, Nils. *Fußball unterm Hakenkreuz: Der DFB zwischen Sport, Politik und Kommerz.* Frankfurt: Campus, 2005.

Hazzard, Shirley. *Greene on Capri: A Memoir.* New York: Farrar, Straus, Giroux, 2000.

Hearnden, Patrick J. *Roosevelt Confronts Hitler: America's Entry into World War II.* DeKalb: Northern Illinois University Press, 1987.

Hell, Jürgen. *Geschichte Kubas.* Berlin: VEB Deutscher Verlag der Wissenschaften, 1989.

Hemingway, Gregory H. *Papa: A Personal Memoir.* Boston: Houghton Mifflin, 1976.

Herring, George C., Jr. *Aid to Russia, 1941–1946: Strategy, Diplomacy, the Origins of the Cold War.* New York: Columbia University Press, 1973.

Herzstein, Robert E. *Roosevelt and Hitler: Prelude to War.* New York: Paragon, 1989.

Hildebrand, Klaus. *Das Dritte Reich.* Munich: R. Oldenbourgh, 1995.

Hill, Leonidas E. "The Wilhelmstrasse in the Nazi Era." *Political Science Quarterly* 82, no. 4 (December 1967): 546–70.

Hillgruber, Andreas. "Der Faktor Amerika in Hitlers Strategie, 1938–1941." *Aus Politik und Zeitgeschichte: Beilage zur Wochenzeitung das Parlament* B19/66 (May 11, 1966): 3–21.

———. *Hitlers Strategie: Politik und Kriegsführung, 1940–1941.* Frankfurt a.M.: Bernard & Graefe, 1965.

———. *Der 2. Weltkrieg: Kriegsziele und Strategie der großen Mächte.* 5th ed. Stuttgart: W. Kohlhammer, 1989.

Hilton, Stanley E. *Hitler's Secret War in South America, 1939–1945: German Military Espionage and Allied Counterespionage in Brazil.* Baton Rouge: Louisiana State University Press, 1981.

Hinsley, F[rancis] H[arry]. "British Intelligence in the Second World War." In *Intelligence and International Relations, 1900–1945* (Exeter Studies in History, no. 15), ed. Christopher Andrew and Jeremy Noakes, 209–18. Exeter: University of Exeter, 1987.

———. *British Intelligence in the Second World War.* Abridged ed. Cambridge: Cambridge University Press, 1993.

Hinsley, F. H., E. E. Thomas, G. F. G. Ranson, and R. C. Knight. *British Intelligence in the Second World War: Its Influence on Strategy and Operations.* 5 vols. in 6 pts. London: H.M. Stationery Office, 1979–1990.

Hitler, Adolf. *Hitler's Second Book, the Unpublished Sequel to Mein Kampf.* New York: Enigma, 2003.

———. *Hitlers zweites Buch: Ein Dokument aus dem Jahr 1928.* Stuttgart: Deutsche Verlags–Anstalt, 1961.

Höbbel, Georg-Alexander. *Das "Dritte Reich" und die Good Neighbor Policy: Die nationalsozialistische Beurteilung der Lateinamerikapolitik Frank D. Roosevelts, 1933–1941.* Hamburg: Lit, 1997.

Höhne, Heinz. *Canaris.* Garden City, NY: Doubleday, 1979.

Holden, Robert H., and Eric Zolov, eds. *Latin America and the United States: A Documentary History.* New York: Oxford University Press, 2000.

Hoskins, Robert. *Graham Greene: A Character Index and Guide.* New York: Garland, 1991.

Humphreys, R. A. *Latin America and the Second World War.* 2 vols. London: Athlone, 1982.

Hyde, Harford Montgomery. *The Quiet Canadian: The Secret Service Story of Sir William Stephenson.* London: Hamish Hamilton, 1962.

———. *Room 3603: The Story of the British Intelligence Center in New York during World War II.* New York: Farrar, Straus, 1963.

Jacobson, Hans-Adolf. "Zur Struktur der NS-Außenpolitik, 1933–1945." In *Hitler, Deutschland und die Mächte: Materialien zur Außenpolitik des Dritten Reiches,* ed. Manfred Funk, 137–85. Düsseldorf: Droste, 1976.

Jakub, Jay. *Spies and Saboteurs: Anglo-American Collaboration and Rivalry in Human Intelligence Collection and Special Operations, 1940–45.* London: Macmillan, 1999.

Jeffreys-Jones, Rhodri. *Cloak and Dollar: A History of American Secret Intelligence.* New Haven, CT: Yale University Press, 2002.

———. "The Role of British Intelligence in Mythologies Underpinning the OSS and Early CIA." *American-British-Canadian Intelligence Relations, 1939–2000,* ed. David Stafford and Rhodri Jeffreys-Jones, 5–19. London: Frank Cass, 2000.

Johns, Philip. *Within Two Cloaks: Missions with SIS and SOE.* London: William Kimber, 1979.

Jones, John Bush. *Our Musicals, Ourselves: A Social History of the American Musical Theatre.* Hanover, NH: Brandeis University Press, 2003.

Jong, Louis de. *Die deutsche Fünfte Kolonne im Zweiten Weltkrieg.* Stuttgart: Deutsche Verlags–Anstalt, 1959.

Judd, Alan. *The Quest for C: Mansfield Cumming and the Founding of the British Secret Service.* New York: HarperCollins, 1999.

Junker, Detlef. "Deutschland im politischen Kalkül der Vereinigten Staaten, 1933–1941." In *Der Zweite Weltkrieg: Analysen, Grundzüge, Forschungsbilanz,* ed. Wolfgang Michalka, 57–73. Reprint. Weyarn: Seehammer, 1997.

Kahn, David. *The Codebreakers: The Story of Secret Writing.* New York: Macmillan, 1967.

———. *Hitler's Spies: German Military Intelligence in World War II.* New York: Macmillan, 1978.

———. "Secrets of the Nazi Archives." *Atlantic,* May 1969, 50–56.

Kannapin, Klaus. "Deutschland und Argentinien von 1933 bis 1945." *Wissenschaftliche Zeitschrift der Universität Rostock* 14 (1965): 107–18.

Keegan, John. *Intelligence in War: Knowledge of the Enemy from Napoleon to Al-Qaeda.* New York: Knopf, 2003.

Keen, Benjamin. *A History of Latin America.* 2 vols. 5th ed. Boston: Houghton Mifflin, 1996.

Kelshall, Gaylord T. M. *The U-Boat War in the Caribbean.* Reprint. Annapolis, MD: U.S. Naval Institute, 1994.

Kimball, Warren F. *Forged in War: Roosevelt, Churchill, and the Second World War.* New York: William Morrow, 1997.

————. *The Most Unsordid Act: Lend-Lease, 1939–1941.* Baltimore: Johns Hopkins University Press, 1969.

Knight, Franklin W. *The Caribbean: The Genesis of a Fragmented Nationalism.* 2nd ed. New York: Oxford University Press, 1990.

Knight, Mary. "The Secret War of Censors vs Spies: Snooping Irked Us, but Paid Off." *Washington Post,* February 3, 1946, B1–B2.

Koop, Theodore F. *Weapon of Silence.* Chicago: University of Chicago Press, 1946.

Kossok, Manfred. "Sonderauftrag Südamerika zur deutschen Politik gegenüber Lateinamerika, 1938–1942." In *Lateinamerika zwischen Emanzipation und Imperialismus, 1810–1960,* 222–55. Berlin: Akademie, 1961.

Kramer, Paul. "Nelson Rockefeller and British Security Coordination." *Journal of Contemporary History* 16, no. 1 (January 1981): 73–88.

Kulshrestha, J. P. *Graham Greene: The Novelist.* Delhi: Macmillan, 1977.

Kunkel, Francis L. *The Labyrinthine Ways of Graham Greene.* Mamaroneck, NY: Paul P. Appel, 1973.

Kurowski, Franz. *An alle Wölfe: Angriff! U-Boote Crews und Kommandanten im Zweiten Weltkrieg, 1939–1945.* Friedberg/H.: Podzun-Pallas, 1986.

————. *Krieg unter Wasser: U-Boote auf den sieben Meeren, 1939–1945.* Klagenfurt: Kaiser, 1979.

Langley, Lester D. "Theodore Roosevelt." In *Encyclopedia of Latin American History and Culture,* ed. Barbara A. Tenenbaum, 4:607. New York: Scribner's, 1996.

Leverkuehn, Paul. *Der geheime Nachrichtendienst der deutschen Wehrmacht im Kriege.* Frankfurt a.M.: Bernard & Graefe, 1957.

————. *German Military Intelligence.* New York: Praegers, 1954.

Levine, Robert M.. "Cuba." In *The World Reacts to the Holocaust,* ed. David S. Wyman and Charles H. Rosenzveig, 782–808. Baltimore: Johns Hopkins University Press, 1996.

Lewis, David H. *Broadway Musicals: A Hundred Year History.* Jefferson, NC: McFarland, 2002.

Lodge, David. *Graham Greene.* New York: Columbia University Press, 1966.

Lübken, Uwe. *Bedrohliche Nähe: Die USA und die nationalistische Herausforderung in Lateinamerika, 1937–1945.* Stuttgart: Franz Steiner, 2004.

Lundeberg, P. K. "La république des États-Unis à la guerre au tonnage." *Revue d'histoire de la deuxième guerre mondiale* 18 (January 1968): 67–96.

Lynn, Kenneth S. *Hemingway.* Cambridge, MA: Harvard University Press, 1987.

MacDonald, Callum. *The Killing of SS Obergruppenführer Reinhard Heydrich.* New York: Free Press, 1989.

MacDonnell, Francis. *Insidious Foes: The Axis Fifth Column and the American Home Front.* New York: Oxford University Press, 1995.

Mader, Julius. *Hitlers Spionagegeneräle sagen aus.* Berlin: Verlag der Nation, 1972.

Maingot, Anthony P. *The United States and the Caribbean.* Boulder, CO: Westview, 1994.

Maney, Patrick J. "Franklin D. Roosevelt." In *Encyclopedia of Latin American History and Culture,* ed. Barbara A. Tenenbaum, 4:606–7. New York: Scribner's, 1996.

Mantle, Burns, ed. *The Best Plays of 1922–1923.* Boston: Small, Maynard, 1923.

Mantle, Burns, and Garrison P. Sherwood, eds. *The Best Plays of 1909–1919.* New York: Dodd, Mead, 1943.

Massari, Roberto. *Geschichte Kubas: Von den Anfängen bis zur Revolution.* Frankfurt a.M.: dipa, 1992.

Masterson, Daniel M., with Sayaka Funada-Classen. *The Japanese in Latin America.* Urbana: University of Illinois Press, 2004.

Mauch, Christof. "Das Dritte Reich und die Politik des amerikanischen Geheimdienstes: Prognosen, Projekte und Operationen im Spannungsfeld von Dilettantismus und Mythenbildung." In *Diplomaten und Agenten: Nachrichtendienste in der Geschichte der deutsch-amerikanischen Beziehungen,* ed. Reinhard Doerries, 162–88. Heidelberg: C. Winter, 2001.

Mazarr, Michael J. *Semper Fidel: America and Cuba, 1776–1988.* Baltimore: Nautical & Aviation, 1988.

McEwan, Neil. *Graham Greene.* London: Macmillan, 1988.

McKale, Donald M. *The Swastika Outside Germany.* Kent, OH: Kent State University Press, 1977.

Mecham, J. Lloyd. *A Survey of United States–Latin American Relations.* Boston: Houghton Mifflin, 1965.

Meier-Dörnberg, Wilhelm. *Die Ölversorgung der Kriegsmarine, 1935 bis 1945.* Freiburg: Rombach, 1973.

Mellow, James R. *A Life without Consequences: Hemingway.* Boston: Houghton Mifflin, 1992.

Messick, Hank. *John Edgar Hoover.* New York: David McKay, 1972.

Meyers, Jeffery, ed. *Graham Greene: A Revolution.* London: Macmillan, 1990.

Michalka, Wolfgang. "'Vom Motor zum Getriebe': Das Auswärtige Amt und die Degradierung einer traditionsreichen Behörde 1933 bis 1945." In *Der Zweite Weltkrieg: Analysen, Grundzüge, Forschungsbilanz,* ed. Wolfgang Michalka, 249–59. Reprint. Weyarn: Seehammer, 1997.

Modin, Yuri. *My Five Cambridge Friends.* New York: Farrar Straus Giroux, 1994.

Mollman-Showell, Jak. *Kriegsmarine, 1939–1945.* Stuttgart: Motorbuch, 2000.

Mordden, Ethan. *Make Believe: The Broadway Musical in the 1920s.* New York: Oxford University Press, 1997.

Morison, Samuel Eliot. *The Two-Ocean War: A Short History of the United States Navy in the Second World War.* Boston: Little, Brown, 1989.

Mueller, Michael. *Canaris: Hitlers Abwehrchef.* Berlin: Propyläen, 2006.

Müller, Jürgen. *Nazionalsozialismus in Lateinamerika: Die Auslandsorganisation der NSDAP in Argentinien, Brasilien, Chile und Mexiko, 1931–1945.* Stuttgart: Hans Dieter Heinz, 1997.

Neufeld, Michael J., and Michael Berenbaum, eds. *The Bombing of Auschwitz: Should the Allies Have Attemped It?* New York: St. Martin's, 2000.

Newfarmer, Richard W., ed. *From Gunboats to Diplomacy: New U.S. Policies for Latin America.* Baltimore: Johns Hopkins University Press, 1984.

Newton, Ronald C. *The "Nazi Menace" in Argentina, 1931–1947.* Stanford, CA: Stanford University Press, 1992.

Norton, Richard C. *A Chronology of American Musical Theater.* 3 vols. New York: Oxford University Press, 2002.

O'Brien, Thomas F. *The Revolutionary Mission: American Enterprise in Latin America, 1900–1945.* New York: Cambridge University Press, 1996.

O'Prey, Paul. *A Reader's Guide to Graham Greene.* Worcester: Thames & Hudson, 1988.

Padfield, Peter. *Dönitz et la guerre des U-Boote.* Paris: Pygmalion/Gerard Watelet, 1986.

Paine, Lauran. *German Military Intelligence in World War II: The Abwehr.* New York: Stein & Day, 1984.

Paredes, Lucas. *Mis 300 Pasaportes.* Tegucigalpa: Ruiz, 1944.

Parry, J. H., and Philip Sherlock. *A Short History of the West Indies.* 3rd ed. New York: St. Martin's, 1971.

Penrose, Barrie, and Simon Freeman. *Conspiracy of Silence: The Secret Life of Anthony Blunt.* New York: Farrar Straus Giroux, 1987.

Pérez, Louis A., Jr. *Cuba and the United States: Ties of Singular Intimacy.* Athens: University Press of Georgia, 1990.

———. *On Becoming Cuban: Identity, Nationality, and Culture.* New York: HarperCollins, 1999.

Persico, Joseph E. *Roosevelt's Secret War: FDR and World War II Espionage.* New York: Random House, 2001.

Phillips, Ruby Hart. *Cuba: Island of Paradox.* New York: McDowell, Obolensky, 1959.

Polmar, Norman, and Thomas B. Allen, eds. *Spy Book: The Encyclopedia of Espionage.* New York: Random House, 1997.

Pommerin, Reiner. *Das Dritte Reich und Lateinamerika: Die deutsche Politik gegenüber Süd- und Mittelamerika, 1939–1942.* Düsseldorf: Droste, 1977.

———. "Überlegungen des 'Dritten Reichs' zur Rückholung deutscher Auswanderer aus Lateinamerika." *Jahrbuch für Geschichte von Staat, Wirtschaft und Gesellschaft Lateinamerikas* 16 (1979): 365–77.

Porten, Edward P. von der. *The German Navy in World War II.* New York: Thomas Y. Crowell, 1969.

Potter, Claire Bond. *War on Crime: Bandits, G-Men, and the Politics of Mass Culture.* New Brunswick, NJ: Rutgers University Press, 1998.

Powers, Richard Gid. *G-Men: Hoover's FBI in American Popular Culture.* Carbondale: Southern Illinois University Press, 1983.

———. *Secrecy and Power: The Life of J. Edgar Hoover.* London: Hutchinson, 1987.

Puhle, Hans-Jürgen. "Unabhängigkeit, Staatenbildung und gesellschaftliche Entwicklung in Nord- und Südamerika." In *Lateinamerika am Ende des 20. Jahrhunderts,* ed. Detlef Junker, Dieter Nohlen, and Hartmut Sangmeister, 27–48. Munich: C. H. Beck, 1994.

Quack, Josef. *Die Grenzen des Menschlichen: Über Georges Simenon, Rex Stout, Friedrich Glauser, Graham Greene.* Würzburg: Königshausen & Neumann, 2000.

Rahn, Werner. "Der Atlantik in der strategischen Perspektive Hitlers und Roosevelts 1941." In *Der Zweite Weltkrieg: Analysen, Grundzüge, Forschungsbilanz,* ed. Wolfgang Michalka, 667–82. Reprint. Weyarn: Seehammer, 1997.

Ranelagh, John. *The Agency: The Rise and Decline of the CIA.* New York: Touchstone, 1987.

Reile, Oscar. *Geheime Westfront: Die Abwehr, 1935–1945.* Munich: Welsermühl, 1964.

Rensselaer Polytechnic Institute. *Transit.* Troy, NY: Rensselaer Polytechnic Institute, 1903.

Rockefeller, Nelson. "Fighting the Traitors Within." *New York Times Sunday Magazine,* January 3, 1943, 6–7.

Rodgers, Richard. *Musical Stages.* New York: Random House, 1975.

Rogozinski, Jan. *A Brief History of the Caribbean: From the Arawak and the Caribbean to the Present.* New York: Meridian, 1994.

Rohwer, Jürgen. *Axis Submarine Successes of World War II: German, Italian and Japanese Submarine Successes, 1939–1945.* Rev. ed.. Annapolis, MD: U.S. Naval Institute, 1999.

———. "The Operational Use of 'Ultra' in the Battle of the Atlantic." In *Intelligence and International Relations, 1900–1945* (Exeter Studies in History, no. 15), ed. Christopher Andrew and Jeremy Noakes, 275–92. Exeter: University of Exeter, 1987.

———. "La radiotélégraphie auxiliaire du commandement dans la guerre sous-marine." *Revue d'histoire de la deuxième guerre mondiale* 18 (January 1968): 41–66.

————. "'Signal Intelligence' in der Geschichtsschreibung über den Zweiten Weltkrieg." In *Diplomaten und Agenten: Nachrichtendienste in der Geschichte der deutsch-amerikanischen Beziehungen,* ed. Reinhard Doerries, 149–60. Heidelberg: C. Winter, 2001.

————. *Die U-Boot-Erfolge der Achsenmächte, 1939–1945.* Munich: J. F. Lehmanns, 1968.

Rössler, Eberhard. *Geschichte des deutschen U-Bootbaus.* 2 vols. Frankfurt a.m.: Bernard & Graefe, 1996.

Rout, Leslie B., Jr., and John F. Bratzel. *The Shadow War: German Espionage in Latin America during World War II.* Frederick, MD: University Publications of America, 1986.

Rubinstein, William D. *The Myth of Rescue: Why the Democracies Could Not Have Saved More Jews from the Nazis.* London: Routledge, 1997.

Ruge, Friedrich. *The German Navy's Story, 1939–1945.* Annapolis, MD: U.S. Naval Institute, 1957.

Ruhl, Klaus-Jörg. *Spanien im Zweiten Weltkrieg: Franco, die Falange und das "Dritte Reich."* Hamburg: Hoffmann & Campe, 1975.

Salewski, Michael. *Die deutsche Seekriegsleitung, 1935–1945.* 3 vols. Frankfurt a.m.: Bernard & Graefe, 1970–75.

Satchell, Tim. *Astaire: The Biography.* London: Hutchinson, 1987.

Scharbius, Manfred. "Zur Politik des deutschen Faschismus in Mittelamerika und Westindien." In *Der deutsche Faschismus in Lateinamerika, 1933–1943,* ed. Heinz Sanke, 145–57. Berlin: Humboldt-Universität, 1966.

Schellenberg, Walter. *Hitlers letzter Geheimdienstchef.* Rastatt: Moewig, 1986.

Schofield, B. B. "The Defeat of the U-Boats." *Journal of Contemporary History* 16, no. 1 (January 1981): 119–29.

Schramm, Wilhelm von. *Der Geheimdienst im Zweiten Weltkrieg: Organisation—Methoden—Erfolge.* 3rd ed. Munich: Langen Müller, 1979.

————. *Der Geheimdienst in Europa, 1937–1945.* Munich: Langen Müller, 1974.

Schrieber, Gerhard. "Der Zweite Weltkrieg in der internationalen Forschung: Konzeptionen, Thesen und Kontroversen." In *Der Zweite Weltkrieg: Analysen, Grundzüge, Forschungsbilanz,* ed. Wolfgang Michalka, 3–24. Reprint. Weyarn: Seehammer, 1997.

Schröder, Hans-Jürgen. "Das Dritte Reich, die USA und Lateinamerika, 1933–1941." In *Hitler, Deutschland und die Mächte: Materialien zur Außenpolitik des Dritten Reiches,* ed. Manfred Funk, 339–64. Düsseldorf: Droste, 1976.

Schuler, Friedrich E. *Mexico between Hitler and Roosevelt: Mexican Foreign Relations in the Age of Lázaro Cárdenas, 1934–1940.* Albuquerque: University of New Mexico Press, 1998.

Schulz, Volker. *Das kurzepische Werk Graham Greenes: Gesamtdarstellung und Einzelinterpretationen.* Trier: Wissenschaftlicher Verlag, 1987.

Sebag-Montefiore, Hugh. *Enigma: The Battle for the Code.* London: Weidenfeld & Nicolson, 2000.

Shapiro, Henry L. "The Infidel Greene: Radical Ambiguity in *Our Man in Havana.*" In *Essays in Graham Greene: An Annual Review,* ed. Peter Wolfe, 83–103. Greenwood, FL: Penkevill, 1987.

Sharrock, Roger. *Saints, Sinners and Comedians: The Novels of Graham Greene.* South Bend, IN: University of Notre Dame Press, 1984.

Sheldon, Michael. *Graham Greene: The Man Within.* London: Heinemann, 1994.

Sherry, Norman. *The Life of Graham Greene.* Vol. 1, *1904–1939.* Vol. 2, *1939–1955.* London: Jonathan Cape, 1989–94. Vol. 3, *1956–1991.* New York: Viking, 2004.

Singer, Kurt. *Spies and Traitors of World War II.* New York: Prentice-Hall, 1945.

Sirios, Herbert. *Zwischen Illusion und Krieg: Deutschland und die U.S.A., 1933–1941.* Paderborn: Ferdinand Schöningh, 2000.

Smith, Bradley. *The Shadow Warriors: O.S.S. and the Origins of the C.I.A.* New York: Basic, 1983.

Smith, Gaddis. *American Diplomacy during the Second World War, 1941–1945.* New York: John Wiley, 1965.

Smith, Grahame. *The Achievement of Graham Greene.* Sussex: Harvester, 1986.

———. "A Burnt-Out Case." In *Graham Greene,* ed. Harold Bloom, 153–64. New York: Chelsea House, 1987.

Smith, R. Harris. *OSS: The Secret History of America's First Central Intelligence Agency.* Berkeley: University of California Press, 1972.

Snell, John L. *Illusion and Necessity: The Diplomacy of Global War, 1939–1945.* Boston: Houghton Mifflin, 1963.

Stafford, David. *Roosevelt and Churchill: Men of Secrets.* London: Abacus, 2000.

Stephan, Alexander. *Im Visier des FBI: Deutsche Exilschriftsteller in den Akten amerikanischer Geheimdienste.* Stuttgart: J. B. Metzler, 1995.

Stoecker, Helmut. "Algunos rasgos esenciales de la política del imperialismo alemán en la América Latina de 1890–1941." In *Der deutsche Faschismus in Lateinamerika,* 187–212. Berlin: Humboldt-Universität, 1966.

Stratford, Philip. *Faith and Fiction: Creative Process in Greene and Mauriac.* South Bend, IN: University of Notre Dame Press, 1964.

Stuart, Graham H., and James L. Tigner. *Latin America and the United States.* 6th ed. Englewood Cliffs, NJ: Prentice-Hall, 1975.

Suchlicki, Jaime. *Cuba: From Columbus to Castro.* 3rd ed. Washington, DC: Brassey's, 1990.

Summers, Anthony. *Official and Confidential: The Secret Life of J. Edgar Hoover.* New York: Putnam's, 1993.

Syrett, David, ed. *The Battle of the Atlantic and Signals Intelligence: U-Boat Situations and Trends, 1941–1945.* Aldershot: Ashgate, 1998.

————. *The Defeat of the German U-Boats: The Battle of the Atlantic.* Columbia: University of South Carolina Press, 1994.

Syring, Enrico. "Hitlers Kriegserklärung an Amerika vom 11. Dezember 1941." In *Der Zweite Weltkrieg: Analysen, Grundzüge, Forschungsbilanz,* ed. Wolfgang Michalka, 683–96. Reprint. Weyarn: Seehammer, 1997.

Theoharis, Athan G. *J. Edgar Hoover, Sex, and Crime: An Historical Antidote.* Chicago: Iran R. Dee, 1995.

Theoharis, Athan G., Tony Poveda, Susan Rosenfeld, and Richard Gid Powers. *The FBI: A Comprehensive Reference Guide.* New York: Checkmark, 2000.

Thomas, Brian. *An Underground Fate: The Idiom of Romance in the Later Novels of Graham Greene.* Athens: University of Georgia Press, 1988.

Thomas, Hugh. *Cuba: The Pursuit of Freedom.* New York: Harper & Row, 1971.

Trefousse, Hans L. "Failure of German Intelligence in the United States, 1935–1945." *Mississippi Valley Historical Review* 42, no. 1 (1955): 84–100.

Trotz, Joachim. "Zur Tätigkeit der deutschen V. Kolonne in Lateinamerika von 1933 bis 1945." *Wissenschaftliche Zeitschrift der Universität Rostock* 14 (1965): 119–32.

U.S. State Department. *Foreign Relations of the United States, 1942.* Vol. 5, *The American Republics.* Washington, DC: U.S. Government Printing Office, 1962.

Ventura Novo, Esteban. *Memorias.* Mexico, D.F.: León Sánchez, 1961.

Volland, Klaus. *Das Dritte Reich und Mexiko: Studien zur Entwicklung des deutsch-mexikanischen Verhältnisses 1933–1942 unter besonderer Berücksichtigung der Ölpolitik.* Frankfurt a.M.: Peter Lang, 1976.

Weinberg, Gerhard L. *A World at Arms: A Global History of World War II.* Cambridge: Cambridge University Press, 1994.

Welles, Sumner. *The Time for Decision.* Cleveland: World, 1945.

West, Nigel. *MI5: British Security Service Operations, 1909–1945.* London: Triad Grafton, 1983.

————. *MI6: British Secret Intelligence Service Operations, 1909–1945.* London: Grafton, 1985.

West, W[illiam] J. *The Quest for Graham Greene.* New York: St. Martin's, 1997.

Wiggins, Melanie. *Torpedoes in the Gulf: Galveston and the U-Boats, 1942–1943.* College Station: Texas A&M University Press, 1995.

Wildbihler, Hubert. *The Musical: An International Annotated Bibliography.* Munich: K. G. Saur, 1986.

Willoughby, Malcolm F. *The U.S. Coast Guard in World War II.* Annapolis, MD: U.S. Naval Institute, 1957.

Wilmeth, Don B., and Christopher Bigoby, eds. *The Cambridge History of American Theatre.* Vol. 2, *1870–1945.* Cambridge: Cambridge University Press, 1999.

Wolfe, Peter. *Graham Greene the Entertainer.* Carbondale: Southern Illinois University Press, 1972.

Wyman, David S. *The Abandonment of the Jews: America and the Holocaust, 1941–1945.* New York: Pantheon, 1984.

Wyman, David S., and Charles H. Rosenzveig, eds. *The World Reacts to the Holocaust.* Baltimore: Johns Hopkins University Press, 1996.

Zeuske, Michael. *Kleine Geschichte Kubas.* Munich: C. H. Beck, 2000.

Index